SELVES, SOCIETIES, AND EMOTIONS

NEW WORLDS
SERIES

A New Series from Paradigm Publishers
Edited by Charles Lemert

CURRENT TITLES

Cities: Unauthorized Resistances and
Uncertain Sovereignty in the Urban World,
Raymond Joshua Scannell (2011)

Deploying Ourselves: Islamist Violence and the
Responsible Projection of U.S. Force,
David A. Westbrook (2010)

FORTHCOMING TITLES

On Time and the World-System, Immanuel Wallerstein

America 3,000, Charles Lemert

Black Men: How Does It Feel to be a "Problem, "Al Young

Virtual Epidemics, Monica Achitoff Gray

SELVES, SOCIETIES, AND EMOTIONS

Understanding the Pathways of Experience

THOMAS S. HENRICKS

LONDON AND NEW YORK

First published 2012 by Paradigm Publishers

Published 2016 by Routledge
2 Park Square, Milton Park, Abingdon, Oxon OX14 4RN
711 Third Avenue, New York, NY 10017, USA

Routledge is an imprint of the Taylor & Francis Group, an informa business

Copyright © 2012, Taylor & Francis.

Library of Congress Cataloging-in-Publication Data

Henricks, Thomas S.
    Selves, societies, and emotions : understanding the pathways of experience / Thomas S. Henricks.
        p.   cm. — (New worlds series)
    Includes bibliographical references and index.
    ISBN 978-1-59451-956-7 (hbk. : alk. paper) — ISBN 978-1-59451-957-4 (pbk. : alk. paper)
    1. Social psychology. 2. Social interaction. 3. Experience. 4. Self. 5. Emotions. I. Title.
HM1033.H455 2012
302—dc23
                                                                      2011031832

Designed and Typeset by Trish Wilkinson.

ISBN 13: 978-1-59451-956-7 (hbk)
ISBN 13: 978-1-59451-957-4 (pbk)

CONTENTS

CHAPTER 1

INTRODUCTION

Social scientists have long been fascinated by what is sometimes called the "miracle of social order"—the fact that human interaction is so orderly and predictable even when the people involved are motivated by diverse, contradictory, and thoroughly partisan interests. With some measure of success, most of us make our intentions plain to others, move briskly through the traffic of human affairs, and find stable vantage points from which to observe the most ill defined of situations. We draw conclusions about the character of those situations, the meanings of the objects we find there, and the intentions of the other people we confront. We pursue lines of behavior with confidence and moral justification. We experience emotions that are recognized—by ourselves and others—to be consistent with what is happening to us. Such feats are accomplished in not only familiar settings before those who know us well but also new, confusing situations in front of complete strangers. How is any of this possible?

Curious also is the degree to which we maintain relatively clear visions of ourselves as we move through our daily activities. That is, we are able to maintain feelings of personal coherence and self-direction at the same time that we embrace obligating relationships with other people, who usually have their own opinions of our character and commitments. As sociologist Georg Simmel (1971, 143–49) argued in a famous essay on "the stranger," most of us are reconciled to the fact that our social relationships never feature complete acceptance or immersion. In one sense we are *a part* of all that happens around us and indeed can only realize our possibilities as persons through the recognition and support that others provide. That set of public recognitions—defining who we are as participants and as persons—is commonly described as our *identity*. However, we also exist in our own private estimations, understandings that are never entirely equivalent to the ways that others see us. In that second sense

1

we have—or perhaps are—*selves*. We maintain our own visions of the world, and those perspectives ultimately keep us *apart* from the settings we inhabit. That tension—between the positions that others would grant us and those that we would give ourselves—is one of the most fundamental matters in the social sciences. That people find and accept their placements in the social world as much as they do is one portion of the "miracle" referred to above. That so many are forced to accept those placements on the terrible terms that are offered them is not only one of the tragedies of the human condition but also the challenge for a compassionate social science.

This book addresses the general issue of how people make sense of their involvements in the world and then behave toward others on the basis of those comprehensions. I will argue that there are different ways of making sense and different resources that are used in that process. My special interest is the tension that has been described above: between the locations that the world offers us and those that we envision for ourselves.

In addition to describing the different ways in which people are placed in the world, I will offer my own models of how those social standings are achieved. Some placements will be shown to be impositions of subjective imagination and desire (what I call "ascending meaning"); others are accommodations to the terms of otherness (what I call "descending meaning"). Most are the curious combinations that lie between these extremes. Most generally, my intention in this book is to show how comprehensible forms organize the movements of people through the world and how people's experiences of those forms are organized in ways that are equally coherent. In that context, this is a book about selves, societies, and emotions.

The question of how people find their places in the world has always been a fundamental theme of social science and, before that, of philosophy, religion, and literature. It persists as a guiding issue for those disciplines and defies resolution because of the vastness of its implications and the inherent complexity of the human condition. Arguably, that question becomes even more pertinent in our contemporary era, especially in those societies that are marked by what is sometimes called "advanced," "high," "late," or even "post" modernity. To cite the view of one prominent observer, sociologist Anthony Giddens (1990, 1991), modern relationships have become increasingly "dis-embedded" and abstract. If once-upon-a-time people managed their lives within the terms of relatively small, stable communities where face-to-face encounters were the dominant settings for meaning making now we have "relationships" with people we may meet once and never again, with those we have never encountered face to face, with faceless abstract organizations, and with the façades of personhood that ever-expanding media forms present to us. Increasingly, we communicate with people through phone calls, e-mails, text messages, webcams, and "tweets." We participate in online video games with players from across the world; we "vote" electronically for the reality show contestant of our choice; we invest money in a stock market and watch our standing rise and fall with the enthusiasms of the millions.

With even less response from the objects of our attention, we understand ourselves to be supporters of professional sports teams, members of celebrity fan clubs, contributors to interest groups, and advocates of political candidates. We feel ourselves to have relationships with the objects of our affection. We trust one television anchor and not another; we follow our favorite actors, musicians, and sports stars—or rather the versions of them that are presented to us—with ardor. By degrees our social connections have been lifted out of their local contexts. In all these ways our current habitation seems to be what Giddens (1991, 16) calls a "runaway world," where social and cultural formations are proliferating and then moving away from one another. By such processes, or so some argue, contemporary people are losing both their sense of being firmly placed in the world and the feelings of assurance that attend those placements.

As important as these qualities of fragmentation and change may be, this book explores the counter-thesis that most of us have not lost our footing entirely. We continue to have selves and identities, although the character of these formations—and the circumstances in which they are made—is now altered. Despite our differences, we behave in patterns that are, for the most part, recognizable to others, and we communicate in ways that make our intentions plain. We understand the world—and share those understandings—through publicly acknowledged formats. Amidst societies marked by increasingly large and mobile populations, social diversity, the proliferation of specialized cultural forms, and new organizations committed to reinventing themselves at every turn, there is still some measure of orderliness and a perception that "meaningfulness" still resides in the world. At least that is the emphasis that is taken in this book. To be sure, disorder, change, and even meaninglessness are fundamental aspects of existence. So are force and fraud. These matters will be considered in due course. However, my abiding concern is to discover how people achieve feelings of coherence and stability amidst the confusions of contemporary life.

FOLLOWING GOFFMAN

In the academic world, books begin where others end. This particular writing takes as its point of departure the contributions of sociologist Erving Goffman regarding the nature of human experience. Like many other writers who I will discuss in this book, Goffman was committed to understanding how people find their way in social settings. More precisely, he wished to describe what he called the "interaction order," the continual forming and re-forming of relationships between people as they encounter one another in face-to-face meetings (1983). Much of Goffman's writing focuses on the conditions or "organizing principles" that make possible these daily encounters. Part of that project means describing the social positions that people hold in these settings and the patterned relationships that exist between people in their capacities as position holders and as persons. In that sense Goffman wished to understand how all of us establish coherent identities before others. However, he also wanted to know how we inhabit those settings subjectively—that is, how we think, feel, and act in our capacities as selves. For such reasons, his work is a valuable point of entry for anyone wishing to integrate the objective and subjective aspects of experience.

That issue of how people inhabit circumstances of many types is central to the discussion of human experience that follows. On the face of it, such a topic is so wide-ranging as to make impossible any attempt to comprehend its various dimensions or even to say anything that has not been said a hundred times before. Better perhaps to read the "classics" of many disciplines and ponder the sayings of those now-distant authors. For that reason, the current book develops a much more limited theme that was given prominence in Goffman's book, *Frame Analysis* (1974). In that writing, which is commonly considered to be his masterwork, Goffman argues that social and cultural patterns that are, for the most part, not of our own making "frame" our experiences of the world—and of ourselves. These frames are essentially typologies of interpersonal encounters. When we "make sense" of the world, we fit its happenings to well-established models that society offers to us. In that way, particular occurrences are comprehended as instances of general types. We process our own, seemingly personal experiences of those events in much the same fashion.

The current book is presented as an extension of Goffman's general approach. In what follows, I argue that the idea of framing can be applied not only to social encounters but also to qualities of persons and to the placement of those persons in social situations (issues that are also central to Goffman's writing). In other words, I describe some additional things Goffman might have analyzed further with his framing perspective had he not died in the midst of his productive career at sixty. However, I also argue that there are other kinds of "frames" and "framing" besides the cognitive or conceptual constructs that are the centerpieces of Goffman's classic book. In that spirit, I try to show the pertinence of physical as well as symbolic patterns to the ways people operate.

Most generally, then, this book, like Goffman's, focuses on how experience is organized. As mentioned above, I place special emphasis on the typology of experience known as the *emotions*, which are shown to be both the results of a series of "framing judgments" as well as a set of labels or narratives that help people make their way through situations. My general position is that human consciousness is located at the intersection of many different kinds of patterns, some physical in character, others symbolic. Effectively, these patterns are frames that permit and channel the varieties of experience. As Goffman (1961b) emphasized, social life can be seen as a series of "encounters" that these contingent frames organize. And our privately managed behaviors can be understood as a succession of movements from one intersection of patterns to the next. Most of the book that follows is a spelling out of ways in which people make sense of those encounters. Ultimately, I develop the theme that experience is a progress through space and time that follows coherent sequences or "pathways"—models for being that connect current events with happenings in the past and future.

ARGUMENTS TO COME

One of my favorite professors in graduate school insisted that writers should never present the structure of their arguments too explicitly. Reading something manufactured with that earnest, plodding spirit is rather like seeing a person's body with the bones poking through the flesh. Writing, even of the academic sort, is not an office memorandum but rather an invitation to reflection. Readers should be encouraged, cajoled, and seduced—they should not be instructed.

That gentleman, no longer with us, was influenced deeply by the tradition of the humanities in which beautiful writing was the ideal. Truth, if such a term can be used in our suspicious contemporary era, was a conclusion people reached through their encounters with well-fashioned cultural expression. To be sure, that general point of view—that our subjective experiences of the world are founded on our encounters with symbolic form—is one prominent theme of the pages that follow. However, against that professor's directives, I set forth in the following pages an overview of the chapters to come. Like most social scientists, I believe that readers—at least of this sort of book—wish to know what it is the author is trying to accomplish and, on that basis, determine if the argument succeeds or fails. That disposition is especially pertinent for a project like the current one, which tries to expose at least some parts of the skeleton that lie beneath the flesh of human affairs. To accomplish that end, it seems appropriate to be both earnest (if such a term means being open and honest about the arguments being made) and plodding (if that means addressing the most familiar matters of life with the most ordinary examples in the least suspenseful ways).

Following this introduction, then, chapter 2, "Framing Experience," details the general approach that I will take in the remainder of the book. The initial portion of that chapter is devoted to an overview of the ideas that Goffman presents in *Frame Analysis*. The remainder of the chapter develops my own vision of how experience is organized. That model, what I call the "ascending-descending meaning perspective," is essentially an arrangement of five principal "fields of relationship" in which people locate themselves. It also describes two opposite processes they follow to appraise and develop their standings in those contexts. A special theme of the chapter is the different ways in which the concept of "meaning" can be understood and the implication of these different meaning systems for action and experience.

Chapter 3, "Selves as Projections of Personhood," considers the ways in which framing activities are applied to persons. The chapter begins with an analysis of the concept of the self as presented by the psychologist William James and explores the specifically social influences on self-development as described by sociologists George Herbert Mead, Charles Horton Cooley, and their modern descendants. Later portions of the chapter shift from descriptions of the cognitive self to descriptions of self-feeling. Seeking to integrate the above views, I develop a general treatment of selves as "projections" of personhood, processes of envisioning the roles that one will play in social settings. By such projections, people are carried into and through events.

Chapter 4 is titled "New Settings for Self Expression." Its general argument is that persons—and their behaviors—are judged also in terms of the settings in which those matters occur. That is, we use understandings of place and time to help us decide what—and who—is going on. The particular focus of the chapter is the new possibilities for self-expression that arise within the "virtual realities" that new media forms create. To put that issue into historical context, I discuss first the changing manifestations of selfhood in premodern, modern, and post-modern societies. The second part of the chapter describes three ways in which persons participate in contemporary media forms—as audiences of electronic selves, as producers of those visions, and as actors who communicate with one another in and around those settings.

Chapter 5, "Emotions as Forms of Self-Awareness," explores the viewpoint that emotions are patterns of awareness produced by the interaction between people's self-understandings and their interpretations of various kinds of circumstances. Focusing initially on the contributions of contemporary psychologists, I review some of the different ways that emotions and emotionality have been understood in that discipline. Using my ascending-descending meaning perspective, I try to integrate what is sometimes described as the dual nature of the emotions—that is, their status as both physical and symbolic realities. The central claim of the chapter is that emotions are the results of a series of "framing judgments," subjective appraisals of the character of situations. In that context, I provide a model that displays this process and indicates how some well-known emotions are related to one another. Those specific emotions are said to be "frames" in their own right.

Chapter 6, "Emotions and Social Order," focuses on how people experience their own placement in social relationships and express that sense of placement through emotions. To support my thesis, I discuss how emotions are both consequences of and contributing elements to our interactions with other people. The chapter begins with some comments on the different meanings of the term "social." The remainder is devoted to describing how these different understandings of the social are addressed in some well-known sociological theories of emotions. Once again, I try to integrate these different theories.

Chapter 7 is called "Dissatisfaction, Disorder, and Desire." People may seek comfortable placements in the world, but they also want to experience movement, excitement, and change. In that light, the chapter begins with a discussion of why disorder is a prominent—and indeed inevitable—feature of personal, social, and cultural relationships. Later portions provide a general theory of satisfaction and dissatisfaction—and more particularly, of pleasure and displeasure—and apply this theory to experiences of stability and movement. The chapter concludes with some comments on how social processes both discourage and encourage the anticipatory feelings called "desire."

The eighth and final chapter is called "Behavioral Pathways." In that chapter I try to show how basic human *behaviors* are framed. I argue that these behavioral frameworks operate as specialized pathways for experience. The chapter begins with a view of emotions as "currencies" or "tokens of exchange" that people use to gain and express social standings before one another. I describe four of those standings— privilege, engagement, subordination, and marginality. The chapter's key theme is the identification of some key interaction trajectories, or "pathways," that lead people to these standings. Four of these pathways—work, play, ritual, and communitas— are given special attention. My argument is that people entering these formats not only have some sense of how the interaction will unfold but also what their role will be in that interaction and what emotions will be relevant. In addition, each pathway is said to feature its own "emotion-sequence." In such ways, the chapter reproduces and summarizes the general theme of the book—publicly recognized formats for personhood, relationship, and behavior move people through space and time. In the final pages I discuss the problems societies create when they hold up certain pathways as ideals while ignoring or discouraging others.

COMMITMENTS OF THE AUTHOR

Creative work of every kind is marked by the dispositions of its producer. Makers decide consciously to confront certain issues and ignore others, work with some materials only, adopt specific styles of expression, and address distinctive audiences. Many times, these "decisions" are not made consciously but instead are consequences of what must be understood to be the proclivities and habits of the creator. Frequently also, there are various external "encouragements"—both social and cultural—to undertake certain kinds of work. And, it must be acknowledged, things are often done a certain way because the maker can manage no other way of doing them. At any rate, in the contemporary era, it has become fashionable for authors to declare at least some of their biases and limitations. Those limitations— some of which are described below—bear notice, not because the author's views are of any general interest but because they give the reader an overview of the specific *style* of reasoning that follows.

An integrative enterprise. The current book aspires to be "integrative" in its commitments and tone (see Boyer 1990). In other words, my task here is to position dispersed bodies of research and theory into frameworks that display the relationship of those studies to one another. On the one hand, this means considering research from different disciplines in the social sciences and, indeed, from outside the social sciences. On the other, it means valuing theoretical perspectives of many different types.

Bridging the humanities and sciences. Many important topics and issues—war, poverty, racism, and environmental degradation come to mind—are simply too important and too vast in their implications for any one discipline to handle. This is certainly the case for the extremely broad subject of the current book, the nature and circumstances of human experience. To be sure, one can choose to focus on experience—or, more narrowly, on emotionality—from the perspective of psychology, sociology, anthropology, biology, or any other discipline, but the results of an inquiry so constricted are only pieces of a much larger puzzle. Although the current book is written by a sociologist and thus tends to emphasize contributions for that discipline, it also signals the importance of research from the other social sciences, the natural sciences, and the humanities.

It is customary for social scientists to operate within fairly narrow theoretical traditions. To take the example of my own discipline, sociologists may declare themselves to be conflict theorists, symbolic interactionists, functionalists, or exchange theorists (to cite some common schools of thought) or, instead, to be the representatives of subtle, specialized versions of those perspectives. Those same sociologists may acknowledge themselves to be "positivists" rather than "constructionists," "postmodernists" rather than "modernists," interpreters of the "micro" order rather the "macro" order, and so forth.

The current writing represents an effort both to recognize and to transcend some of the above differences. Readers of a disputatious nature will be disappointed to find that in almost no case is one line of thought declared to be superior or correct and another simply ill considered or wrong. That conciliatory spirit is perhaps out of place in the academic world, where disciplines, subdisciplines, schools of thought, and even individual authors routinely trumpet their own virtues and decry or ignore other forms of work (see Abbott 2001). However, an integrative approach seems appropriate—to this writer at least—for broad-ranging subjects like selfhood and emotionality, which no one field or point of view can contain.

In that sense, the current work takes prominent arguments from psychology, sociology, anthropology, literature, philosophy, and other disciplines and then emphasizes what aspects of those arguments the author considers useful. Those ideas become centerpieces of the schemes that follow. What originality I claim is in the reconsideration and the theoretical integration of those perspectives.

Theoretical leanings. In a somewhat mocking reproof, Goffman (1974, 13) described his own writing as "mentalistic." That is, his work is filled with concepts (by which to see the social world in a new way) that are frequently elaborated in extensive lists or typologies. Most of his scholarly energy is spent explaining how daily behavior meshes with these characterizations.

The current book possesses similar limitations. I emphasize ideas and their implications, including the development of various categories of experience. As noted above, I hold that most of the world's occurrences can be interpreted as the intersection of patterns of different types, each of which seems marked by its own distinctive "logic." Much of the book is devoted to identifying the character of these different logics. None of this is said to deny the tremendous importance of empirical research or the generation of theory through summaries of human behavior. However—and somewhat in opposition to current scholarly trends—I believe in the possibilities of general theory, especially as this enterprise creates an array of concepts through which to see the world. Theories are both models (in the sense of organizing perspectives) and explanations (as descriptions of how one set of occurrences leads to another). This book emphasizes the former theme somewhat more than the latter.

I will also acknowledge here that I am very impressed with the theoretical diversity and vitality of the social sciences and see no need to categorize myself as belonging to one school of thought rather than another. Many of those different traditions appear at different places in the book. However, I should admit that Simmel, who sought to describe the basic "forms" of human association, has influenced strongly my own thinking about the human predicament. Although he was an extreme formalist, Simmel has in recent years been taken up as one of the progenitors of postmodernism (see Pescosolido and Rubin 2000; Weinstein and Weinstein 1993). That is because Simmel emphasized such currently popular ideas as the expansion, objectification, and decontextualization of culture; the "pluralization" of symbolically organized worlds; the importance of social interaction; and the imperfect intersection of personal forms with social and cultural forms (see Henricks 2006). In the spirit of Simmel and Goffman (who, in my view, carries forward Simmel's general approach), the current book tries to show how the human enterprise involves not only the erection and habitation of form but also the resistance to that which has been erected. Pointedly, I argue that the study of the formal and stable qualities of life is a route to understanding the alternatives to those qualities, specifically change, informality, and even formlessness.

Games as examples. A study of human experience has as its subject matter all kinds of behaviors and encounters. For a project so construed, examples can be taken from anywhere. Although I will use a range of examples in this book to make my points, I will rely especially on examples from games and sports. This is done partly because Goffman's own writing is dominated by what anthropologist Clifford Geertz (1983, 24) calls a "game analogy." But I do this also because games are familiar matters to most people (see Perinbanayagam 2006) and because much of my own writing has focused on the nature of human play and how that activity differs from other forms of expression (see Henricks 2006).

I could of course restrict myself to a relatively narrow set of playful activities to show how frames operate, as Gary Alan Fine (1983) has done in his noted study of role-playing games. Clearly, there are readers who prefer detailed ethnographies—featuring the language of the subjects involved in those settings—as ways of showing how human experience operates, and it is arguable that all the elements to be discussed in what follows are at issue in any one of those contexts. However, the purpose of the current book is to develop a vocabulary for describing situations of many types, and for that reason examples are taken from wide varieties of settings.

Audiences. Finally, I should mention the intended audience—and as a consequence, the writing style—of this book. As indicated, this book is presented primarily as a commentary on the possibilities for human relating. It seeks to describe patterns and processes that I propose are of some use to those who wish to characterize the architecture of experience. In that sense, it is directed toward any reader who is interested in developing his or her own view of how people operate. Because the book presumes no scholarly background with regard to these issues, it can be considered an introduction to them. However, as the reader will quickly discover, this does not mean that I will shy away from the complexities that are inherent to this topic, nor is my use of the term "introduction" intended to suggest that more advanced scholars—who tend to be specialists in distinctive fields of study—will not profit by reflecting on the lines of thought developed in other disciplines. For the uninitiated, the following pages are an opportunity to think *of* these fundamental matters. For those who are well versed, they are an opportunity to think *against* the models I am presenting.

Because of the multiple audiences that are addressed—and because the topic is pertinent to every moment of every life—I try to adopt a conversational tone in this writing and use examples of the most familiar sort. In addition—and as the reader will already have noticed—I often abandon third person, neuter pronouns for the language of "I," "we," and "you." That strategy seems appropriate for a topic in which no one writer can claim authoritative insight and where the encouragement to think about these issues deeply is much more important than any perspective the author supplies. That dialogical style is also consistent with my considered belief that the challenge of the modern social sciences is to return to—and reconsider—what is most basic about human relationships. In that enterprise, I take my inspiration from the fundamental enquiries—and the plain speaking—of the classic thinkers who are given some emphasis in the pages that follow (see also Mills 1959). In my opinion, every new venture starts with a backward glance. Scholarship is inevitably a rethinking of what has come before.

CHAPTER 2

FRAMING EXPERIENCE

This book discusses the ways in which people make sense of the world and then act on the basis of those understandings. To begin that discussion, consider the following example. A man approaches you on a city street and says something you don't understand. What just happened, and what should you do about it? A number of interpretations go racing through your mind. Perhaps the man is asking for help. Is he lost? Does he want money? Maybe the man is a foreigner who doesn't know the local language and customs. Perhaps he is hard to understand because he has a disability that affects his speech. Could he be emotionally disturbed? Is he disoriented by alcohol or drugs? Perhaps *you* are the one who is having difficulty hearing or is disoriented for the reasons stated above. Maybe it is just too noisy on the city street for you to catch what he said. All these are possible evaluations of an ambiguous event. Once you've decided what the person is trying to communicate, you can respond to him, if only to ask him to repeat his comments. Or you can decide to ignore his remarks and walk away.

All of the above interpretations presume that the man is attempting to communicate with you in earnest—that is, that he believes himself to be a petitioner of some type who is asking for your help. But what if things are *not* as they seem? Perhaps the petitioner is only pretending to be a person asking for something. Perhaps he has other ambitions in mind. You think of some possible explanations. Could our stranger be a con artist or pickpocket? That is, the encounter is possibly a distraction or ruse that will lead to the loss of some possession. Perhaps the mysterious conversation is a practical joke or trick of some type, somebody's response to a dare or an initiation rite for a club. Still another possibility is that *you* are being tested or subjected to some dramatic scenario that in a moment will be revealed and have everyone—including knowledgeable bystanders—laughing.

Could it be that you are unwittingly participating in some scientific study, perhaps about helping behavior in anonymous settings? Perhaps the whole affair is only a dream—or, quite differently, a daydream.

As will be shown, this question of how people make sense of situations was central to Goffman's *Frame Analysis*, and it is also the guiding concern for my own interpretations. In that spirit, the current chapter addresses three aspects of the preceding sentence. The first of these is the issue of what it means to say that something is a "situation." After all, aren't there innumerable sorts of occurrences going on at any time? How does a person decide to focus on just some of those happenings—and to see them as elements of a situation—rather than on the thousands of others that could claim one's attention? A second issue is what it means to say that something "makes sense." Is sense making essentially a cognitive affair, a process by which people somehow fit the happenings of the world into concepts they hold in their minds? Or are there other kinds of sense making, including some that feature primarily physiological patterns of recognition and response? Surely, experience is a not a simple affair but instead a complicated integration of different forms of awareness.

The third concern is *how* people make sense—that is, what roles they play in their own acts of sense making. Is sense making an activity that people recognize and regulate? Is it a process they conduct on their own terms, or are other, external factors also determinants of the "sense" that is made? To repeat all these questions in the most high-sounding language, do people manage the terms of their own existence, or is participation in the world—and our awareness of that participation—largely an accommodation to forms and forces that range across the moments of life and that we are relatively powerless to control?

It may seem that questions of the above sort are best left to professional philosophers and that other studies of experience—at least in the social sciences—should avoid them. My view is the opposite, for social theories always include tacit assumptions about these very matters. Indeed, I believe that the challenge for any study of experience is to show how the world is organized, how people become aware of their placements and movements in that world, and how they organize their responses to the happenings they behold. To begin the process of considering these matters, the first part of this chapter describes how Goffman answers these questions in *Frame Analysis*. I then offer my own extensions of those views.

GOFFMAN'S FRAME ANALYSIS

In establishing the foundations for *Frame Analysis*, Goffman (1974, 8) asks his readers to accept the following proposition: "I assume that when individuals attend to any current situation, they face the question: 'What is it that's going on here?'" As I've suggested above, this is no small problem, for all kinds of things are going on at every moment of our lives. In fact, there are so many of these that the problem of human existence becomes one of selecting a manageable set of these occurrences to focus on and use as reference points for behavior. And this problem is accentuated when we find ourselves in the company of other people who have their own patterns of attention and interest.

Goffman's answer to his own question is essentially this: people's experiences of the world are "framed" by socially supported definitions. These definitions—essentially conceptual devices all of us use to put our comings and goings into communicable formats—help us banish some of the uncertainties and ambiguities that are inherent to our interactions with others. Once we have decided that a situation is of a certain "sort," we can move ahead—or stay behind—with confidence. In other words, people must quickly comprehend the character of events so that they can operate assuredly within those events. This is particularly important in situations that are just beginning; are characterized by divisions of interest, belief, and skill; or are otherwise ambiguous. Once we've identified a situation—like my example of the man on the street—as a plea, a test, a con, a joke, a dramatic performance, the ravings of an unstable person, and so forth—we can orient ourselves to an ensuing chain of events.

Goffman's colleague at the University of California, anthropologist Gregory Bateson, was an important influence on the development of this perspective. Bateson (1972, 171–93) was interested in not only human cultural expression but also the patterned behavior of animals and the similarity between these two kinds of regularity. Observing zoo animals, Bateson was drawn to the issue of how creatures like monkeys are able to distinguish when certain behaviors are to be taken seriously (e.g., as "real" threats) and when those behaviors are recognized as being nonserious or playful. As Bateson described, the animals signify their intentions to one another through distinctive "play-faces," bodily gestures, and verbal calls. By such devices, they effectively reframe the encounter—that is, they indicate their intention to follow a sequence of behavior that will be of a certain type, rhythm, duration, and consequence. Thus, what looks like real fighting to an untrained human observer may be understood to be play fighting by the participants themselves. In Bateson's famous formulation, a bite is not a bite when it's a nip.

The issue of how people create and sustain the idea systems under which they live is a general theme of the sociological tradition known as symbolic interactionism (see Blumer 1969). However, Goffman's work sits uneasily in that tradition. Whereas symbolic interactionism emphasizes the role of individuals as active agents in the development of situational definitions, Goffman, at least in *Frame Analysis*, emphasizes the opposite view—that people do not interpret reality just as they choose. Drawing inspiration from the concept of culture as developed by anthropologists, he argues that social life should be understood as the recognition and habitation of publicly established meaning systems. In other words, people do not create their own interpretive schemes but instead employ well-established, publicly recognized frameworks. If all the participants in an encounter understand an activity in a similar way, then they can move through it with some efficiency. Everyone involved will have some sense for how the affair will start and how it will end, how long the whole process may take, what goals and manners are pertinent to the occasion, and what roles each of them must play. Once the encounter is over, the participants can remember it as an "event" of a certain type. They can go home and discuss it with family and friends, who in turn can tell their own stories about it coherently.

To illustrate this with one of Goffman's own examples, people who conclude that they are the victim or "butt" of a (relatively harmless) practical joke know that they should be a "good sport" about it by controlling their emotional reactions to the experience, not seek immediate retaliation, and allow the people "in" on the joke to have their moment of fun. Participants know that the ordeal should not last too long or be too painful, that bystanders should "keep a straight face" and not gang up on the victim, and that some gentle teasing or consoling words may be needed to restore equanimity. After it's over, everybody is expected to discuss the matter in a lighthearted fashion that makes plain the absence of "hard feelings."

At nearly six hundred pages, *Frame Analysis* is by far Goffman's longest and perhaps most difficult book. Its initial portions discuss the nature of framing and then catalog some of the different kinds of frames people use to comprehend their encounters. Subsequent parts focus on the ways in which frames are "anchored" in social structure and on the ways in which these frames may be disabled or otherwise fail to operate. A final chapter applies the idea of framing to the conversations that people have with one another, a theme that Goffman pushed forward in his final book, *Forms of Talk* (1981). A detailed summary of *Frame Analysis* at this point would sorely tax the reader's patience. For such reasons, I present in the following paragraphs Goffman's basic ideas about "frames" and list some of the different frameworks that people use. A discussion of "anchoring" follows that. I introduce other themes from the book in the chapters that follow.

Goffman's (1974, 10–11) concept of framing is built on the proposition "that definitions of a situation are built up in accordance with principles of organization which govern events—at least social ones—and our subjective involvement in them." The term "frame," he states, is simply "the word I use to refer to such of these basic elements as I am able to identify." In that light, he declares that people typically make a very basic distinction between two different kinds of circumstances: nature and the social world. The perspectives we take toward them he calls the two "primary frameworks." Natural frameworks are used to describe seemingly undirected, physically determined occurrences. Social frameworks describe matters that are thought to be products of human intervention and will.

Goffman's book is almost entirely about social occurrences—actions, encounters, and events that involve two or more people—but he is quick to point out that the two kinds of interpretive systems are both prevalent and may even collide with one another. For example, a traffic accident is both a physical and a social event. On the one hand, it sets off interpretations of what happens when large, fast-moving objects collide; on the other, it invites ideas about the mentality of the people operating the machines and of those who watch and respond to what occurred. Furthermore, he points out that some kinds of events are not well explained by either of these frameworks. Examples of hard-to-explain or mixed activities include what he calls the "astounding complex" (occurrences involving visitors from outer space, religious healing, and the like); the exhibition of seemingly impossible stunts (by acrobats, magicians, etc.); "muffings" (where the body slips from conscious control as in fainting or flatulence); "fortuitousness" (occurrences of incredible coincidence); and "tension" and "joking" (the uncomfortable overlay of idea systems, as in the treatment of nakedness in medical procedures). In all these cases, people try to place the occurrence into some publicly accepted idea system so that those participants (and bystanders) know how to respond appropriately to what is happening.

The reader might imagine that Goffman at this point lists the fundamental kinds of social encounters. However, he doesn't do this, nor does he describe some basic kinds of social behavior such as fighting, asking for help, giving orders, withdrawing support, and so forth. Instead, he moves to a discussion of how any social occurrence, which on the face of it looks like a fairly basic or straightforward affair, may in fact be transformed into something rather different—and therefore be the basis for a quite different interpretation.

Keys and fabrications. Probably the best-known section of Goffman's book is his treatment of "keys" and "keying." As noted above, Goffman shared Bateson's fascination with the ability of creatures to make very subtle discriminations in comprehending and executing behavior. An occurrence that looks like a fight may not be *quite* what it seems. For their part, humans have spectacular capacities to approach behavior from slightly different interpretive stances. Actions can be staged, fantasized, analyzed, written about, enjoyed retrospectively, practiced, dreaded, and so forth. Adopting a musical analogy, Goffman states that behaviors can be transposed into slightly different "keys." He then lists some basic keys, including "make-believe" (including such specific forms as playfulness, fantasy/daydreaming, and dramatic renditions); "contests" (essentially games of various descriptions); "ceremonials" (all manner of ritualized or formally administered movements), "technical re-doings" (a number of "run-throughs" that include simulations, rehearsals, exhibitions, replays, role playing, and experiments); and "re-groundings" (quasi-real events, as when a member of a royal family "serves" food at a homeless shelter). In other words, something that looks like a "real" fight—with possibly lethal consequences—may in fact be a play-fight between two good friends, a fight on stage with cardboard swords, a sporting event, a form of practicing or training, or even a historical reenactment.

The "keys" listed above are based on relatively "open" communication between participants and observers—that is, the people involved are operating with a shared understanding. What Goffman (83) calls the "fabrication" is a different kind of transformation. Fabrications are based on the "intentional effort of one or more individuals to manage activity so that a party of one or more others will be induced to have a false belief about what is going on." Some of those deceptions, he explains, are relatively benign: they do not harm the interests of the person who is being duped; indeed, the deceptions may help him. Examples of benign fabrications include various forms of "playful deceit" (e.g., practical jokes, surprise parties, and hoaxes done in the public interest); "experimental hoaxing" (i.e., forms of trickery and spying performed by scientists); "training hoaxes" (e.g., fire drills); "fabrications to test character" (e.g., ploys to check the loyalty and efficiency of employees), "paternal constructions" (done in the best interests of the child); and "purely strategic fabrications" (e.g., the accepted bluffs and feints of games).

Quite different are "exploitative fabrications"—chicanery that is intended to harm the interests of the person who is fooled. That list of frames (which will not be developed here) features cons, schemes, blackmail, and other forms of mischief and bamboozlement. Finally, Goffman notes that these patterns of misdirection and bamboozlement can go on within the person herself. Examples of this latter pattern include dreams, dissociated states, psychotic fabrications, hysterical symptoms, and hypnotism. All these cases make clear his general point that, although people sometimes agree on the definitions that will be in play, quite often patterns of disadvantage, deceit, and discord mark the search for common terms.

Laminations. When people *transform* situations through the use of keys and fabrications, they substitute one way of thinking about a situation for another. Sometimes, those transformations do not require much knowledge of the primary definition that is being transformed. For example, when we play board games like "Risk" or "Monopoly," we don't need to know much about the *real* military strategies and capitalist business practices on which these games are based. However, at other times we need to keep in our heads some knowledge of earlier situational definitions, and our actions become a "take" or "perspective" on those previous understandings.

An example of this is Simmel's (1984, 133–52) essay on flirting and the most artful practitioner of that act, the coquette. As I believe most people would acknowledge, being in love sometimes involves requests for affectionate attention. Flirting is a specialized form of such requesting, which features exaggerated expressions of romantic interest. Flirting can be done in earnest—that is, to give and receive affection from another; it can also be done just for fun or, rather, for the gratitude that comes from commanding the attentions of another. In its most heightened versions, however, flirting swings loose from such consequences and becomes an art form in itself. For Simmel, the coquette is a woman who practices this art with such elegance that the objects of her attention can never quite determine if she is serious. Her exaggerated but always ambiguous gestures and proclamations keep her admirers dangling in a state of confused desire. And the social form of flirting is best realized when both participants are equally skilled in these effusive, ambiguous displays. Are the two practitioners the least bit interested in one another romantically, or are they only trying to show how well they play the game of love? Who can tell?

In his essay Simmel does not consider the person who pointedly *pretends* to flirt in this artificial, high-toned way because he or she is actually quite serious about the other person. Such persons are playing at the play-form, perhaps because they do not wish to be hurt (by a rejection of "real" flirting) and because interaction based on silly high spirits is better than no interaction at all. However, complexity of that sort is Goffman's long suit. In that regard, he argues that people's understandings of their current actions and relationships stem from previous understandings about what has been going on to this point. Some of those understandings or "definitions" have perhaps been shared publicly. Other understandings of what people really think—or thought—about past events have to be surmised from their words and behaviors. In either case the task for interpreters is much the same: they must make judgments about the *kinds of knowledge they think other people have*. Because social relationships are often built off previous ideas about what was said, done, and thought at the time, definitions of situations may feature what he calls "layers" or "laminations."

That potentially terrifying degree of complexity is described by Thomas Scheff (2006, 42–43) as levels of "mutual mind-reading" that he sees as being an important basis of the social bond. Social relationships move forward with assurance when people believe that they know what others know. To illustrate this, Scheff recalls a fragment of a song from his childhood ("I know that you know that I know that you know" . . . that we're in love?). Readers with an appetite for this sort of thing are directed to Umberto Eco's "postscript" to his novel *The Name of the Rose*. There, Eco (1984, 32) describes the contemporary predicament

> as that of a man who loves a very cultivated woman and knows that he cannot say to her "I love you madly," because he knows that she knows (and that she knows that he knows) that these words have already been written by Barbara Cartland. Still there is a solution. He can say, "As Barbara Cartland would put it, I love you

madly." At this point, having avoided false innocence, having said clearly that it is no longer possible to speak innocently, he will nevertheless have said what he wanted to say to the woman: that he loves her, but he loves her in an age of false innocence.

Gratefully, most of life's interactions do not feature such complicated referencing. When we say, "Please pass the butter," we expect only that. But when we ask, "Do you think you have enough butter on your bread?" we are not really asking but rather insinuating and surely working off earlier assignations and resentments as well.

To help his readers understand this process of transformation and retransformation, Goffman offers images of "brackets," as used in mathematics and written discourse (254–55). Inside those brackets—or frames—certain understandings or "operations" are thought to occur. However, those bracketed patterns may be placed inside other brackets that have different rules of operation and thus effectively modify the meaning that would apply if only the first pattern were followed. The idea of using mathematical brackets to describe how people frame experience—and to note progressions in time—has been developed further by Baptiza (2003) and Scheff (2006, 87–88).

Anchoring. By this point the reader may have concluded that what Goffman offers us is a subtle and fluid perspectivism, a chameleon-like shifting of the meaning of events as people introduce one privately harbored understanding after another. Visions of Kurosawa's *Rashomon* apply. To be sure, different people can see a murder and rape, as in that film, in quite different ways, and even a seemingly harmonious relationship—like a friendship or marriage—can feature quite different "realities" for the persons involved. Anyone picking up a handful of modern novels will discover quickly enough that the isolation of the participants' thoughts and instances of failed communication that result from this state of affairs often haunt relationships. Misunderstandings, it seems, lead to other misunderstandings—and to the resentments that spring up when one's wishes are not honored.

Goffman probably understood these qualities of distance, failure, and incompletion as well as any social scientist ever has, but his theme—at least in *Frame Analysis*—is precisely the opposite point. Against the tremendous complexity, divisiveness, and ambiguity of the world, people are able to establish and then follow (together) lines of thought and action. They are able to do this not because people function as isolated individuals who somehow pool their insights but because they recognize each other as coparticipants in publicly acknowledged endeavors. We make our way through the social world as well as we do because there are some fairly basic—and widely shared—definitions that societies use to describe encounters. To be sure, few people can name and list these categories of human relating as Goffman does, though most of us get the gist of situations quickly enough. And once we have done so, we are able to draw conclusions about the directions of any particular event, its expectations for us, and the likely abilities and motives of the people we meet there.

Moreover, these interpretive frameworks do not "float free" as cultural categories that we can pull down and apply whenever and however we like. Quite the opposite: the understandings we follow are "anchored" in the material and social world. To quote Goffman's own language (247), the frameworks described in his book are

> not merely a matter of mind but correspond in some sense to the way in which an aspect of the activity itself is organized—especially activity directly involving social agents. Organizational premises are involved, and these are something cognition arrives at, not something cognition creates or generates. Given their understanding of what it is that is going on, individuals fit their actions to this understanding and ordinarily find that the ongoing world supports this fitting. These organizational premises—sustained in both the mind and the activity—is what I call the frame of the activity.

In such ways, Goffman carries forward Simmel's theme that the various forms of social interaction take shape as the logical workings-out of their own preconditions and premises. To be sure, any individual is capable of thinking about a situation in any fashion she chooses—images of Thurber's daffy character Walter Mitty or an eccentric street person come to mind—but idiosyncratic interpretations are usually blocked quickly by other people or are otherwise found to be untenable. In other words, our interpretations of the world tend to be more successful—and more satisfying—if we *adapt* them to the logic of the event that is unfolding before us and when the other people involved reaffirm our judgments.

In the first instance, then, using models for behavior and interpretation that are in common currency and that seem to fit the "logic" of the event is helpful. However, interpretation is anchored in other ways as well. To illustrate this with an example, consider the ways in which a game of chess is "made real." Chess—at least in its face-to-face version—is facilitated by such material elements as playing pieces, a designated playing board, and a surface to hold this equipment. There must be recognized rules for the activity as well as two players who know something of those rules. Indeed, the players should have some preexisting skill in the movement of the pieces. At the very least, they must share a psychological disposition, specifically a willingness to play each other at that time. A group of spectators, with some knowledge of chess, may help reaffirm the players' commitment to start and then continue the game. In such ways the game is *realized* for the participants, if reality means that a particular way of looking at the world is put into operation. When people come together to conduct an activity, they bring to that situation the legacy of who they have been as persons—and as practitioners of the form in question—a range of material objects, and a set of cultural directions for their performance in that occasion. These elements transcend the moments of their interaction. That is, in almost every case, these objects and patterns exist before the event occurs and continue to exist after it ends.

Moreover, events are pushed forward by their own sequencing devices—sets of cultural markers or symbols that Goffman calls "episoding conventions." For example, when we go to the theater the official gatekeepers allow us into the building only within a certain span of time before the play begins. We see the soon-to-be audience bustling through the lobby, all dressed up and chatting in animated ways. We are ushered into the auditorium and find our seats. Suddenly, the room darkens, the crowd quiets, and a vast curtain is drawn. The play begins. All these elements make real the sense that we are at the theater. The darkened room keeps our attention focused on the brightly lit stage. Actors parade across that stage and speak in artificially loud voices. Usually they speak to one another, but sometimes they break that pattern by talking—in an even more oddly elevated way—to themselves, something that is not permitted in regular life. Once in a while, they move to the front of the stage and offer knowing comments—again, in a very stylized way—to the audience. At various points the curtain is drawn, the lights come up, and the crowd returns to its bustle. Most human events, it seems, use tangible devices—bells, whistles, sirens, clappers, altered tones of voice, changes of posture, movements of officials in and out of spaces, changes in lighting, and so forth—to announce that the event as a whole—or merely some segment of that event—is beginning, is over, or has moved into a different version of itself.

Every space and portion of life—or so it seems—has its regimens. When our theater crowd moves to the lobby, they find that only certain behaviors are permitted (perhaps no smoking) and that queues have already formed to obtain refreshments and use the restrooms. Each of those destinations is organized in its own way. Using certain stock expressions, we tell our companions that we are going to one or the other of those locations. They seem to understand what we will do there and why we have chosen to go. They seem confident that we will rejoin them after a certain period of time. Again, the point here is that we are led through the moments of living by a support system of established cultural, social, and material configurations. These configurations constrain our choices, but they also make it possible for us to imagine those choices in the first place and then to make those visions real. As Goffman puts the matter in his book *Interaction Ritual*

(1967, 3), his interest in the sociology of occasions is "Not, then, men and their moments. Rather moments and their men."

To summarize, Goffman's sociology is an account of how people move within and between a series of situations that are effectively little worlds (see also Collins 2004). When we enter one of these settings, we put on the costumes, gather the equipment, and adopt the mannerisms that are deemed appropriate. We are able to do this assuredly because there are a limited number of publicly identified—and thereby communicable—formats for situations. The ritualized directives of those formats transcend (in space and time) our uses of them. By such processes smaller elements—like individual roles, specific types of encounters, and even narrow "strips" of behavior—are set into wider patterns of meaning. Such meaning systems are the vehicles by which we characterize others and are characterized by them. They allow us to converse with one another and stay focused on joint endeavors.

As individuals, we cannot escape or modify these public frameworks in significant ways, and our paltry efforts at creativity and uniqueness are always evaluated in those terms. We spend much time and energy pondering strategies that will accomplish the goals that each particular world holds out to us. When our actions are over, we usually rely on that world's terms to determine whether we succeeded or failed. Whatever strategies we choose and ends we attain, those practices have already been defined publicly as acceptable or unacceptable ways of behaving in settings of that type. Within such predefined occasions people "encounter" one another. Understood in this context, human interaction is less a bubbling up of playful ingenuity than it is a practiced maneuvering along well-worn public walkways.

Beyond Goffman. Goffman's *Frame Analysis* is one of the classics of modern sociology because it demonstrates, in a way that is both imaginative and powerful in its implications, how individual experience is located in socially supported contexts. Of course, that book—and Goffman's writing more generally—has had its critics (see Ditton 1980; Manning 1992; Lemert 1997; Fine and Smith 2000). Goffman's approach is sometimes said to overemphasize processes of consensus building and normative regulation—the so-called "miracle of social order" referred to in the opening lines of this book—and to deemphasize the themes of power and privilege that influence the character of these public definitions and generate all kinds of resistance to their establishment. Some critics see his portraits of the cultural forms that people use as being an overly static view of how people actually behave. In that light, one commentator (Sharron 2000) has dubbed Goffman's book "Frame Paralysis" because it takes the themes that Goffman says he cares about—that is, people's comings and goings in the ever-changing moments of life—and then shoves them into a set of frozen conceptual models for how such people *should* think and behave. Others (see Gouldner 1970) have pointed to the somewhat culture-bound character of Goffman's ideas. Does Goffman's writing reflect a hyperawareness of the conditions of late-twentieth-century industrialized societies, which featured capitalist economies, large-scale bureaucracies, and individualist mythologies? Perhaps people should not be seen as crafty, self-interested actors who perform before others and try to build fragile agreements with them. Still others criticize Goffman's heavily cognitive emphasis. Do people really operate on the basis of these "definitions" of events, roles, identities, and so forth, or is social participation just as much a physical or even sensual affair?

My interest here is not to defend Goffman's writing against such claims; instead, I want to show how his general approach can be pushed forward in a way that addresses at least some of these concerns. Some of these "extensions" Goffman addressed clearly in his other books. Some he recognized implicitly but did not develop in his writing. Some he would not have approved.

WHAT IS IT THAT'S GOING ON HERE?

Consider for a moment the example of a woman walking along a city street. What kinds of things are occurring as she makes her way? To say that walking is simply a physical act, a case of putting the body into motion is easy enough. In that sense, how a person walks is a biomechanical event. Each of us has a distinctive gait based on length of legs, flexibility of muscles and joints, the structure of the foot, height and weight, age, sex, and so forth. Add to this the physical condition of our walker: she may be tired, have a sore foot, or be nursing a cold. All of these matters are "going on" as she makes her way.

What about the physical environment that is the setting for her movements? Whether the weather is hot or cold, rainy or windy, or too dark to see clearly influences dramatically how our walker proceeds. The challenge of going uphill or down, the roughness of the pavement, and the prospect of that pavement's being covered by ice and snow also influence her. Consider also the physical artifacts our walker possesses. Do large packages or a heavy coat encumber her? What kind of shoes is she wearing?

The cultural definitions for walkers in her society and the current "situation" in which she finds herself represents still another range of circumstances. A mature person is expected to walk differently than a child; a woman may be held to different standards than a man. Furthermore, a woman in professional attire walking during working hours may be expected to conduct herself differently than the same woman in leisure attire at night. Such public visions for our own and others' behavior guide most of us. We have learned—sometimes painfully—how to behave before others. Do these codes "exist"? Are they "going on"?

Yet another set of events concerns the social behaviors that are unfolding. Is our woman walking alone or in the company of friends? Are other people on the street, and how are they behaving? Will she have to greet some of these people and avoid others? To be sure, she can fail to acknowledge a person she knows, but snubbing a person is quite a different matter from ignoring a building or a mailbox. Can the resulting social practices—that affect the way she stands and moves—be said to be occurring now?

Finally, there are the myriads of psychological preoccupations. Is she feeling rushed or anxious? Is the setting familiar to her, or does it demand unusual attention? Is she going to an important meeting or home to relax? Does she enjoy walking on city streets or detest that activity every step of the way?

As the reader can see, the seemingly simple act of walking is a quite complicated event that involves great ranges of occurrences. Experience is the process of becoming aware of such occurrences and of our relationship to them. As our walker moves down the street, she realizes that her feet are hurting, that the pavement is slippery, that she is late, that a person ahead of her is acting suspiciously, and so forth. Suddenly, her attention shifts from present-time circumstances— what is happening before her now—to considerations of past and future. She tries to anticipate how the meeting she is approaching will play out. She broods about some ill-chosen remarks she made yesterday to a colleague.

Consciousness finds its end points in these ways. Sometimes our experiences of the world proceed without our being especially conscious of the processes that are occurring or even of the steps we are taking to address these matters. Other reflections—perhaps a sense that the weather is turning cold or an image of our child playing at home—we pull into awareness and subject to all the scrutiny of which our species is capable.

Are all of the above described matters "real"? Some readers may be inclined to accept as real only the physical aspects of the world, others only the happenings of mind. The view that I maintain in this book is that all of them are real enough—that is, that they can be recognized as patterned occurrences and those patterns have demonstrable consequences for the ways people think, feel, and act. Generations of social scientists have labored to demonstrate that cultural and social patterns are real (in their own ways) and that those realities stand beside bodily, environmental, and psychological patterns. Those "five fields of relationships," as I call them, will be important to the discussions that follow.

KEEPING ONE'S FOCUS

Most remarkable is the speed and fluidity by which people notice what is occurring. Psychologist Mihaly Csikszentmihalyi, in his own studies of human experience, has pondered some of the possibilities for human awareness. Basing his calculations on information theory, Csikszentmihalyi (1991, 28–29) suggests those possibilities in the following way. Most humans are able to manage about seven "bits" of information—visual stimuli, distinctive sounds, and so forth—at any one time. The mind can jump from one organized "set" of these seven bits to another in about one-eighteenth of a second. Making no allowances for weariness or inattention, it follows that people can process about 126 bits a second, 7,560 bits per minute, or nearly one-half million bits per hour.

Because people have such inherent abilities to be alert to their surroundings, that they stay focused on any one line of behavior as well as they do seems miraculous. And the challenges of living in a postindustrial society, where people are exposed to a firestorm of electronically generated signs, sounds, and images that request their attention at seemingly every waking moment, surely compound these difficulties. How do people maintain their concentration? Why is attention deficit disorder not more prominent than it is?

Such questions have been central to Csikszentmihalyi's (1975, 1991) own studies of "flow"—that quality of experience in which people are engaged only with the immediacies of the moment and keep their attention riveted on the task before them. Based on his observations and interviews with practitioners of a variety of activities—including surgeons, rock climbers, chess players, and artists—Csikszentmihalyi concludes that people keep their concentration best when—among other factors—their abilities match the level of the challenges that lie before them. Too much or too little challenge causes one's attention to drift—toward anxiety (in the case of overstimulation) or boredom (the case of understimulation).

The issue of how people stay focused on a chosen line of behavior is also a key theme in Goffman's writing. In his book *Encounters* (1961b), he describes the factors that help people stayed engaged and even "have fun" in social situations. To accomplish this end, he stresses the degree to which those situations can be seen as "games."

For Goffman (1961b, 19) games are "world-building activities" in which people voluntarily adopt a restricted field of vision and follow specialized norms. Such norms include "rules of irrelevance," whereby certain themes and issues are deemed inappropriate to the activity at hand, and "rules of realized resources," whereby certain elements are defined—or redefined—as appropriate elements or themes of play. Thus, for an informal game of baseball, the external social status of the participants, the food they just ate, or the cost of their mitts is deemed irrelevant. Oppositely, a rock or piece of wood becomes newly "realized" as first base or an out-of-bounds marker.

In such ways games exhibit a quality of "make-believe" that people impose on many of life's moments. Make-believe is not simply fantasy, for the activity of the game is as "real" as any other human activity; rather, it is the sense that people are given permission to be and do certain kinds of things in this setting that would have little credence in the other moments of their lives. Indeed, it is not simply "permission," for people are obligated to act in these ways if the game is to go forward: players must accept the responsibilities of being shortstop or catcher, take their turn at bat, offer encouragement to teammates, and, more generally, take the whole affair "seriously." Not to do so is to be a "spoilsport," someone who declares the occasion unimportant or ridiculous and thus destroys the social pretense that is the game. Deviants of that sort are much more dangerous than "cheats," who curiously reaffirm the importance of the game by wanting to win so badly that they are willing to use any method to do so (see Huizinga 1955, 11). In that sense games—like most other social occasions—are moral orders. They are bounded events when people pledge to follow publicly agreed-upon lines of action.

Although Goffman emphasizes that games—and, by extension, most social situations—are cut off from other activities by this framework of rules, he is clear that these little worlds must also be guarded from outside activities and concerns. In that light, his most distinctive contribution is his concept of "transformation rules." As he argues, participants also develop and employ rules that help begin—and end—the game and handle the inevitable claims of the outside world that threaten to disrupt its processes. As he (1961b, 29) notes, when a guest at a British country house asks, "Anyone for tennis?" that "anyone" does not include the butler and the maid. Instead, there are rules about inclusion/exclusion and other transitional practices to help the event get started. And although people's social status in the outside world is not supposed to be addressed directly in playful events, it often is, as in seating arrangements at dinner parties or by orders of precedence in play.

Even more interesting is his point that procedures must be put in place in order to keep external matters from breaking into or even destroying the frame. Because we know that these interruptions will happen from time to time, rules of this type are sometimes stated at the outset or are otherwise made explicit. Such guidelines may include prohibitions against answering telephone calls or discussing "business" during the game or feature rituals of consolation and teasing to soothe injured—or, conversely, overinflated—psyches. As the reader can see, Goffman's general point is that people live in many different—and intersecting—social worlds. For each world to maintain its integrity—and to ensure that it will continue to dominate the person's attention—participants must enact boundary-maintaining procedures.

However important this framework of rules may be, keeping people focused—or helping them have "fun"—is not enough. Human engagement is also facilitated by various *situational determinants*—environmental and sociocultural factors that make possible certain kinds of interaction and block other kinds. In that light, Goffman argues that people stay focused better when they are placed directly in another's gaze (e.g., face-to-face across a table or in an intimate embrace). Another person not only responds to and monitors our behavior (thus keeping us "in line") but also reaffirms—or disaffirms—the importance of what we are doing. Similarly, games may entrance us when they are institutionalized (in a fashion that presumes their legitimacy, even if it is only in their status as "games") and when they present us with sets of interesting challenges. However, pleasurable engagement also depends on two additional factors: "uncertainty of outcome" and "sanctioned display."

Much like Csikszentmihalyi, Goffman argues that people seek some optimal balance between familiarity, which can be boring, and novelty, which can be disorienting or stressful. Thus, games are structured to produce manageable levels of competitive tension and uncertainty of outcome. Commonly, this is accomplished by procedures to equalize the strength of opposing sides, to allow luck to affect the outcome, and to alter the course of lopsided games. Every child knows what it means to pick even sides or make one team play with a "handicap." However, even perfect equality of competition and uncertainty of play—as the example of a coin-flipping contest illustrates—are not enough to sustain interest. Ideally, games showcase not only skills, such as physical and mental abilities or traits of character, but also personal and social identities that have some currency in the wider world.

Furthermore, people routinely sweeten their encounters by introducing "stakes," or external incentives that specify the relationship of the game to outside identities and life opportunities. Besides monetary stakes, there are other common forms of risk (e.g., threats to physical safety or social reputation). The level of these stakes must be set carefully. Stakes set too low will not keep people motivated through the more boring moments of play; stakes set too high will create degrees of anxiety that effectively distract the players. In other words, the best games are those that draw people into somewhat curious, uncertain situations that display or otherwise put at risk qualities or possessions that are useful in the wider world. In such ways Goffman develops the theme that the play-world exists at a strategic distance from the other settings of life. Some themes are brought in, some are left out, and many others are transformed to make our experience of them seem fresh and alive.

Goffman is famous for his ingenious use of metaphors—social life as drama, as information game, as asylum, as ritual, and so forth—but he was well aware of the limitations of these comparisons. Social life is not, in the final analysis, a game; however, forms of human interaction and organization do display game-like features. Thus, even a bureaucratic organization uses rules (of irrelevance, realized resources, and transformations), problematic tasks, competitive formats, exclusive social memberships, external incentives, and so forth to keep people focused on their business. These limits, uncertainties, and rewards—the setting and direction of which is the art of management—are the structural conditions of human interest.

All these external constraints and encouragements are not happenstance affairs; instead, they are built into that setting as publicly recognized outcomes and are supported by established social agents and procedures. When we win a large amount of money in a poker game, it is understood that the other players will pay off and that the payment should be in "real money" that can be used at occasions outside the game. To say all this is only to repeat Goffman's general theme that the momentary events of life—such as our poker game—are tied or "anchored" to other moments by the use of social and cultural forms that allow one to pass from one setting to the next. Those transcendent forms are considered next.

APPRECIATING CONTEXT

Goffman's somewhat undeclared challenge to his readers, as Scheff (2006, xi) argues, is to come to terms with the contexts of their own awareness. We attend to the never-ending flow of occurrences that pass before us by placing them into conceptual arrangements, or "definitions," that we impose on those events. Equipped with such perceptual filters, we notice some things with much acuity and disregard others entirely. Typically, we are unaware of the many implications of the perspectives we are using or, indeed, that we are using perspectives at all!

The idea that people "know" the world through their own perceptual systems was made famous in philosophy by Kant. The view that people can become aware of those perspectives (and perhaps move past these to less mediated forms of subjectivity) is associated with the writings of Husserl. Many writers, including the philosopher Schütz and sociologists Berger and Luckman, developed the position that societal arrangements mark heavily these systems of personal perception. Like many other members of his discipline, Goffman operated with a kind of sociological Kantianism, the belief that we format experience with patterns of conception that our host societies supply to us. Furthermore, he was influenced by a theme that runs through the writings of Hegel, Marx, the American pragmatists, and many contemporary philosophers. Namely, people do not simply regard the world from a distance and strategically "use" its forms; rather, they live deeply inside that world, and their actions shape its character.

I do not wish to review here the history of philosophical opinion on these matters, though some of those views will find their way into the chapters that follow. Instead, I want to place some of the previously introduced ideas into a general discussion of the ways in which "occurrences"—both *processes* we see going on around us and those that have taken more or less stable form as *objects*—are placed into "contexts." Those contexts are patterns that help us identity the elements of those occurrences and tell us how to deal with them. My argument is that people place occurrences into contexts in at least four ways: (1) by recognizing them to be elements of identifiable "events"; (2) by recognizing their connection to occurrences in other, external events; (3) by recognizing them in terms of "structural" patterns that transcend those events; and (4) by employing ideas of time—that is, by seeing how they are connected to past and future occurrences.

I'll begin by citing a truism of anthropology. Human beings have a special ability to envision the character and implications of the "situations" in which they find themselves. This ability—which allows people to step back and reflect on circumstances in an abstract, dispassionate way—is called the capacity for "displacement" (see Friedl 1981, 71). Many species, or so the argument goes, have their consciousness centered on a concrete, sensuous present. They move through their environments by responding to the immediate needs and urges of their bodies and by confronting the challenges that appear before them. Much of their behavior is said to be sudden and unreflective, the expression of well-established biological programming.

Humans may not possess some of the wonderful sensitivities of those species, but we can move or displace consciousness into less action-focused modes. That is, we can think about our situation—and our position in that situation—without becoming aroused or motivated to respond. Moreover, we can envision that situation as a matter of its own sort, which may or may not involve us directly. In a related way we can redirect consciousness toward objects and events that are no longer occurring (or at least toward our memories of those events) and toward things that have not yet happened (or, again, toward our mental images of those possible futures). Yet, more impressively, we can turn consciousness toward entirely imagined scenarios, events that have never happened and never will. In such ways we think of things that are absent or nonexistent as easily as we do of things that are happening now. However, our greatest ability may be our capacity to think about the processes we are following to create those visions in our minds. Not only can we become conscious of some of the frameworks we use to categorize and analyze happenings, but we can also become aware of the experiences we are having while we are making those mental calculations. And with the use of widely shared symbol systems, we can communicate something about those forms of awareness to other people.

By such processes all of us attribute complex kinds and levels of meaning to events. We do not simply act and react; instead, we ponder the implications of our actions and then readjust those actions in term of our thinking. Frequently—and with an importance that cannot be overestimated—we decide to take no action at all. In other words, we employ—and then inhabit mentally—fully fledged visions, models, or templates that organize how we will move through the event at hand. With that background, let me say something about each of my four points. And to make my points plain I'll use an example that may be familiar to many readers, the goings-on of a professional baseball game.

Connecting occurrences to events. A first way in which occurrences are "contextualized" is through their being recognized as constituent elements of the events in which they are found. This viewpoint—that aspects of situations are set into broader definitions of situations—is a key theme for Goffman as well as for Scheff (1997), who describes it as the "part/whole" analysis.

To begin our example, imagine that you are seated in the bleachers at a baseball game and you have just heard the home-plate umpire shout out the word "Strike!" and watched him raise his arm in an exaggerated way. That action, what Goffman calls a little "strip" of behavior, is meaningful only to those who have some knowledge of baseball. Indeed, to understand what a "called strike" means, one must know what a "pitch" is and understand that the umpire's action is part of a longer interaction chain involving the umpire and three other characters: the pitcher, batter, and catcher. That interaction sequence—which features the taking of a "stance" (by pitcher and batter), the "wind-up," the "pitch," the "take" (by the batter), the "catch," the umpire's "call," and the "return throw" to the pitcher—is the central unit of baseball and occurs a couple hundred times each game. However, that unit is itself part of a wider unit called a "time at bat" that may involve many pitches. The "time at bat" is, in turn, one component of an "inning," which itself is a fundamental part of a game.

In much the same way the physical objects used in the game—such as balls, bases, and uniforms—take on their best-known meanings only when interpreted in this game context. The same can be said for valued skill sets (like throwing a curve ball), positions on the field (like first-base coach), arcane rules and terms (like a "balk"), or distinctive behaviors (like the "stealing" of the catcher's signs by a runner at second base). Like our theater patron who applauds a famous actress at her first appearance on stage, buys refreshments at the end of each act, and uses the restroom, most of us find that the little behaviors of life tend to be coherent responses to the happenings of particular events.

Connecting occurrences in events to occurrences outside events. I've argued that people impute meaning to occurrences—both objects and processes—by seeing the connection of these to the broader events in which they happen. However, they also locate the meaning of those occurrences by seeing their relationship to other kinds of things that are going on in the world outside the event. The reader may recall that both Simmel and Goffman emphasize the degree to which events—like parties or games—are not isolated but rather semipermeable worlds. Some of the issues, objects, ideas, and customs from settings outside the game may be brought into that "magic circle"; others are kept out. When these matters are brought in, often they are redefined and then re-presented in altered ways, such as in a lighthearted or teasing fashion. How these external concerns are treated is the subject of Goffman's analysis of "rules of irrelevance," "rules of realized resources," and "transformation rules" that were described above. These specified linkages make clear the relationship of the event to the outside world. As I've said, they "anchor" it and make it "real" in the wider world's terms.

Although Goffman does not develop this point in *Frame Analysis*, it should be emphasized that events also sustain their distinctive identities through what post-modernists call the "presence of absence" (see Derrida 1981). That is, participants in an event usually know that other people have been pointedly excluded from that setting, that other commitments have been set aside for the duration of the event, and that they are allowed to behave in ways not normally permitted. This sense of exclusivity and difference gives the event much of its character and dynamism.

An interpretation of this sort is pertinent to our baseball example. As we loll in our seats, we are quite aware that we could be attending to more pressing matters. We know that many people cannot afford the tickets we purchased and that others who can are now at work. We are conscious of the various activities that are going on around the game—the directing of traffic, the parking of cars, the selling of hot dogs, the amplified voices of the announcers, and so forth. These give the game a curious excitement and importance. We gaze at the spectators in our section of the crowd to see what they are doing and how they are dressed. After the game is over we watch them head homeward. We know that we will be able to read about the game's occurrences in tomorrow's sports pages or hear that "news" discussed on television. We anticipate that the matter will be treated with some seriousness, and we look forward to hearing official media representatives tell us what we already know. All this makes us feel that we are attending something special. More profoundly, it makes us feel that the event we just witnessed was "real," for surely it must be real if so many people declare it to be so.

Connecting occurrences in events to structural patterns. Another important way in which events are anchored and given meaning is through their connections to structures that enable and regulate those events. Those firmly established patterns—which are of several types—are frameworks to which people are committed. When people participate in an event, they honor and enact those frameworks.

To return to the example at hand, "a baseball game" is quite different from "the game of baseball." The former is an occurrence in space and time. The latter is a pattern of culture, featuring a set of rules for activity of this type and a vast range of "lore" about the history of the game and its players. Moreover, our baseball game is understood to be an instance of "sport," as that social institution is practiced in a particular society. Our baseball game is also an event in which recognized cultural artifacts—bats, bases, uniforms, and the like—are employed. These artifacts are objects that exist before the game begins and after it ends. Indeed, the umpire puts particular balls "in play." In the same way, players and the field itself are only potential elements of games until the umpire shouts "play ball."

We should also emphasize that the participants in our professional game do not just "happen" to be there; rather, they hold clearly defined roles in organizations that are equally well defined. Those organizations are elements of a wider structure, a league. Our umpire is part of an umpire's association. His activity on the field is also his occupation. That occupation is both a source of income and a crucial element of his wider identity. Commitments to family and friends buttress that identity. Although it may no longer be common for the crowd to shout that the umpire should be "killed," it is still the case that he—like the other participants in the game—feels a great deal of pressure to perform his role well. His activities must be seen in this much wider context.

Connecting occurrences to past and future occurrences. Events are not snapshots of activity but rather movements of people though space and time. And definitions of situations commonly include directions for those movements and incorporate ideas about proper beginnings, middles, and ends. Participants are typically aware of this model for their activity and judge its progress in those terms. Moreover, any occurrence in an event tends to be evaluated as part of a series of occurrences. There are things that have already occurred, things that are occurring now, and things that are projected to occur in the moments ahead. In that light, Goffman's guiding question for situations—what is it that's going on here?—should be amended to include concerns with past and future. That is, what is it that *was* and *will be* going on here? At any rate, it should be apparent that people contextualize their activities with ideas of time, and that these time frames can involve a few seconds or many years.

Certainly, our baseball game illustrates these matters. The "time at bat" that I referred to above is composed of a series of pitches. A called "strike one" is a matter of little consequence; a called "strike three" is an entirely different affair. "Innings" are not simply game units; they are numbered. An individual game is commonly part of a three- or four-game "series"; the "season" is composed of a defined number of games. People understand this progression clearly, and occurrences toward the end of games are usually accorded more attention than those in beginnings or middles.

In a similar way participants understand their own activity as a movement in time. Our umpire, like the other participants, surely sees his job as part of a career. That career may have its ups and downs, but such an idea typically features the expectation that one will be moving toward positions that feature higher levels of pay, status, and responsibility. Such notions of progress apply to our sponsoring organizations as well. Successful organizations prominently display banners that indicate championship seasons as well as a variety of other artifacts—monuments, plaques, photos, and so forth. Their purpose in doing so is to make clear to their patrons that they are entering "storied ground." Unsuccessful teams—and especially their patrons—grumble noisily about the years that have passed since they were champions. Baseball, as most people know, is awash with statistics. Those records permit rough comparisons between contemporary and past players as well as set standards for future generations to live up to and then surpass.

Through the four processes described above, people displace their awareness to matters that surround or "transcend" the settings in which they find themselves. On the one hand, this practice is a flight from the concrete, intimate experiences that many creatures know. On the other, displacement can be seen as a process of "placement," a relocating of the subject in much more expansive—if more abstract—circumstances. For humans, life is considered to be "meaningful" in ways that most other creatures cannot imagine.

THE MEANINGS OF MEANING

To this point, I've emphasized how people interpret occurrences by placing their perceptions of those occurrences into systems of concepts or ideas. To decide what something "means," we place that something into a context or pattern that makes clear its relationship to something else. By discovering and applying those patterns, we make or *impute* meaning to the things we've identified.

But is this the only way in which meaning is made? Are there other forms of "connection" between the elements of the world that do not depend on people's uses of ideas to mark their existence? And if there are more or less coherent connections between those aspects of the world, is it possible to say that those relationships are "meaningful," even if the people involved do not understand what is happening in them?

In the following section I argue briefly that the terms "meaning" or "meaningfulness" can be expanded to describe a general quality of relationship that exists between two or more elements of the world. One thing is said to be meaningful to another when that former element can be recognized through patterns possessed by the latter. Consistently with what I've argued above, I believe that there are five primary "fields of relationships" that are used to map occurrences: the psyche, the body, the environment, sociality, and culture. Things "make sense" when they are fitted to established patterns operating in those fields.

I am also claiming, controversially, that meaningful relationships are of two general types: symbolic and physical. My argument is that, just as there is the sort of meaning in which people place events into existing idea systems—and then try to respond to the resulting understandings—so there are processes of recognition and response that occur in unrecognized, involuntary, and almost entirely *physical* ways. Said differently, I believe that meaningfulness is not just a matter of *conception* but also of *sensation*. To take this viewpoint is to suggest that there are meaningful occurrences that go on in the world that we humans—at least in our capacities as consciously aware subjects—know little about. Let's look first at three fields of relationship that feature primarily symbolic meaning, and later we will consider those more mysterious, physical matters.

Fields of symbolic meaning. The first of these symbolic meanings is *cultural* meaning. As I claimed in my example of the woman walking along a city street, I believe that culture "exists" as the publicly accessible patterning of information. When we look up the definition of the word "apple" in a dictionary or consult some mathematical formula in a physics textbook, we are acknowledging that one concept can be recognized—or, perhaps better, "cognized"—in terms of other concepts. I'm not claiming that these concepts and their linkages are equivalent to the physical elements to which they often refer—that is, that our word "apple" is the same as a tangible apple. Nor am I arguing that cultural idea systems provide some tightly specified and logically interrelated set of concepts that effectively define all that goes on in the world. (Postmodern theories of culture have shown our public meaning systems are much more loose, contradictory, and "unsystematic" than that.) However—and this is crucial—I do believe that cultural meanings are coherent trails of symbolic connection and that these concepts effectively narrow the ways that people think and behave. In the United States at least, a red octagonal sign beside a roadway has a publicly recognized meaning: people are to stop their vehicles.

There was a time when cultural meanings depended on people—as culture bearers—to bring them to life as elements of action. In an advanced industrial age dominated by computers, this is less clearly the case. Information processing machines both "read" occurrences and instigate responses to those occurrences. A nation's strategic defense system, stock-market trading, medical procedures, and the like are increasingly dependent on computerized information systems. In such ways culture exhibits its own patterns of recognition and response.

If cultural meanings operate as a public referencing system—which distinguishes the elements of the world by placing them in patterns of conception—then *social* meanings are something else. Objects, events, and other occurrences have social significance when they pertain to the ways in which persons present or "locate" themselves with regard to one another. To a large degree social life is a trading of symbolically organized intentions. People have "interests" in one another and act willfully toward them. Those actions are most effective when there is a shared communication system that allows them to make clear their intentions. In other words, things mean something socially when they have implications for people's actions before others. When someone says, "If you do that again, it will *mean* the end of our relationship," the social significance of that statement is clear.

The third setting where symbolic meanings operate is the *psyche*—the patterning of individual thought and behavioral disposition. Things mean something to us psychologically when they affect the ways we understand ourselves and move about the world. These movements are not just of the social type—that is, what we do in the presence of other people—but also include all manner of thoughts and actions. When something happens, all of us call up images and ideas based, in part, on our distinctive experiences with the world. What a practical joke or retirement party means to one person may be quite different from what an event of that sort means to another.

This last idea—that people come to their own conclusions about what something means—is the theme of Ogden and Richards's classic work, *The Meaning of Meaning.* Ogden and Richards (1923) argued that although language is a system that establishes connections between *symbols* and their *referents*—for example, between words/concepts and the elements of the world to which they refer—it often fails to communicate the meanings the speaker intends. That is because symbols also invoke *reference*, the trail of psychological meanings that go on in the mind of the listener. Thus, when two siblings reminisce about their childhood, they may talk of "Mom," their pet cat "Fluffy," or "that summer at the lake." Use of such symbols directs people's attention to the objects or events identified, but the participants call up quite different thoughts about these forms. When we play out the implications of things in our minds, we are engaged in psychological meaning. When people are involved in events, then, they bring to bear upon those events these quite different types of understandings.

The ways in which these patterns intersect makes the event quite complicated. Something said or done at one moment may have a different meaning from the same thing said or done a few moments later. That "situational" viewpoint was taken by the philosopher Wittgenstein in his later writings (1968). For him, the meaning of words or actions is not to be found in dictionary definitions but rather in the ways people *use* language. That is, as individuals we decide what words and phrases mean by interpreting their pertinence to the situations in which we find ourselves. The same word—for example, "hot"—can mean many different things and we decide which connotation applies. Furthermore, words have many different purposes besides simple description. For example, the word "mother" can be uttered as an exclamation, a request, a demand, a complaint, an answer to a question, a cry, and so forth. And, to continue with this example, "mother" can refer both to a tangible person who stands before us, to an abstract category embracing many kinds of women, or to various combinations of the particular and abstract, as in the case of one's deceased mother. Furthermore, many words seem to refer to no classes of objects at all—as in the examples of "and," "happy," "still," "curiously," and so forth. In summary, words and sentences have many possible meanings, and the listener's job is to make sense of what is said.

Most of us are not philosophers, though we understand these matters well enough. When we try to tell someone a funny (to us) story about something we've witnessed, we sometimes receive a blank stare. Our response to them is to say,

"You had to be there." That is, we know well that occurrences are contextualized profoundly. Each moment is the working out of cultural directives, social imperatives, and the participant's ideas about what should be done in specific settings.

Fields of physical meaning. Do occurrences also have physical meaning? Some philosophers (see Grice 1957) have discussed what they call "natural" meaning. When we say, "The rising of the sun above the horizon *means* that the local environment will start to lighten and warm up and that many different species will increase their activity levels," that sentence may well be a comment on how humans perceive things, but it is also a way of saying that a chain of events is going to occur with or without human consent. The physical world follows its own patterns; occurrences there set off patterns of recognition and response from other organisms. The idea systems we humans possess may well help us "understand" or "adjust" to those processes or even help us block or buffer their effects on us, but the bulk of those processes are going to go forward without us, and in many cases they will force us to respond. Dark and light, heat and cold are not abstractions for the finest philosophical minds to debate; they are physical conditions that open and close the possibilities of living.

As great as Descartes's thoughts on the centrality—and isolation—of human consciousness may be, we must acknowledge that psychic awareness is nested in a body that is itself nested in an ever-changing environment. That body must somehow "read" or "know" its circumstances in ways that prefigure—and in that sense are more fundamental than—the conceptual or analytical frameworks that have been emphasized to this point (see Turner 2000).

This general approach has been developed by what is called bio-semiotics (Hoffmeyer 1996). Against the view that "meaning" is something that should be reserved for thinking, human subjects, students of bio-semiotics hold that the capacity to recognize and respond is a more general feature of organisms. Only some of these processes occur in ways that we would consider conscious. More interestingly—and more problematically—many response patterns do not involve the organism as a whole but instead are quite localized. When one's finger is cut, many physiological processes rush into operation. If the cut becomes infected, other kinds of reinforcements arrive. Indeed, most physiological processes that balance and rebalance what goes on inside the body and regulate its interchanges with the outside world can be seen in this way. In that quite expanded sense, then, our cut finger is "meaningful" to the body, and processes of recognition and response may be in full swing before we even realize that we are bleeding.

Because this book focuses on how humans, as conscious subjects, make sense of things, it is not crucial that the reader accept the extremist viewpoint that internal bodily reactions of every sort are "meaningful." However, a study of experience must at some point confront the idea that subjective "understandings" involve unconscious, physical patterns of recognition. This is in fact the position that has been developed in the writings of neuroscientist Antonio Damasio.

According to Damasio (1994, 1999), mental functioning must be understood in a way that admits of many brain-body relationships and several *levels* of consciousness. Although neuroscience historically has been devoted to the task of identifying which parts of the brain are pertinent to which patterns of thought, feeling, and behavior, contemporary scientists recognize that different parts of the brain communicate with one another in complicated ways and that what we call thinking and feeling are the expressions of those integrative processes. Tremendous ranges of interaction—both with external objects and events as well as with the internal happenings of our bodies (as "homeostatic" or dynamically balanced systems)—go on without our awareness. We do not "decide" how we are going to recognize our child's face, how we will code and decode a conversation with our neighbor, how we will blink our eyelid in response to a gnat, and so forth. Instead, the brain develops neural patterns that "dispose" us to recognize and respond to the world. Some of these patterns are in-born or species-specific, some become deeply familiar through learning, and some demand conscious attention and behavioral control.

To illustrate these different levels of consciousness, Damasio (1999, 82–106) discusses examples of patients with different kinds of brain injury or dysfunction. Thus, being awake but functionally immobile (as in an "absence seizure") is not the same as being stirred up by "background emotions" (i.e., being in a "mood"), which is different again from "low-level attention" (being dimly aware of the elements in our surroundings) and from "focused attention" on bodily events and external happenings. More sharply focused yet are "specific emotions," "specific actions," and the conceptualized or "verbal reports" of those feelings and actions. In other words, the brain takes care of its business in many different ways and organizes responses (to matters it recognizes) with different levels of awareness.

Many of those processes of recognition and response are immediate or extremely transitory. Damasio terms this level of awareness "core consciousness," a quality of mental activity that we share with many other species. Other, more abstract patterns of recognition he calls "extended consciousness." This latter pattern—people's minded and focused awareness of "circumstances" in the broadest meaning of that term—is the theme usually emphasized in the social sciences and in my own account of human experience. Whatever the importance of conscious thinking, we should not forget the general point of neuroscience: that "rational" consciousness is ultimately dependent on foundational, species-specific relationships involving brains and bodies.

If the above arguments are persuasive, then occurrences can be said to be meaningful in at least three *physical* ways. Events take on *environmental* meaning when they lead to patterns of recognition and response by communities of life forms. Events are meaningful to the *body* when that body finds that it must adjust its form and movement to what has occurred. And events are meaningful in a *psychological* way when they set off unconsciously monitored processes of noticing within the brain that lead to subjectively managed behaviors.

By exploring the concept of meaningfulness in this way, I wish to make only the very modest point that people are physical creatures and that the social sciences must address this physicality. Physical structures condition human subjectivity: we are able to operate as conscious beings only because of the relatively stable qualities we share with the other members of our species. Whatever the lingering appeal of nineteenth-century ideas about the body being a mechanism composed of highly interdependent parts, twentieth-century biology has shown that bodies are also informational systems whose processes are attributable to underlying codes. Brains and bodies function as well as they do because of constituent systems of physical-chemical recognition. We exist within these patterns and depend on them completely.

The Death of Ivan Ilyich. Differences between physical and symbolic meanings can be illustrated with the example of a serious medical condition. Diabetes, cancer, brain tumors, and the like are almost always significant events in a person's life. People typically become aware of these conditions in the form of "symptoms," the multitude of ways in which illness expresses itself within the body. When we are afflicted in one of these ways, we notice certain departures from our customary modes of feeling and behaving, which are the reasons we go to a physician. Whether or not we go to a doctor, those occurrences are "meaningful" to the degree that they challenge us to recognize and respond to what is happening to us.

A somewhat different process of recognition is the symbolic interpretation performed first by ourselves (and perhaps by our families) and then by a series of doctors. A diagnosis—correct or not—lays a framework of symbolic meaning on a series of events. The present condition, now named, is given a past as well as a range of possible futures. One can argue, of course, that the condition is not meaningful until physicians and patients "comprehend" it with symbols. However, in my view an undiagnosed condition is still meaningful to the degree that it refocuses patterns of subjective orientation. When we are ill, we sense that something different is occurring; we are frequently disturbed or even frightened. We "feel" ourselves in a new predicament, even if we cannot explain that condition cognitively to either ourselves or others.

To continue this example, consider the case of a worsening condition—heart disease or cancer perhaps—that goes undetected in the person. Perhaps because the person is older or has other serious conditions, the undiagnosed illness will never become a matter that the person must confront. He or she will die of other conditions first. However significant that condition may be to the organism as a whole (in which processes of resistance are already in full swing), it is not defined as "subjectively meaningful" until it invites processes of recognition and response at some level of awareness.

All this suggests that there are different "avenues" of meaning for human subjectivity. To continue our example, consider two friends—youthful, callow spirits—who are sitting in their apartment discussing the prospect of their own deaths at some point in the distant future. That exercise—a largely symbolic enterprise—is quite different from a conversation in which one or both persons know they are about to die, perhaps from chronic illness. In that latter instance death has an *import* that resounds throughout the possibilities of personhood. This is the theme that Tolstoy (2004) develops in *The Death of Ivan Ilyich*, where the protagonist must confront the various meanings of his own death.

To return to my five fields of relationship, the prospect of death can be meaningful at a largely cultural level—that is, as a playing out of conceptual implications. To die is to no longer exist—or at least to no longer exist in a physical way. What does continue are the artifacts of oneself—the forgotten coat in a closet, the picture in a drawer, the entries with your name on them in the company records. Moreover, people no longer think of you in the same way. You become an idea or a memory, someone who cannot intervene in their affairs as you once did.

Much different is social death. Tolstoy's protagonist is the unhappy witness to the dramatically altered behaviors of this wife and friends, who are already plotting their responses to his impending death. Someone else must assume his position (as a judge); his wife must secure her finances. Sadly, his friends have started to treat him as if he is already dead. He realizes that he is only someone who occupies a spot in the social order, and that spot is about to be taken.

Impending death is also profoundly meaningful at the psychological level, where all manner of thoughts go racing through the mind and new visions of self are sometimes grudgingly assembled. The aging or chronically ill person knows she is not the same person she once was. Troubling indeed are the circumstances in which the person must ask herself, "Am I still me?" More horrifying yet is the point when this question can no longer be asked.

Equally profound are the bodily meanings. People recognize changes in appearance and manner. Internal support systems fail; sick persons feel themselves to be different. Finally, there are a host of environmental meanings. A person so discomforted cannot go about as she once did: climbing stairs, negotiating city sidewalks, operating household devices, driving automobiles, and the like become impossibilities. New objects—canes, wheelchairs, hospital beds, and so forth— become prerequisites for living. Ultimately, the physical world closes in and becomes an interior affair. Such observations are commonplace to anyone who has experienced the chronic illness of a loved one.

Tolstoy's example shows clearly that issues of meaning—in which the elements of the world invoke processes of recognition and response—go on at many levels. On the one hand, dying people find that they must reevaluate their relationships with cultural, social, environmental, bodily, and psychological elements. On the other, those external elements find that they must also adjust. Spouses and children must reestablish their lives. There are pets to be fed, bills to be paid. Memos at work "demand" response. And at the courthouse, forms await completion.

Ascending and descending meaning. Although meaning can be described as I've done above—as a quality of recognition and response that exists between the elements of the world—this book centers on a somewhat narrower theme: how people themselves actively "make" meaning. In other words, I'm concerned primarily with processes of *subjective* meaning, ways in which people recognize what is occurring (at some conscious level) and then respond to it.

I'll begin by saying that a long-standing concern in the social sciences is the *extent* to which people administer situations or even direct their own thoughts and behaviors. Although Western societies tend to celebrate the role of individuals as willful agents, social scientists have emphasized also the extent to which cultural and social structures over which the individual has relatively little control bind personal choice making. This issue is sometimes described as a tension between "agency"—the ability of subjects to manufacture and control the terms of their living—and various forms of "structure," which confront those subjects and make demands on them. In psychology that opposition is often envisioned as the distinction between an internal and external "locus of control."

My way of thinking about this tension is to identify two different approaches people take to *understand* their placement in the world. I emphasize the word "understand" here because I'm saying that there are different kinds of patterns—effectively, principles that people operate with or "stand under." Some of those patterns can be said to be external matters—that is, the bodily, environmental, social, and cultural relationships described above. Others seem to be more internal—or closely linked—to consciousness; psychological patterns are of this latter type. When we make meaning, we look to one or the other sort of pattern as the guidelines for how we—and the other elements of the settings we are in—will behave. To that degree, our subjectivity almost always involves some act of deference to the frameworks that filter and organize experience. The issue becomes: which patterns will become those organizing principles?

I describe people's quest to find those organizing principles as a "movement" of meaning because whether external or internal sources of control will prevail is very often unclear. That is, we must decide whether we will adhere to a recognized—or "dictionary"—meaning of a word when we talk or whether we will make up and use our own meaning. A breakfast-table conversation may turn on whether one's own plans for the day will rule or whether one's partner will provide those terms. Frequently, people contest and negotiate those meanings, a theme that will be considered in subsequent chapters.

The first of these movements is what I call the project or path of "ascending meaning." When people apply their own personal formations—both symbolic and physical—to occurrences, they do so with the ambition of interpreting and controlling those occurrences according to those internally derived principles. To that degree, experience is a kind of psychic imperialism. We impose our will upon the object world so as to make it serve our needs. As a purely symbolic enterprise, ascending meaning refers to our effort to "fit" the world into our preexisting interpretive frameworks. At the level of action, it means that we try to alter or rearrange external patterns.

This process of subjective assertion also "goes on" in the psyche itself. Inside that field of relationships, ascending meaning refers to the ways in which the ego resists the psyche's own ideas and feelings and then tries to regulate and direct them. At its purest, then, ascending meaning represents the rebellion of self—and more precisely, the rebellion of consciousness—against the forms and forces of the world. Action and experience are conducted on the person's own terms.

The opposite movement, what I call "descending meaning," features an acceptance of or accommodation to external frameworks and patterns. Action becomes a compliance with or adjustment to the directives of otherness. Personal action and experience are conducted on the basis of schemes that are *not* the subject's own. Inside the psyche descending meaning occurs when the ego capitulates to cognitive and emotional demands. Our thoughts and behaviors become acts of deference to these claims. Although this movement of meaning features compliance, it should not be seen simply as inaction or passivity, for often it involves the most energetic realignments or reinventions of the self. In that sense, sense making of the descending type is people's attempt to realign their thoughts and action strategies with the regularities of the world. This process of recognizing and adjusting oneself to the *logic* of external happenings is, the reader may recall, a guiding theme of Goffman's *Frame Analysis*.

To state this difference as simply as possible, the self sometimes seems to determine, control, or even cause relationships; at other times, other people or external circumstances are what seem to define the character of that relationship (see Oatley 1992). That tension between rival organizing principles is a key theme in the cognitive psychology of Piaget (1962), who described it as the conflict between "assimilation" and "accommodation." That issue is also prominent in Goffman's writing. At times Goffman's actors seem to be self-interested schemers who manipulate other people and social settings to get what they want. At other times his actors seem trapped by the cultural scripts that define social situations and everyone within them. My own approach differs from these two theorists in that I'm interested in both conception and sensation as themes of meaning making. I also stress the importance of the five different contexts of meaning, and in the relationship of those contexts to one another. That general picture of human experience is restated—and shown graphically—in the chapter summary below.

SUMMARY: A GENERAL MODEL OF EXPERIENCE

In this chapter I've tried to bring together many concerns of social scientists into a general view of how people comprehend the character of "situations" and then act on the basis of those recognitions. One form of conclusion is to present those earlier arguments—or at least many of them—as a visual model. That model— what I call the "ascending-descending meaning perspective"—is shown in figure 1.

As the reader can see, human experience is centered in a "psyche" that is itself positioned at the juncture of two different kinds of "realities": physical and symbolic. That meeting point or eye-of-consciousness is represented in the figure by the "ego." On the left side of the figure are fields of "social" and "cultural" relationships. These are said to be primarily symbolic or conceptual formations—that is, they exist as patterns of information available for public use (culture) and as

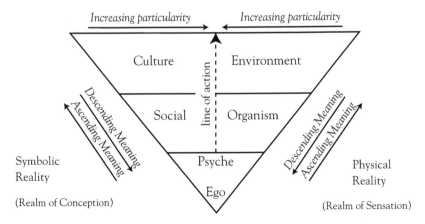

FIGURE 1. **Fields of Human Action and Experience (The Ascending-Descending Meaning Perspective)**

arrangements for personal interaction (social structure). Notably, culture is placed higher up (i.e., above) the social in the model. This is because culture is the more suprapersonal and abstract of these two fields of relationships. Sociality, by contrast, is a more *interpersonal* realm that stands between these patterns of public conception and the private, "psychic" inspirations of individuals. Similarly, the social is said to be an intermediary reality because societies customarily make cultural resources available to their members and then sharply regulate the ways in which those resources can be used.

On the right side of the diagram are physical patterns of recognition and response. The "organism" is presented as being situated in a wider physical "environment," but that body is also a distinctive—and relatively self-directed—field of relationships that interacts with that environment. The physical environment has object-relations of its own sort; the preponderance of these occurs without the influence of any individual organism. However, the environment strongly influences the character and functioning of any individual organism; indeed, environmental patterns transcend and make possible the very nature of that organism. For such reasons, the body—somewhat like social formations—is an intermediary context that stands between the psyche and wider fields of physical object-relations.

At the bottom of the figure the psyche is pictured as a "triangle" that partakes of both physical and symbolic contexts. That image is intended to remind many readers of Freud's great contribution to the social sciences. For Freud (1952), consciousness must come to terms with the fact that there are psychic forces of different sorts—both the psycho-organic drives he named the "id" and the internalized and morally charged ideas he called the "superego." In addition to dealing with these internal challenges, the ego must confront the challenges of external reality (occurrences within the four other fields of relationships I've discussed). In the face of all these rival schemes, people ask themselves to determine courses of action that honor their personal interests and integrity.

Although I do not wish to identify this writing with some of the older, indeed Victorian ideas and images of psychoanalysis, I do take from the Freudian tradition its guiding themes that people are "conditioned" or "embodied" from both these directions simultaneously and that those demands are not easily resolved. All of us live amidst these influences and try to apprehend them in what ways we can. Some challenges are presented by external physical and symbolic forms; others arise from patterns located in ourselves. In either case we make accountings of the patterns we recognize, and we produce behaviors directed toward the more concrete elements of those patterns. When people are able to assert their own claims on external patterns—both symbolic and physical—the arrows of "ascending meaning" represent that pathway. When consciousness defers to external patterns, "descending meaning" prevails.

The process of focusing one's attention on some element of the world and then acting in relation to it is displayed as a "line of action" running through the center of the figure. Significantly, that center line is also the place where relationships from the different fields converge. Thus, a cultural artifact like a flag is both a physical thing and a symbolic pattern; a social interaction is both a movement of human bodies in environments and a set of symbolic arrangements formalizing those movements. When people "act," they address elements that these different fields of relationships have shaped.

The line of action also runs through the center of the figure—in a way that touches all the "fields of relationship"—because I want to emphasize two points. First, most actions—like our woman walking along a street—feature inputs from all five fields. When patterns from these different fields intersect, they effectively "create" the settings in which we operate. Second, the line of action is in the center of the triangle to emphasize the point that although action is fed by more general elements of the world, it is also intensely particular. People do not behave generically. Rather, they engage in specific thoughts and actions at specific times and places; the people they speak to and the objects they handle are equally specific. When a baseball player picks up and throws a baseball, that act of throwing—however many thousands of times it is done—can never be repeated, for each moment is set in circumstances that continually change. In the model, two arrows of "increasing particularity" (across the top of the triangle) show the ways in which external patterns, processes, and objects are brought into events to make them "real." Even though these elements are "brought in" to define or specify the situation at hand, they do not lose their status in the wider world; indeed that continuing status is what serves to "anchor" and give direction to our momentary behaviors.

Of course, models, like the one I present here, are just heuristic devices: they are "helpful" only to the sorts of people who appreciate visual depictions. My ascending-descending perspective is simply one way to envision the contexts of action and experience. I make no claims that the settings in which people operate can be simplified so easily. To be sure, "situations" are filled with many elements that can be analyzed in many ways. *Experiences* (how we conceive and sense our involvement in a situation) are different from *actions* (the behaviors we actually produce). Both experience and action are complicated affairs, and as we've seen, consciousness can flash from one aspect of the world to another in an instant. And despite my persistent focus on the degree to which events are "meaningful," we must acknowledge that sometimes the incomprehensibility—and putative meaninglessness—of what occurs stuns us.

The misfortune of the social sciences is that reality should be so complicated—and of such different types. Nevertheless, explaining the intersection of such patterns is the problem confronting any student of human experience. To my mind, the challenge of such analysis is to indicate specifically how these different movements of meaning operate in situations. What is accepted, and what is resisted? In what ways do people seem to be in charge of their circumstances, and in what ways do they seem to be out of control? And what are the objects that become the bones of contention of these alternative interpretative schemes? The following chapter explores one of the most hotly contested settings for all these issues—the context of personhood termed the "self."

CHAPTER 3

SELVES AS PROJECTIONS
OF PERSONHOOD

This chapter addresses an aspect of situations that people are keenly interested in: themselves. To consider that theme, I change Goffman's guiding question in *Frame Analysis*, "What is it that's going on here?" to a different, if somewhat ungrammatical, one: "*Who* is it that's going on here?" My argument is that people are framed in much the same ways as we frame other aspects of the world. And it is not just other people whose characteristics and intentions we are determined to understand; it is ourselves.

In what follows I describe the ideas of "identity" and "self" as contexts within which people operate. In this chapter I focus on the foundational conception of the self provided by psychologist William James and then show how sociologists Mead and Cooley extended this view. The ideas of Goffman and other sociologists are added to the mix. Ultimately, I try to integrate the various perspectives into a comprehension of self as a *projection* of personhood, a pattern of commitment and connection that carries individuals through events.

HUMANS AS PERSONS

To be sure, people are organisms with distinctive physical forms and processes. However, we imagine ourselves to be much more than that. We may be creatures, but we are also "minded" creatures who maintain quite complicated patterns of psychological orientation and judgment. Furthermore, we are social and even cultural beings. That is, we live in communities of fellow humans who rely on shared symbol systems to regulate their thoughts, feelings, and behaviors. Indeed, most of us are expected—and expect ourselves—to spend large portions of our lives interacting with the other members of our species.

Because we participate in human communities, we are said to be "persons" (Cahill 2000). To be a person is to be granted certain publicly acknowledged rights and responsibilities. The bulk of those proscriptions have to do with how we are allowed to behave toward others and, conversely, how they are allowed to treat us. A crucial element of personhood is the idea that the various members of this community of persons share similar kinds and levels of awareness. "Persons" are able to use those shared abilities to communicate with one another. When we interact with other persons, we believe they have some prospect of understanding our interior reflections, as we do theirs.

Human bodies are not always granted personhood. For example, when we die, our rights and responsibilities as a person may pass with us. In the period just after our deaths, we retain the right to have our body treated in a certain way, at least when it is being displayed before others who care about us. After that, the body's rights may decline. In a similar way, developing life is sometimes accorded more and more privileges as it nears the moment of birth. In both cases the concept of personhood is connected to ideas about subjectivity—that quality of awareness and self-determination that allows one to appraise her position in the human community and direct her own course in that setting. When we lose our ability to manage that course—as when we are severely ill or have lost certain mental functions—our status as persons may once again be challenged, sometimes irrecoverably. And because personhood is a social attribution, many categories of people—set apart by designations of age, sex, ethnicity, class, sexual orientation, and so forth—historically have been denied "full citizenship" as persons. When people are persons, they are recognized to be not just the objects of other's people schemes but also social subjects, who have acknowledged rights to conduct themselves in certain ways and have their thinking processes honored.

There are three sometimes-competing contexts for interpreting personhood. The first of these contexts is *culture*. At one level, personhood is an abstraction—a set of publicly circulated ideas about the character and implications of being human in the society in question. However, persons are not just categories or abstractions; they are individuals. Those individuals are also defined culturally, as seen in the various "identity cards"—driver's licenses, credit cards, and the like—that people carry in their wallets.

However, being a person is much more than having the proper papers. Rather, persons hold specific positions in relationships, groups, and organizations that we share with others. In other words, being a person is a *social* matter that features the key question: how do other people think, feel, and act toward me? When those other persons and groups regard us in a certain way, we are said to have a social identity (see McCall and Simmons 1966). That is, those people have attributed to us certain characteristics—distinguishing physical features, personality traits, occupation, biographical details, and so forth. They see us in a distinctive way and probably treat us in a way that is consistent with those understandings. And because our personal identity—as a composite of those imputed traits—is different from anyone else's, the way they treat us may be very specialized indeed. That special standing is made clear at the time of our deaths, when it may be necessary for those who know us well to "identify" our body.

The third context for interpreting personhood is how we think, act, and feel toward ourselves. Social scientists commonly call this subjectively monitored version of the person the "self" (see Branaman 2007; Hewitt 2000). As will be shown, people self-identify. That is, they assemble complicated visions of themselves and try to see that these visions are honored in social relationships. Much of the dynamic of social life features the tension between the social and cultural versions of ourselves (identity) and the versions that we ourselves maintain (self). People want to know how others are identifying them and, if possible, to change those definitions to conform to their preferred visions of themselves. And they also know that others are engaged in the same scrutinizing procedures.

At any rate, people are keen to appraise the characteristics—and behavioral possibilities—of one another. With that eye, let us return to our example of the mysterious stranger, the man who approached us on the street and made a remark that we did not quite understand. In the earlier version of that example, our attention was directed entirely toward his actions: what does this person want or, more darkly, what is he "up to"? What was not said before is that we rely heavily on our judgments about the man's appearance and manner to help us figure out his actions.

For us to conclude that the stranger who approaches us on the street is indeed a person in need of help, he must fit the role of what (we think) a petitioner of that sort should be. In particular, he should seem—at least during our exchange—to be somehow less socially competent than ourselves. That is, we more readily attribute the person-in-need role to those who appear to be very young or old, injured, disabled, shabbily attired, or disoriented. Moreover, we expect petitioners to exhibit the demeanor of a properly needy supplicant, traits that they can reveal to us by politeness, a somber countenance, softness in the eyes, and other marks of receptivity and deference. If they do not present themselves in this way—for example, if they seem to be healthy, wealthy, and wise—we may have difficulty believing that they are indeed a person in need. What we do then—at least in Goffman's view— is to flip quickly through our other "definitions of situations" to see if there is one that better matches the person's characteristics with what he is doing.

Just as we identify other persons in terms of their placement in contexts or meaning systems, so we also apply those same processes to ourselves. That is, we must also decide "who we are" in the situation at hand and, by extension, how we should act. For a helping situation to be fully realized, someone must play the role of benefactor. That person should be someone who has the resources to help. Ideally, benefactors should give in a way that is both generous (not asking for repayment or assistance themselves) and courteous (so that they affirm the dignity of the person who is being helped). To be sure, there are cultural differences in the way socially advantaged people are expected to help others; however, Goffman's general point—that societies offer their members publicly acknowledged models for such occasions—seems sound. When both parties to a situational definition recognize the event they are in and play their roles appropriately, matters can move ahead quickly. However, just as our potential beneficiary may destroy the frame through his failure to live up to the appropriate model, so we ourselves may block or destabilize those understandings. Who of us has not at times simply ignored such petitioners or has "begged off" with claims that we cannot help because we have no money or time or because we do not know enough to provide the proper guidance?

WILLIAM JAMES AND THE SELF

If selfhood is something we ourselves work to establish and maintain, of what materials is it constructed? Perhaps the classic answer to this question is the one that William James presents in his 1890 book, *The Principles of Psychology*. As he (1952, 188, emphasis his) defines his subject: "*in its widest possible sense, however, a man's Self is the sum total of all that he CAN call his,* not only his body and his psychic powers, but his clothes and his house, his wife and children, his ancestors and friends, his reputation and works, his lands and horses, and yacht and bank-account." This list of possessions and affiliations—however class ridden and patriarchal it strikes the modern reader—is James's way of explaining that the line between that which is "me"—the self as some recognized presence in the world—and that which is "mine" is very difficult to draw. Moreover, he makes clear his view that human beings understand themselves through their attachments to objects. Frequently, we see those objects as extensions of ourselves, and when those objects are damaged or threatened, we feel those injuries in a deeply personal way. Losing a loved one through death, a part of one's body through injury, or even a cherished possession through theft or fire may cause one to feel violated and diminished. Oppositely, seeing those attachments prosper produces feelings of satisfaction and pride.

James's listing of self-related objects also makes clear the point that the self is not merely a psychological territory—that is, some way in which we *think* about ourselves—but is instead a pattern of connection to real objects in the world. Certainly, this is the case with one's body. People do not simply think of themselves as possessing bodily characteristics and then operate on the basis of that mental vision. Quite the opposite, we have a real body that serves as a set of tangible boundaries for who we are. That body "speaks" to us through its registration of needs and urges as well as the ways in which it both enables and restricts our movements. Ideally perhaps, our mental image of the self—or at least those aspects of self that focus on bodily qualities—corresponds to this physical entity, but complete correspondence is never the case. Most of us have some idealized vision of height and weight (honored on our driver's licenses) that differs from those heresies that the measuring devices in doctors' offices perpetuate; and many other persons—such as those suffering from anorexia—exhibit even more radical departures from "reality." Less clearly, perhaps, but just as substantially, we are connected to family and friends, jobs, clubs, churches, and even to our presumed "horses and yachts." Whatever their status as mental possessions may be, objects of these kinds define the possibilities of concrete behavior. A man with a yacht can go about the world differently than a man without one can. When we have a self, we sense our bodies and minds moving coherently amidst these elements of the world.

Fields of self-experience. James argues that there are four constituent elements of the self: the material self, the social self, the "spiritual" self, and the "pure ego." The material self has its primary residence in our bodies. That body is commonly thought to provide the boundaries for what is "me." However, James (1952, 189) expands this purely bodily view of self with his claim that we feel an almost "material" connection to our close kin, "bone of our bone, flesh of our flesh." As noted above, we also identify deeply with such material objects and surroundings as our home, clothing, and other forms of property. In such ways, he establishes the theme that selfhood involves connections to elements of the physical environment. We recognize our distinctive placement in the world when we open our front door, sit in a chair in our living room, or look across that room to see curios we have acquired over a lifetime.

A person's social self is the "recognition which he gets from his mates." Human beings, in James's view, are gregarious creatures who desire to be noticed or, rather, who desire to be noticed in positive ways. As he (189–90, emphasis his) puts it, *"a man has as many social selves as there are individuals who recognize him* and carry an image of him in their mind." To damage any of these images is to damage the self. Such a viewpoint raises the question of where the self resides—in our own minds, in the minds of other people, or perhaps in other realms that exist outside these two forms of subjectivity. My own view, as noted above, is that the term "identity" better describes this more external or publicly acknowledged version of personhood—what other people and organizations consider us to be. However, I support James's general point: there is some "empirical" or publicly accessible basis to the self. All of us are aware that others have opinions of us, and we feel diminished when we sense the disapprobation of persons we love and admire.

James admits that having as many selves as there are persons who regard us is too complicated a notion for any of us to manage. For that reason we tend to organize our selves through our relationships to the different groups of our belonging. As he puts it, a child will act demurely in the company of his parents and five minutes later behave like a "tough" before his friends. All of us have access to a variety of social selves and adopt the manner (we think) appropriate to each as we move from one interpersonal context to the next.

The "spiritual self" is James's term (1952, 191) for a person's "inner or subjective being, his psychic faculties or dispositions." He argues that these psychic dispositions are the "most enduring and intimate part of the self" and that "we take a purer self-satisfaction when we think of our ability to argue and discriminate, of our moral sensibility and conscience, of our indomitable will" than when we think of our other qualities and possessions. We can focus either on these qualities abstractly—in the manner of "faculties"—or more concretely, as on the mental contents that present themselves to us in the stream of consciousness. In either case, we understand ourselves to be thinkers and feelers and have some knowledge of the moments when we are performing these activities.

Is there an internal point of judgment that stands apart from—and then connects with—the various attributes and possessions described above? Is there a "pure ego," a "self of all the other selves"? Following Kant, James believes that the person does not simply register and record her experiences in the world; rather, there is a fourth element of the self, an active "nucleus" or principle of subjectivity that reaches out toward, receives, and organizes experience. Religious people sometimes refer to this principle as the "soul"; more secular types describe it as the "ego."

In his book James acknowledges that many scientists of his time neither accept this postulate of a nuclear self nor embrace his "introspective" approach to psychological functioning. Nevertheless, he argues that people can feel the workings of the psyche. This "palpitating inward life" is experienced as a series of "mutual inconsistencies and agreements, reinforcements and obstructions, which obtain amongst these reactions of my spontaneity upon them, welcoming or opposing, appropriating or disowning, striving with or against, saying yes or no" (194). He goes on to say that these "acts of attending, assenting, negating, making an effort are felt as movements of something in my head." Even more precisely, he claims that mental life is experienced as a set of changes in respiration, contractions of the jaw muscle, opening and closing of the glottis, furrowing of the brow, and so forth.

James is quick to note that these motions are only the physical manifestations of our inner deliberations and that the greater part of psychic functioning, in his view, is not open to observation or even introspection. Still, he advances the opinion that this pure or nuclear self should be seen as a set of "adjustments" to experience, somewhat in the manner of physiological reflexes. Said differently, there is some very basic structure for human functioning that directs "sensorial and ideational processes" and serves as a framework for the various feats of mental and emotional gymnastics that humans perform.

Can these different contexts for the self be arranged in an orderly way? James (202, emphasis his) claims that there is a hierarchy of self-regard *with the bodily Self at the bottom, the spiritual Self at the top, and the extracorporeal material selves and the various social selves between.* Setting aside James's rationale for such a ranking, his scheme conforms to a long tradition in Western philosophy that celebrates the psychological self as the ultimate controller of human affairs (see Seiger 2005). Furthermore, James promotes the equally favored view of philosophers that the more enduring or abstract referents of the self—especially those occurring in the spiritual self—are more important than transient thoughts, sensations, and possessions. In that regard, he is interested ultimately in the ways in which the psychological realm—which has its center in the pure ego—creates and directs the "potential" self in all its varieties. For people live in the future and the past as fully as they occupy the changing moments of the present.

Essentially what James offers his readers is a sketch of the basic contexts of self-experience. I have presented that sketch at some length here not only because it is a classic account but also because I want to contrast it with my own view. Consistently with what I argued in the preceding chapter, I believe there are *five* contexts for self-experience. In addition to the contexts that James describes—psyche, society, body, and the material world—people also locate themselves culturally. That is, our personal "possessions" include public conceptual forms. We hold certain understandings of the world (e.g., that our own country has specific qualities), we stand for certain principles (e.g., "individual freedom" or "respect for older people"); we acquire specific skills (e.g., the ability to speak the language of our society); we are committed to wide varieties of custom and law (from traffic laws to every other manner of regulation). We commonly define ourselves in terms of our relationship to these publicly acknowledged symbol systems. People who describe themselves as "religious," "libertarian," "traditional," and the like are making claims about the ways in which they connect themselves to well-known ideas. Some of these public ideas (e.g., political or religious tenets) we wholeheartedly endorse, others we despise, and others yet are matters of complete indifference to us. That process of public, symbolic location is a centerpiece of Goffman's sociology.

One can argue that these symbolic possessions are entirely psychological affairs that are covered adequately by James's "spiritual" category. To be sure, we do possess our own ideas—and are possessed by them. But we also have knowledge that these ideas exist in some broader cultural sense. We know that some of our favorite beliefs are widely shared by others and that some are not. We have some sense that we are good or bad at certain publicly recognized skills, such as watercolor painting or ballroom dancing. We usually know when we are breaking the law. We feel ourselves engaged with—or alienated from—those shared informational resources. Our own beliefs are comprehensible—to ourselves and to others—only in terms of this public system.

My own arrangement of these contexts was displayed in the preceding chapter's "ascending-descending meaning perspective." There I presented my justification for that arrangement—essentially a claim that some fields are more proximate to consciousness than others. Whatever the appeal of that model, the general theme I am developing follows that of James. To have a self is to be located amidst patterns associated with these different fields. To be self-aware is to be cognizant of those connections.

Still, much is to be considered. How are these comprehensions of who we are—both in the moment and across time—established? And what is the role of the ego, that "self of selves," in managing this process? In the following, I present some classic sociological answers to these questions.

SELVES AS SOCIALLY SITUATED

Is self-awareness the sense that we are bounded entities or "objects" in relationships with other objects? Or is it, quite differently, the sense that we are psychic "vantage points" who appraise circumstances and then act willfully from moment to moment? As indicated above, James emphasizes that personhood is to be understood in both ways. On the one hand, we are "empirical" beings who have a concrete presence in the world and observable relationships with that world's elements. On the other, we possess intangible, interior qualities—represented in the "pure" self—that allow us to reflect on and process those relationships.

Mead's interactive self. In sociology, perhaps the greatest commentator on the simultaneous presence of these objective and subjective qualities of the self is George Herbert Mead. Although James discusses the division of the self into its more active and passive components—called the "I" and the "me"—Mead develops this theme more fully. And much more than James, Mead discusses the degree to which these comprehensions are dependent on our relationships with other people. For Mead (1964), the "me" represents the internal organization of the more or less objective aspects of the self. Through their experiences in the social world, people develop an understanding of what is expected of them as participants in social situations. In that sense, the "me" is a kind of residue of past social encounters and attitudes, an awareness of what society is like and how the subject herself fits into its various patterns.

Quite differently, the "I" represents the ongoing responses of the person to those expectations. For Mead, then, selfhood is not simply an internalization of preexisting social patterns and positions, a viewpoint that Dennis Wrong (1961) describes as the "over-socialized" concept of the person. Instead, selfhood is a dialogue between one's own judgment and the perceived judgment of others, a moving back and forth between private and public expectations—or to put matters differently again, between the placements that we seek for ourselves and those that other people would confer upon us.

Mead developed this viewpoint as part of a broader theory of mind (see Mead 1964, 83–196). Mental activity, he argues, is largely an imaginative working through of alternative courses of action, an internalized conversation of gestures. Particularly when we are deciding how we should act before others, we try out different behavioral scenarios in our minds, including the likely responses of other people to those projected actions. We first imagine what we might do or say to someone; then we imagine what they might do or say to us in return.

How can we possibly anticipate the reactions of others? After all, people vary so much in terms of personality, background, and current circumstances. One person may respond angrily to what we've done whereas another may laugh out loud and another still will exhibit complete indifference. Psychological anarchy of this sort cannot be explained away, but Mead's answer is similar to the one that Goffman supplies many years later. People can anticipate the reactions of others because they live in a world that is socially and culturally organized.

To address the latter of these two contexts first, our ability to anticipate others' thoughts and actions depends on the existence of symbolic—that is, publicly established—meanings for words and gestures. That patterning of meanings places a frame on all we do. In that light, most of us understand that our behaviors are not simply exhibitions of private intentions but rather public declarations. In other words, we know that our behavior will probably be "read" in terms of this public meaning system. If we can anticipate how people are likely to interpret our actions, then we can anticipate how they are likely to respond.

Explaining how these public meaning systems help people understand and communicate with one another is an important contribution. But Mead's argument is much more focused than that. Public meanings are specified to various kinds of social situations and to the social positions that people hold in those situations. Those positions can be seen as "roles"—publicly recognized understandings for how a person in such a position is expected to think and act. To operate effectively in society, people must know more than how "any sort of person" will respond; they need to know how a person occupying a specific social position will respond.

How do people develop the ability to inhabit the various social positions in society and then to see their own qualities and behaviors from the vantage point of those—quite external and quite abstract—positions? Mead's answer is that this process of self-awareness occurs in stages. A first step is the young child's development of reflexive consciousness, the ability to see oneself as an object in a world of other objects. Possessed of this ability, we have some sense of what is "me" or "mine" and what belongs to the external world. A second stage features the ability to "take the role of the other." This is the capacity to occupy mentally one of society's roles—say, that of police officer or mother—and then to think and act toward the world using that abstract perspective. More astoundingly yet, children at play can engage in private dialogues featuring two or more roles. That is, they can pretend to be both a police officer, who is rescuing a baby, and the baby who is being rescued and then create the chain of interaction—and the dialogue—that would be produced in such a situation.

More impressive still is older children's ability to see themselves as members of wider groups. As in a game of baseball, a person playing the role of shortstop must understand what all the other positions on the field expect of him. This complex of rights and responsibilities indeed defines his social standing. Other members of the team not only think of him as the shortstop, but they also judge how well he, as a person, is meeting the requirements of that position. On the basis of these public expectations, he may be judged to be a good or bad shortstop. More profoundly, his performance as a shortstop may influence the qualities that people attribute to him as a person. To be sure, these general evaluations are important, but our assessments are also intensely particular. When a ball is hit into the "alley" in right-center field and runners are flying around the bases, the shortstop must do what his teammates expect of him *now*.

Children—and the rest of us—belong to many groups and play various roles in those groups. How do we develop some broader understanding of ourselves as "persons," a pattern of self-regard that transcends those temporary commitments? Although there is surely some truth to the claim that people are social chameleons who adapt their self-concept to whatever setting they in, Mead emphasizes the opposite point. He believes that we take on the monumental task of putting together all our various group experiences—essentially understandings about how others have seen and treated us in those settings—into some overall view of who we are. In this final (widest) perspective, we decide what society as a whole—the "generalized other"—thinks of us. Surrounded by understandings of ourselves as extroverted, fat, amusing, or socially inept, we move from one setting to the next.

Still the question remains: can we really know what others think of us? Because consciousness is largely an interior affair, we cannot. Still, we are determined—even desperate—to know. How we achieve that knowledge is the subject of Charles

Cooley's (1964) famous "looking glass" theory of the self. In fairy tales, books, and poems, a common theme is the desire of people to possess some "mirror" that will reflect them as they truly are. Unfortunately, this mirror does not exist. Nor can we pass "through the looking glass," in the manner of Lewis Carroll's Alice, to discover another reality that stands behind the world of everyday affairs. What we must do instead is use people's reactions to us as that reflective surface.

Because we cannot know others' thoughts directly, we rely on what we can see: the physical manifestations of those thoughts—that is, people's words and behaviors—as these are presented to us. On the basis of those "appearances" we make judgments about what we *impute* to be people's judgments of us. Like readers of a letter, we interpret what the writer means by analyzing the words, sentences, style of writing, type of stationery, and so forth they use. Once again, our ability to draw these conclusions depends on the existence of accepted cultural meanings of those patterns, and our confidence in the success of that analysis hinges on our belief that others use these forms in ways similar to our own. Without that shared symbolic language, we cannot scrutinize the motives of other people, nor can we communicate our intentions to them. For Cooley, then, the best that life offers us is a kind of sympathetic, if ever distant, speculation about the minds of others. Our similarity to other people—as well as our possibilities for intimacy with them—is dependent on our possession of shared circumstances and tools.

Both Cooley and Mead emphasize the degree in which self-awareness arises through our interactions with other people. The world is not a frozen lake on the surfaces of which people walk for either writer, nor do people stare at those surfaces—and ponder what lies below—in the manner of philosophers. Quite the opposite, we are deeply immersed in settings that are constantly changing and whose general patterns individuals are powerless to control. For such reasons, we do not adopt the philosopher's practice of mentally sorting and grading the various abstract qualities of the world so as to produce some general account of "reality" and of our relationship to it. Instead, we form those conclusions—and become ourselves—through the direction and encouragement of other people. Society gives us publicly communicable frameworks to internalize; flesh-and-blood people tell us how these standards should be applied to ourselves. In that sense our project is unlike that of the wicked queen in *Sleeping Beauty* who used her mirror to gain absolute knowledge. Instead, we desire only practical (socially validated) understandings, which will guide us through our relationships with others.

CONTEMPORARY CONCERNS

The social sciences have moved on since the days of the great pragmatist thinkers who have been considered to this point. However, interest in the study of the self remains strong (Baumeister 1999). One the one hand, an endless stream of books and articles suggests the continuing importance of the self in contemporary society and the many aspects of this theme that can be studied. On the other, it suggests that the problems the classic thinkers raise remain unsolved. Because the literature on this topic is so extensive, my approach in this section of the chapter is simply to highlight some of the challenges that continue to confront scholars of the self.

Structure and agency in self-experience. The distinction of James and Mead between the "I" and the "me" has inspired two rival traditions of self-study in sociology (see O'Brien 2006). The first of these emphasizes the nature of the self as a more or less stable arrangement that people occupy and then rely on to direct their lives. This approach, which is sometimes termed the "structural" or "identity" tradition, centers on the way in which people are connected to both internal patterns (e.g., psychologically sustained ideas about oneself) and external patterns (e.g., current social roles and group memberships). Such formations are said to stabilize and channel personal expression.

Structural approaches to the self also emphasize the extent to which subjective understandings are tied to more objective or public kinds of identity (see Rosenberg 1981). That is, people's understandings of who they are—as members of groups, as role actors, as persons—arise out of their involvement in publicly supported frameworks that exist in the social world. Participation in those external structures reaffirms our identity before others and, by consequence, our understandings of and commitment to that identity. In such ways, public experience channels private experience. Said a little differently, people build identity as a series of commitments to these forms, take pride in the more successful of these commitments, and even make some of these aspects of self the most important or "salient" to them (see Stryker 1968). In such ways, the expectations surrounding public identities are a touchstone for self-understanding and a motivator for action.

The opposite point of view is that selfhood is not a settled or stable matter but is instead a continually negotiated enterprise, a process of personal assertion and response in specific social situations. If the "identity" tradition emphasizes the extent to which thoughts, feelings, and behaviors are largely instances of role or identity *conformity*, then this latter "agency" tradition emphasizes the quality of *reflexivity* that people bring to the moments of their lives (see Hewitt 2000). Said most basically, people generally think before they act. Having thought, they may or may not do what is expected of them. That much more fluid, unpredictable view of self is associated especially with the writing of Herbert Blumer. In Blumer's (1969) view, the self arises out of a social dialectic in which interested individuals attempt to establish preferred "lines of action." As part of that process, such individuals seek to define situations—and themselves—in ways that forward those interests. At times they succeed, at times they fail, and many more times the standings that result are compromises between these extremes. In such a view social relationships do not simply emerge; they are "produced" through the actions of energetic individuals (O'Brien 2006). In other words, selfhood is less a static entity than it is an ongoing process that is dependent on a willful and resourceful "I" that seeks to maximize favored versions of the person (see Blumstein 1975).

Most social scientists live in the territory between these camps. To use my own terminology, sometimes action—and the awareness that attends that action—occurs along lines that some energetic, strong-minded individual dictates, a condition I have called "ascending meaning." Sometimes action and experience are capitulations to lines that others have established—my "descending meaning." More often, self-experience is a process of negotiation among the individuals involved and between those individuals and the challenges of the world. Sociologist Carolyn Ellis (1995) has developed the view of social and personal reality as an intensely negotiated enterprise. Both in situations that are quite ordinary and in those that are profound, such as the impending death of a loved one, people endeavor to write narratives collectively that make sense of what is occurring. Some parts of those stories are accommodations to matters that cannot be controlled; others are manifestos of hope against the patterns that confront them.

Is the self a social artifact? Although the perspectives of the classic thinkers remain important, contemporary scholars have challenged their "one size fits all" account of the self. Those earlier writers tended to see the quest for selfhood as an attempt to develop an independently controlled personal framework. That framework should be well fashioned, integrated, and abstract enough to allow the occupant to comprehend wide varieties of situations. That occupant should also be able to control the way in which this framework is connected to society. Ties to valued social entities should be strengthened; ties to devalued people and circumstances should be cut loose. Perhaps, it is sometimes suggested, this earlier version of the self is a historical artifact, a portrait of how upper-class men in Western industrial societies have been encouraged to think and behave. Perhaps a better sociological contribution is to show just how deeply contextualized the self is, to show how its configurations vary according to the settings and circumstances of the people involved.

Although I would argue that people have always had selves, clearly the historical development of societies has altered the ways in which people comprehend their characteristics, capabilities, and placements in the world. People are now less deeply embedded in the groups that once defined and oriented them. That relative liberation of the individual (see Kahler 1956: Nisbet 1966) has led to people becoming—or at least to their seeing themselves as—quasi-independent agents who establish contracts with other social agents. This process of individualization started at the top of society and worked its way downward. Such changes had repercussions for the character of groups as well. If in the distant past social bodies were understood to be long-enduring entities that shaped the character of their members, ultimately they became what Kahler calls "collectivities"—artifices put together and sustained by the commitments of their members. Society has moved, to continue his language, from a "pre-individual" to a "post-individual" stage.

Such changes put a different sort of pressure on individuals, who now find it necessary to achieve or negotiate many of their more important statuses. If the self is to be seen as a more independent—even isolated—affair, then people must be attentive to its presentation, management, and protection. A similar theme has been developed by Giddens (1991), who argues that "high" modernity creates conditions of "ontological insecurity" and "existential anxiety" at the personal level. Not only are cultural and social formations proliferating at unprecedented rates, but every social organization now seems committed to "reflexively" evaluating and then modifying its practices. Abstract plans and policies of increasingly wide scope are the order of the day. Distant processes that individuals themselves can neither control nor understand now drive the small, local worlds that once sustained people and provided feelings of stability and comfort. In such a fluid, diverse, and vastly configured world, how can any of us know who we are or what we should be doing with our lives?

Postmodern writers have also pushed forward ideas about the changing conditions of self-experience (see Rosenau 1992). Because modern society and culture are so diverse and complicated, using a single "grand totalizing narrative" to describe those settings or the people who inhabit them is no longer possible. In that light, accounts of the self have shifted from descriptions of integrated, relatively permanent structures that explain much of human behavior to descriptions of multiple selves or even to the many "masks" that people wear (Gergen 1991). People are said to move from one situation to the next and realize themselves in that succession of moments.

Such themes—related to the fluid, fragmentary qualities of contemporary life—will be developed in the next chapter. For now, I wish to emphasize that Mead's pursuit of an integrated self is dependent on the social counterpart of that self—that is, on the integrated set of public "attitudes" that he terms the "generalized other." Part of the charm of the game stage, he informs his readers (1964, 223), is games have a publicly recognized "logic, so that an organization of the self is rendered possible. There is a definite end to be obtained, and the actions of the different individuals are all related to one other with reference to that end so that they do not conflict." However, modern society as a whole is much less clearly "agreed upon" and integrated, and its participants do not possess the relatively equal status of Mead's ballplayers.

For such reasons sociology is now committed to the thesis that self-experience is a multifaceted affair that the more important statuses of the individual influence dramatically. However, it is probably also fair to say that sociology historically has tended to emphasize—and continues to emphasize—the struggles for selfhood by people from the middle classes (see Bellah et al. 1985), who operate from distinctive platforms of occupation and wealth and have similar social biographies, ranges of public contacts, opportunity sets, and visions of their own movement though those contexts. A poorer or less well-connected person may rightly see such preoccupations as the whining of someone who cannot fall asleep in a comfortable bed. Just as working-class people are connected to society differently from their richer counterparts (see Sennett and Cobb 1973; Kusserow 2004), so the upper class—by all accounts our clubbiest and most internally reinforced group—has its own visions of personhood and styles of expression (Domhoff 1998).

In much the same way, feminist scholars (see Landes 1998) have criticized the cult of the isolated self as a theme of male experience that cuts into women's experience in many different ways. Perhaps, as philosopher Carol Gilligan (1982) has claimed in a well-known argument, women more often focus their views of self on participation in social relationships and evaluate the quality of their life in those terms. Perhaps they dream less of inviolate power. Furthermore, one should not expect the possibilities of selfhood for children to be the same as those for adults, a category that is itself broken into various settings and stages (see Denzin 1977). Ethnic groups vary in their histories and traditions, social locations, and feelings of security and hope. Individual societies—and historical periods of those societies—provide distinctive frameworks for self-experience, as do the various regions, communities, schools, and occupations of those societies (see Lamont 1992). Gay and lesbian people face challenges different from those of heterosexuals; an immigrant's experience of a country varies from that of a citizen. Individuals do not operate out of any one of these statuses alone but instead live amidst multitudes of intersecting locations. Whether a particular status will be brought into play at a particular moment of life—or be held in abeyance—is difficult to predict. Describing just how these matters will play out—as a set of actions and reactions—is more difficult again.

Finally, we should acknowledge that the sociological approach I am emphasizing in this chapter should itself be contextualized. As I have tried to show, there are at least five fields of relationships—culture, society, body, environment, and psyche—that provide the "mirrors" by which we understand the implications of our actions. Are some of these mirrors more important than others, or are they simply more valued by society's members? As we've seen, sociologists give primacy to the influence of other persons and groups in matters of self-definition (see He-witt 2000). However, romantic writers and artists have long stressed the impor-tance of encounters with the natural environment as pathways to selfhood (see Oerlemans 2002). In sharp contrast, postmodernists emphasize the importance of encounters with culture, particularly in its more artifactual and transient ex-pressions (see Simpson 1995). Recently, Westerners who study the "embodied self" (see Williams and Bendelow 1998; Featherstone, Hepworth, and Turner 1991) have taken up the awareness of the body, for centuries a theme in Eastern philosophy. And of course, psychologists continue to point to our psychic com-mitments as the ultimate crucible of human awareness (see Baumeister 1999).

Some of the relationships that develop in those different contexts are firmly established and transcend our normal activities and events; others are the most evanescent constructions that afford glimpses of the person and then are gone. Our own comprehension of ourselves in these contexts, like all acts of autobiog-raphy, changes as we move from setting to setting through the life course. From this tremendous array of encounters and placements—a telling observation from a stranger, a broken arm in eighth grade, a sense of being shorter or fatter than other children, residence in a certain house on a certain street, a lesson learned in school, the loss of a loved one, and so forth—emerges the patterned understand-ings of who we are now, who we have been, and who we will be in the years ahead. Each day involves small or large acts of redefinition, both by ourselves and by those "others" with whom we live.

Self as a pattern of feeling. This chapter has described the self as a pattern of awareness that people have about their own qualities, capabilities, and commit-ments. For the most part, I have emphasized patterns of cognitive understanding. Most of us, I would argue, have strongly held conceptions of who we are. Typi-cally, also, we tell stories or "narratives" about the situations that (we believe) have shaped us and about our most important experiences. We live our lives against the backdrop of those ideas and stories. Certainly, this is the approach Mead takes. As he (1964, 228) sees it, "the essence of the self, as we have said, is cognitive."

But is this an adequate description of how we "understand" ourselves? As I ar-gued in the preceding chapter, experience involves an integration of symbolic and physical meanings. When we make sense of occurrences, we combine thoughts and feelings. In my view, we comprehend the self in much the same way.

The view that the self should also be seen as a pattern of feeling was clearly ex-pressed by James. As we have seen, his argument (James 1952, 195, emphasis his) is that people feel themselves as a series of "*adjustments* and *executions*" pertinent to their own actions. Stated at greater length, people are involved in activity in the world, this activity produces sensory experience, and our selves both adjust to these patterns of sensation and instigate new lines of action. Seen in this light, psychic life is a kind of interplay between action and reaction, both in our contacts with the external world and with the goings-on of our bodies and minds.

In discussing "self-feeling," James (197) focuses on two primary forms of feeling: *self-complacency* and *self-dissatisfaction*. These are, as he puts it, "two opposite classes of affection." The first refers to such positive estimations as pride, conceit, and vanity, and the latter to more restrained appraisals like modesty, humility, and diffidence as well as to more strongly negative ones like shame and despair. Although the "associationist" psychologists of his time connected feelings to transitory sensations of pleasure or pain, James does not follow that course. In his view, emotions like shame and pride are broader and more enduring types of self-evaluation, or what he (197) calls an "average tone of self-feeling which each of us carries about with him." That tone is to some extent "independent of the objective reasons we may have for satisfaction or discontent." In other words, our feelings about ourselves are relatively stable patterns that we carry across situations.

Although self-feelings are said to be relatively stable, James is clear that these feelings are dependent ultimately on the experiences we have with the external world. Self-esteem rises through a pattern of personal success and social regard, whereas "he who has made one blunder after another, and still lies in middle life among the failures at the foot of the hill, is liable to grow all sicklied o'er with self-distrust, and to shrink from trials with which his powers can really cope" (197). However pitiable this latter state of affairs, James offers his readers a certain comfort with his view that the self is not only a recipient of the judgments of the world but also an active prosecutor of its own standing. People are involved in what he terms "self-seeking" and "self-preservation." That is, we aspire to self-improvement—or at least self-maintenance—with regard to bodily, material, social, and spiritual identity: his "constituent" elements of the empirical self described above.

The position that ideas are tinged with feelings was also central to Cooley's vision of the self. In Cooley's view, shared ideas as well as shared feelings hold together persons and groups. He calls those shared feelings—which unify and give direction to action—"sentiments."

Cooley's understanding of this latter term is instructive. As he (1962, 177) explains: "By sentiment I mean socialized feeling, feeling which has been raised by thought and intercourse out of the merely instinctive state and become properly human. It implies imagination, and the medium in which it chiefly lives is sympathetic contact with the minds of others." In that sense, he argues that lust, rage, and "animal terror" are basic or lower feelings that express the physical heritage of our species. Their more complicated counterparts—love, resentment, and the fear of disgrace or ridicule—are true sentiments, that is, feelings that have been shaped by social experience. Such feelings must not be seen simply as *consequences*

of social experience. Feelings are equally *causes* of behavior; that is, they provide
the energy that drives social life forward. As Cooley (177) continues: "Sentiment
is the chief motive power of life, and as a rule lies deeper in our minds and is less
subject to essential change than thought, from which however, it is not to be too
sharply separated."

How do people acquire these fundamentally "social" feelings? Much like
Mead, Cooley (1962, 7) argues that each member of our species has an unusual
capacity for "sympathetic introspection," which he defines as a person's "putting
himself into intimate contact with various sorts of persons and allowing them to
awaken in himself a life similar to their own, which he afterwards, to the best of
his ability, recalls and describes." By that process we can appreciate—if not comprehend entirely—"any phase of human nature not wholly alien" to us. By placing
ourselves imaginatively in other people's circumstances, we create an avenue to
not only their thoughts but also their feelings—that is, to their broader awareness
of their situation. We ourselves know what it feels like to be in love or resentful,
and we imagine that others feel those sentiments in similar ways (see Clark 1997).

Because we can feel "with" people (*sympathy*, in one of its meanings), we can
more effectively realize three other common meanings of that term. That is, we
can commiserate with or feel "for" others, we can stand in agreement "with" them,
and we can feel loyalty or allegiance "to" them. Moreover, that ability to feel with
others leads to a much more expansive understanding of the self that Cooley calls
the "we." That concept is addressed later in this chapter.

THE SELF AS ACTION IN THE WORLD

I've argued that the self is a frame that features both thought and feeling. Just as we
have ideas about the nature of the world, so we have ideas about ourselves. Some of
those beliefs about our character and capabilities are of no special importance to us;
others we are attached to passionately. For example, James himself was very committed to his standing as a psychologist; not knowing something in his field embarrassed him terribly. Oppositely, he declares himself "contented to wallow in the
grossest ignorance of Greek" (James 1952, 200). When ideas become "sentiments,"
to use Cooley's term, they become encouragements—and discouragements—to attach ourselves to the objects before us. Seen in that light, the self becomes a pattern
that permits and enables behaviors, a way of leaning into situations.

This final section considers the ways in which the self readies a person for action and then monitors her experiences as she acts. My special interest is the idea
of self as a "projection of personhood," a process by which we imagine ourselves
moving through events. That movement is not only a transition from one physical
setting to the next but also a progress along what Perinbanayagam (2006, 36) calls

"the arrow of time." To have a self is to experience continuity in those movements. People operate with understandings of who they have been, who they are now, and who they will be in the moments ahead. To rely once again on James's (1952, 214) imagery, this sense of persistence through time and space can be compared to the reaction of a woman who looks at herself in the mirror each day and concludes that she is the same person she was yesterday and will probably be much the same tomorrow. Without that feeling of coherence and confident anticipation, the self cannot be claimed to exist.

How long must those feelings of continuity last? Consistently with what I presented in the previous chapter, I believe that experience focuses both on events—and on our "lines of action" in events—and on the patterns that transcend those events. Self-experience also exhibits this double quality. We think of ourselves as possessing general qualities (the transcendent self); we also recognize ourselves as actors in particular events (the situated self). Sometimes these two kinds of understandings—who I am generally and who I am in this particular situation—correspond; sometimes they don't. Most of us imagine ourselves to be good at certain skills; however, on some days we fail terribly.

Typically, the transcendent self establishes the pattern of expectations that people hold for situations ("I've been treated this way in the past, so today I expect to be treated the same way"). But humans are much more ingenious than that. There is also a set of "shadow" selves hovering about. These are the versions of the imagined self, the self that *might* be realized. All of us have idealized versions of ourselves, essentially portraits of who we would like to be. At the same time, we harbor visions of despoiled selves, what we fear becoming. Somewhere between those highest hopes and darkest fears lie all manner of intermediate stations, including our more reality-based "expectations" for what is likely to occur. When people act, they match these various levels of expectation against their understandings of what is actually happening to them. Who we are, have been, and will be is set against who we might be.

All this is just a way of saying that human experience is quite complicated and that the self moves forward on different fronts. And I should note that the comments here parallel my discussion of "displacement" from the previous chapter. People do not simply inhabit situations; they interpret those situations by seeing them as contributing elements to "contexts" of many types. I will illustrate this by describing briefly the ways in which two sociologists have discussed these issues.

The presentation of self. The first of these is Goffman, who figured so prominently in our first chapter. Goffman's later writing may have focused on the ways in which social situations are defined, but his first and most famous book focused on the self. In that work, *The Presentation of Self in Everyday Life*, Goffman (1959) explores several of the themes that I have discussed above. Conspicuous among these is the tension between the understandings that other people and groups have of us (our identity) and how we understand that same person (our self). Another tension is between the general identities we operate with (our transcendent self) and our perception of the ways that we are being treated at any particular moment (our situational self). Still another tension is between the way we would like to be treated (our idealized self) and our experience of the treatment we receive (our actual self).

Following the example of the literary theorist Kenneth Burke, Goffman develops a theatrical (or "dramaturgical") metaphor to explain how people address these tensions. People are said to be actors in the theater of life. Like accomplished actors, we have a wide repertoire of roles we know how to play; some of those roles we understand to be better—or at least more socially valued—than others. The challenge of social life, not unlike that of an actor who has been given a role she really wants, is to put forth an entirely convincing portrayal, in effect to show that we really *are* the character we claim to be (and not some hack who is ill equipped for the part). To convince our audiences, we realize our characters with all manner of stagecraft—language, gesture, costumes, props, and so forth. At times, we sense that we are "off-stage" (and can relax a bit). But when we feel the spotlight, we know the task before us: to make others accept this version of ourselves. In the best of times audiences do accept our portrayals and even applaud the person behind the role. But one small misstep—perhaps a forgotten line or an errant gesture—can destroy in an instant everything we have labored to create.

Every metaphor has its limitations, and Goffman was well aware of the limits of his. Life is not a theater. In a stage play people have written scripts they follow; their fellow actors know precisely what is coming. More importantly, stage actors do not have to convince one another; rather, they have to convince an audience whose only job is to witness the scenes. Even more to the point, everyone knows that actors are not "really" the characters they play; we accept that their performances should be false to this degree.

Normal social behavior is unscripted—at least in formal ways—and the job of the actors is not to convince some distant audience but rather to convince one another that they are who they claim to be. Indeed, people move back and forth between their roles as actors and audiences. To be sure, there are times when we know our performances to be false—for example, that we are not really up to the job that we are applying for—but more frequently we believe the parts we are playing. Indeed, we are as interested in convincing ourselves that we are who we claim as we are in convincing other people. For such reasons, Goffman titles his book the "presentation" rather than the "performance" of self.

The more general point to be taken is that, for Goffman, the social world is not a stage but rather a moral order. That moral order works well only if people are who they say are. Those who deceive us—liars, cheats, and frauds—will be dealt with severely if we can catch them in the act. Offenders so captured frequently receive a temporary reduction in their social standing; the worst offenses will result in a permanent reduction, including the possibility that we will never "trust" them again. All of us are a little unsure that we are who we claim, and we may be even more doubtful that others should recognize us as the person we aspire to be. So we manage information very carefully, presenting some matters and withholding others. In part, we do this for fear of social consequences, but we also do this for our own self-regard. Who wants to think of herself as a fraud or liar?

Goffman's work, as I have argued, is mostly about the ways in which people create and sustain focused lines of action. As actors in situations, we want to see ourselves—and be seen by others—in certain, agreed-upon ways. But is it possible for people to be involved with their circumstances in several different ways at the same time? Can they run out and then sustain quite different "lines of action" with regard to different persons or objects? This is the theme that Gary Alan Fine has developed in his (1983) study of personal involvement in role-playing games like "Dungeons and Dragons." Fine, who draws inspiration from Goffman's *Encounters* and *Frame Analysis*, emphasizes that individuals participate in these games at several different levels. The first of these levels is the level of the *person*. When kids play such a game they are likely to be friends who have many kinds of connections outside the game setting. That wider setting is usually described as the "real world." They recognize the "fantasy world" of their game to be something quite different.

The second level, in Fine's view, is that of the *player*. A player is a particular version of the person that is put into operation for the purposes of that setting. Whether we know anything about role-playing games or not, we know that players are to follow the rules, obey the referee or judge if there is one, try to do their best and—perhaps—win, and so forth. The third level is different again: persons in games of this sort inhabit *characters*. We become, to use one of Fine's examples, Sir Ralph, the doughty knight. These different versions of the individual— essentially three presentations of self—occupy three distinct and sometimes intersecting realities: the friendship circle of the kids, the gaming circle of the players, and then—although Fine himself is disinclined to overbuild this world—the specific fantasy world that these fictional characters populate. Fine's book explores the tension that arises from these different kinds of participation—being a friend, being a gamer, being Sir Ralph. And he is especially intrigued by very subtle questions about what kinds of knowledge a character in a role-playing game is expected to have (e.g., what Sir Ralph should know and how he should act) and where this knowledge comes from. All this raises more general issues about processes of role identification and personal involvement in events (see also Stromberg 2009). Following both Simmel and Goffman, people seem to stand both inside and outside their roles at the same time.

Just as we can see encounters or events as contexts that are situated inside other contexts, so it is that personhood is framed and anchored in these complicated ways. We interact not only as role performers but also as persons. Recalling Mead's treatment of self-development from earlier in the chapter, we are able to see ourselves as elements of a social situation—both as actors and as persons—from our own internal view, from the more external view of another person, from the view of the group as a whole, or even from some wider societal viewpoint. We are able to imagine all these different perspectives, and we refer to them as we make our way through situations.

Self as a grammar of possibilities. Any treatment of the ways in which people put themselves forward should consider one final matter. When people interact, do they simply think of the "self" in some narrow, private way, or do they include other people in their sense of who they are? Is selfhood more than a matter of "I" and "me"? As we have seen, James's vision of the self seems very possessive and controlling, a matter of "my" friends, horses, and bank accounts. And Goffman, although he struggles to find the sources of moral order, also seems haunted by the vision of the alienated but enterprising individual who seeks favor with his associates. The current section describes briefly some other, more participative patterns for experiencing personhood.

One of these is Cooley's "we" or "us." When we care deeply about the welfare of others, we do not act as solitary agents; instead, we include them in our plans. To think of ourselves and other people as a "we" is to endorse the idea of shared subjectivity; such people are expected to work together to achieve a common goal. To use the term "us" is to acknowledge that all of those so included are subject to a common fate. Such ideas are pertinent not only to what Cooley called "primary groups"—such as our family and friends—but are also essential, he (1964) argued, to the possibilities of a democratic society.

A rather different version of the self is what is called the "you." Sociologist Norbert Wiley (1994) describes well this version of personhood in his extension of the ideas of James's colleague and friend, Charles Peirce. Peirce was concerned with how people project themselves into the future. In that sense, his approach differs from that of Mead, who focused on reflexivity as a process of thinking about the "me" as a set of well-established personal traits, attitudes, and capabilities. In Wiley's view, Mead's self is preoccupied with the past—that is, with the "me" that is essentially a residue of past social experiences. On the basis of those life lessons—internalized now as attitudes—the "I" decides how to act. In other words, the Meadian self tends to look backward before it looks ahead.

By contrast, Peirce was interested in experience as a kind of dialogue between two different locations of subjectivity. When we talk to others—or to ourselves—and invoke the term "you," we are asking the individual so addressed to respond. That is, we are recognizing others as persons who will express agency in the next moment. Their "I" is expected soon to emerge as a considered action, but for now it is only a hypothetical "you," a set of latent possibilities for which we must ready our responses. That we can confidently engage the "you" at all suggests the existence of some commonly shared communicative structures that allow us to make hypotheses about what will occur. Peirce's commitment to practical, forward-looking action is the basis for his status as an additional founder of pragmatism. His attention to the intersubjective, anticipatory forms of personhood (represented by the "you") provides an important counter to the more psychological (or I-me) line of thought James developed.

For Wiley, then, the self is both "retrospective" (represented by the "me") and "prospective" (represented by the "you"); it also lives intensively in the present that the "I" dominates. I would continue this line of thought by saying that if selves can be put forward in these different ways, clearly we can also attribute different qualities of personhood to other people. That is, we can treat those others as "they," "them," or even "it" (see Rose 1996). When we describe people in such third-person terms, we are thinking of them as subjects and objects that have no direct connections to us. What happens to them is their business. This general issue—how we should consider ourselves and others—was the subject of philosopher Martin Buber's (1996) famous book, *I and Thou*. We "create" the personhood of others by the way we treat them; they create us through their reciprocating actions.

As we have seen, people move certain versions of themselves forward in social situations. The relationships they have with the people they find in those settings either confirms or disconfirms those understandings. Although we focus on what is occurring before us in the moment, we also look to both the past and the future for guidance. We also rely on models for how occurrences of that type *should* be conducted, standards that defy ideas of space and time. We live both in situations and in the contexts that frame those situations. I refer those readers with an interest in exploring the extremely complex personal meanings that arise within these multifold relationships to Wiley's (1994) book, *The Semiotic Self.*

Striking out. Having stated the issues so abstractly, I will end with a simplifying example. Let's go back to the pitcher-batter confrontation that we considered at several places in the preceding chapter. Imagine that our batter coming to the plate is an expert hitter, much like Casey of Mudville, the protagonist of Thayer's popular nineteenth-century poem (see Thayer and Bing 2000). Such a fellow understands himself to be a star batsman and has the statistics to prove it. Those understandings—held both by himself and by others—have been translated into a set of expectations. Thus, Casey expects to do well nearly every time he comes to the plate; others expect this of him as well.

However, the current time at bat is of special importance, as Mudville is behind that day (the score being 4 to 2) and they are in the last inning. Indeed, there are two outs. Moments before, there had been little hope, for the two batters preceding Casey were Flynn and Blake ("a lulu" and "a cake," our poet tells us). Incredibly, they have gotten on base. Indeed, Blake is safe at second and Flynn's "a-hugging third." The home crowd is wild with anticipation. In much the same fashion, Casey's focus becomes that of the anticipated self. Will he perform well in this pressure-laden moment? He has a vision for how he will perform and gives evidence of this by the confident way he strides to the batter's box.

Now he is at the plate and deeply immersed in his role as an actual rather than potential batter. The expectation system sharpens to a very fine point. He must hit at least one of this pitcher's deliveries into the outfield away from a fielder's reach. Even this (for him) minor accomplishment should mean that the hapless Flynn and Blake will make it home and the game will be tied.

Casey watches dismissively as the first pitch passes the plate. He hears the umpire call "Strike one." He must now understand himself to be a batter who has one strike against him. But he comforts himself that he saw the ball well and that this offering was simply not "his style." Another pitch comes and goes with the same result. Now he becomes a quite different character, a batter with two strikes against him. Still he expects to do well. After all, one swing is all he needs. The final pitch is confronted with a tremendous swish of the bat.

Surely, there are happy lands where birds sing ever sweetly and where local heroes perform mythic feats without exception. Perhaps our Casey still considers himself a great batsman and remains confident about the summer days to come. Perhaps he feels he did his best and that his character is beyond reproach. But for now, he has struck out. That failed self will be the subject of his own recriminations that night, as it will be also for the joyless Mudville fans.

CHAPTER 4

NEW SETTINGS FOR SELF-EXPRESSION

So far, this book has discussed how people make sense of their circumstances. I've argued that we do this by addressing two issues: *What is it that's going on here?* and *Who is it that's going on here?* In other words, we determine the character of situations by placing their people and activities into general or categorical understandings about those elements of the world. Furthermore, we try to integrate our assessment of those two issues. That is, we may decide what qualities people possess by examining the things they are doing; we decide what they are doing based on our evaluations of their personal qualities. A shabbily dressed man who approaches us on the street and says something we do not understand is probably asking for a handout, and a well-dressed man is probably asking for something else—or so we think.

Still, something is missing from this account. Doesn't our evaluation of situations depend also on the *settings* in which the activity occurs? Aren't we sensitive to issues of time and place? To consider this matter, go back to our example of the man who approaches us. Arguably, whether it is 3:00 in the afternoon or 3:00 at night influences dramatically how we interpret that situation—and how we respond. That is, night and day are understood to be different regimes; each presents its own prospects and perils. Similarly, the time of year may affect our judgment. Surely appeals made to us during holiday seasons—or at least those holidays associated with charitable giving—will encourage us to make sense of the man's comments in this way. A request to us on a freezing winter day may be greeted differently from the same words spoken on a balmy summer one. And, of course, there is our own psychological—or subjective—sense of time. That is, we may be more disposed to help if we have recently been helped ourselves or have otherwise become conscious of our own good fortune. People read events through prisms of time and timing.

Perceptions of place also influence judgment. If the stranger approaches us while we are walking down an otherwise deserted street, we may read his behavior differently from if he comes forward in a crowded plaza. Would our reaction be different if he came to the door of our house or into our backyard? What if we find him seated in our bedroom? Clearly, the various spaces of the world are defined by systems of expectation that make plain our understandings of who should be there and what they should be doing.

All my examples have maintained the emphasis that Goffman follows in his own books—that the man confronts us in a face-to face way. But surely there are other ways the man could address us. What if he sends us a letter, an e-mail, or a text message? What if he telephones and we engage in a conversation? Still, these examples continue to presume that the man is contacting us directly, in a personal or one-to-one way. Quite differently, he may "broadcast" his appeal to us through a newspaper, magazine, or television advertisement. He may present his concerns on a personal homepage or an organizational website. We may encounter him in a documentary film about persons sharing his condition or, instead, as a fictional character in a play, TV show, or movie. Arguably, we have understandings of each of these media forms and of our obligations, as viewers, to the matters presented there. And we may evaluate the man's presentation of self—who he is and what he is doing—differently because of those contexts.

As the reader can see, the book's previous questions—about who and what is going on—must be amended once again. Now we ask, "When and where is it going on?" To summarize my previous examples, a telephone call received at 3:00 in the morning at home is dealt with differently from a face-to-face encounter with someone in a busy city plaza at 3:00 in the afternoon. An e-mail is different from a text message or a note left in a mailbox. A sad-eyed stranger in a documentary film is to be distinguished from the same man appearing suddenly in our bedroom.

I've introduced the current chapter in the above way because I want to make clear just how *contextual* our interpretations of self and identity may be. However, I also want to stress that if selves are "projections" of personhood, as I've argued, then one must be attentive to the effects of settings—understood here as arrangements in space and time—on those projections. In that light, this chapter focuses particularly on the possibilities of selfhood that new media forms create. In what follows I describe first (and briefly) how historical changes in societies—including changes in media forms—have influenced the way people experience selfhood. The second part of the chapter discusses how current—and quickly evolving— forms of electronic media create new opportunities for self-expression.

CHANGING SOCIETIES, CHANGING SELVES

As stated previously, it is my view that issues of self and identity are fundamental concerns of human beings in every age. We are social creatures who look to one another for confirmation and support; we form alliances with selected categories of people and occupy publicly recognized positions in groups—and we understand ourselves in terms of those placements. That general point having been made, I emphasize now that *how* people experience selfhood is a matter of cross-cultural and historical variation.

That self-experience should vary across societies—and within societies—is not surprising. The human predicament is to live inside circumstances of many sorts. Some of those circumstances we try to notice, define, and confront as "situations," constellations of occurrences that seem pertinent to us *here* and *now.* Those occurrences have their origins in the various *fields of relationships* described in chapter 2. Those fields, the reader may recall, include cultural matters (great ranges of humanly created resources), social patterns (arrangements of and for persons), environmental factors (expressing the physical properties of the earth), bodily conditions (such as our capacities for physical activity), and psychological orientations (people's learned and unlearned proclivities to think, feel, and act in certain ways). Our processes of thinking, feeling, and acting are attempts to identify particular occurrences that seem pertinent to us as well as to develop strategies to deal with those occurrences. We do this by comprehending them as instances of abstract patterns, arrangements, or frameworks. As Goffman argued, particular situations are understood to be examples of *types* of situations.

In their broadest meaning human societies are the ways in which populations define and regulate situations of the above types. Those regulations, which are frequently the residue of important economic and political struggles, open and close the possibilities of living. For the most part, people experience personhood in the terms that their host societies offer them. In the following I describe some arrangements that have been important to self-development in three broad types of societies: premodern, modern, and postmodern. My argument will be a simple one: in each type of society certain versions of personhood are encouraged.

Chopping up the history of societies into three (or four or five) categories is, of course, a questionable enterprise. As the reader may already have considered, even particular societies at particular points in time do not fit neatly into any such scheme. Some categories of people—distinguished by age, gender, class, occupation, ethnicity, urbanity, and so forth—may be more "modern" than others. Furthermore, communities and regions of a society vary, as do social institutions, such as the family, economy, religion, and polity. In other words, societies do not march into the future in a resolute, integrated, and consistent way. Nor do they march alone, for economic, political, social, and cultural contact among societies is the rule rather than the exception. Finally, the very idea of determining some stages of history as more modern than others is questionable, for that idea usually contains the assumption that there is some uniform—and perhaps irreversible—path of progress for social change (see Carneiro 2003).

Those concerns having been noted, I do employ ideas of modernity here. In part I do this because this approach conforms to the practice of many scholars (see Parsons 1966; Giddens 1990; Hall et al. 1997). But I do it also because I am interested in a broad set of interrelated changes—social, economic, political, and cultural/technological—that have characterized the development of European and European-influenced societies. My goal is to show how these changes have supported changing visions of self. I make no claims that one period is better than another; indeed, the last chapter of this book questions that Western trajectory.

Selfhood in premodern societies. For almost all the time our species has existed, people have lived on fairly intimate terms with the natural world and with small communities of other humans. Although the primary economic strategies of those societies have varied historically—from hunting and gathering to horticulture to herding to the more "intensive" kinds of agriculture featuring irrigation, draft animals, and plows—all of these strategies have emphasized the need for people to work together and to distribute the goods and services they produce (Lenski 2005). In part because of the severe difficulty in making a living through solitary effort, in ages past people centered their existence in tradition-bound communities, tribal affiliations, and kin groups. In addition to economic sustenance, such groups offered social support, political protection, health care, education, and spiritual guidance. The extent to which those groups offered their members stable public identities and equally stable comprehensions of self was also critical. Individuals understood themselves to be the living representatives of social bodies that had long preceded them and would exist for generations after their deaths.

As anthropologists have emphasized, ascription (or the assignment of immutable social status) was a key theme (Linton 1964). Neither ideas of personal achievement—in the sense of purely *individual* success or mobility—nor a mythology of individual rights was well developed. Rather, people were encouraged to embrace the five R's of the traditional society: ritual, respect, responsibility, religion, and routine. Seen in that way, individual success was embedded in group success; pride and shame were collective as much as personal matters. To summarize, the members of premodern societies presented themselves less as private agents and more as the representatives or guardians of their sponsoring groups (Kahler 1956).

If there was little occupational specialization (to make social mobility of that sort meaningful), so there was little geographical mobility. That latter circumstance was due to the quite limited resources for communication and transportation. Although there might be some movement associated with seasonal migration, expanding population, warfare, and religious pilgrimage, most people found little reason to travel great distances. This meant that individuals spent the greater portion of their lifetimes with a small, relatively unchanging community of people. The members of that community typically got up at the same time each morning, followed similar pursuits, possessed common skills, worshiped collectively, spoke a shared language, and circulated a narrow range of ideas. If "identity confusion"— to use Erikson's (1968) term—was not a paramount danger in those days, threats of social shunning and banishment were; even higher-status people were largely captives of their localities.

For all these reasons the sociologist Ferdinand Toennies (1963) argued that people in these intensely local, collectively monitored communities acted with a different kind of "will" from their modern counterparts. For Toennies, traditional communities featured *wesenville*, decision making based on the unreflective expression of communally shared values. People thought *out* or *through* those values, and they felt comfortable expressing those understandings with powerful emotions. By contrast, modern people followed a more halting, deliberate style that Toennies called *kurville*, the relatively dispassionate (and reason-based) consideration of alternative actions. To complete his portrait, earlier village communities—in German, *gemeinschaft*—were traditional, communal, informal, religious, personal, and sentimental. The world that he saw as their replacement—*gesellschaft*—was impersonal, contractual, specialized, secular, individual, and hard boiled.

Much of the character of premodern societies can be attributed to their paucity of communicative devices or "media." For the most part, an oral tradition dominated societies of this type (see Ong 1982; Havelock 1988). This meant that information could only be passed from person to person in social gatherings. Without the means of writing—at least for most people—emphasis was placed on memory and on such memory-instilling devices as songs and stories. Crucial also were social gatherings in which people established public beliefs by means of animated dialogue, teasing, ranting, and other forms of persuasion. A somewhat different setting was the ritual ground that is emphasized in so many anthropological accounts. In an age without written records, periodically people needed to reenact the great moments of their group's history so as to remind themselves of what was important and unimportant, right and wrong. Ceremonial occasions also were opportunities for individual persons to display *publicly* their own commitments to those traditions. In a fashion that many modern people find difficult to understand, those reenactments could also be experienced as entries into eternity, movements into timeless realms of being that transcend day-to-day affairs. In the rituals of traditional societies, people did not simply identify with sacred beings in some imitative way; rather, they *inhabited* those characters and settings and, through their actions, made those powers real (Huizinga 1955; Eliade 1957). To that degree truth was danced. Whatever the difficulties of developing "we" feelings in the modern world (to recall Cooley's concern), these problems were less prominent in ritualized, community-based societies.

Again, none of this is meant to imply that people were not passionately concerned about issues of personal identity (i.e., their standings in groups) and of self (their comprehension and enactment of those standings). Nor am I suggesting that premodern people refrained from being selfish or grasping. However, I am arguing that people had little ability to separate themselves—physically, socially, and psychologically—from their sponsoring groups. Moreover, they had few opportunities to develop rival idea systems to analyze their worldview. And they had almost no reason to align themselves with groups from outside their communities. To be sure, differences in age, sex, kinship, and social status were recognized, but selfhood was largely an extension of one's commitment to those locations. Even specialized occupations—which became important with the development of intensive agriculture—were seen less as personal accomplishments and more as connections to communities of similarly situated people who protected one another's interests. Much like the characters in Chaucer's *Canterbury Tales*, people took pride in being recognizable human "types." For such reasons I would describe the premodern period as the age of the *embedded self*.

Selfhood in modern societies. There is no single point at which the world—or any part of it—can be declared "modern." However, European societies did experience a series of changes that manifested themselves as new forms of social and cultural organization and shifted the allegiances of persons. Some of the better known of these changes are the rise of the nation-state, capitalism, empirically based science, bureaucratic administration, public education, and an individualistic, calculating style of religion called Protestantism (Weber 1958; Eisenstadt 1970). Many of these changes can be traced to the European Renaissance of the fifteenth and sixteenth centuries—itself a rediscovery of some themes of classical societies. Others were extensions of the systematizing, universalizing procedures of the Catholic Church that had lasted for some centuries. Those patterns came into sharp focus during the Enlightenment of the eighteenth century, when commitments to rational inquiry and freedom of expression challenged older ideas about divine right and communal obligation. Accompanying those political and cultural shifts were the economic transformations of the Industrial Revolution, which profoundly altered the character of life during the nineteenth century. In earlier times people tended to be rurally situated, dependent on agricultural trades, immersed in family and community, and obligated in a personal way to firmly established authority figures. With the Industrial Revolution, they found themselves moving to towns and cities, negotiating for places to live and work, participating in money-based relationships, and otherwise pursuing their "private" interests.

The old world—represented by the extended family, peasant community, occupational guild, and monastery—had simultaneously restricted and sheltered its members. The emerging world, however, adopted the credo of an abstract, law-driven economic "market." People were free to succeed or to starve.

It is important to note that modernism exhibits two seemingly opposite movements. On the one hand, social life is marked by increasingly large organizations and the application of those organizations' operating principles to wider settings and numbers of people. For example, during the feudal period people expressed loyalty to their immediate superiors, who in turn were obligated to those above them in great chains of personal service. The rise of the nation-state meant a shifting of loyalty—expressed in the collection of taxes, acknowledgment of legal jurisdiction, military service, and so forth—to the king and, later, to the nation-state itself as a vast, publicly maintained abstraction. More narrowly, modern people expressed their commitments to congregational churches, schools, businesses, and voluntary associations.

Because they were humanly created, politically motivated groups could evaluate, criticize, and even change those organizations and their guiding principles. Seen in that light, the new social forms exhibited both tremendous strength and weakness. On the one hand, organizations found that the institutions of politics, education, business, medicine, and even sport had an administrative reach that placed the population as a whole under standardizing beliefs and practices. On the other hand, those new organizations were understood to be artifices that interested parties could reform.

The other element of modernism is the rise of the individual as a coherent social entity (see Kahler 1956). If in earlier times people were embedded deeply in long-established groups, now they were cut loose from many of those obligations and involvements. One consequence of this change was that people were less likely to see themselves through the lenses that their host community, church, family, and guild provided. Beliefs about responsibility, accommodation, and servitude became less central; instead, individuals were expected to manage their own affairs, defend their "rights," and participate in acts of popular sovereignty. If once people were *subjects* of the king, now they were expected to be *citizens*, who applied ideas of town governance to national issues. In other words, new standards for self assertion, or ascending meaning, came into favor.

As in the premodern period, social and personal possibilities were responsive to technological shifts, especially changes in transportation and communication. During the eighteenth and nineteenth centuries inventions related to the control of steam power and iron making not only revolutionized economic production, but they also created undreamed-of capacities for moving people and goods. Railroads and steamships became the vehicles of worldwide imperialism. Mechanized warfare was its protector.

For our purposes, a key theme was the development of print culture (see McLuhan 1964; Ong 1982). During the fifteenth century the invention of a printing press with movable type made possible the widespread dissemination of complicated ideas and directives. That device led to the cheaper production of books, pamphlets, and, ultimately, newspapers. When combined with the new focus on public education, this meant that the rising middle classes could now read about—and imitate—the manners of their social superiors. An even more important consequence of print culture was the rise of individualistic, reflective religion. A reading public might have imagined itself no longer to need beautiful churches and stately ceremonies, nor did they require the guidance of a highly trained priesthood. Instead, they could communicate with God directly through acts of reading and reflection.

To summarize, modernism is very much associated with the development of a reflective and analytical but also somewhat isolated self. Writers in a print-based culture are able to revise continually and then make permanent their thoughts. Having done this, they can disseminate those thoughts across time and space. Because it is deliberate, written discourse can take the form of quite complicated argumentation (Postman 2005). However, writing does not easily overwhelm its audience, for each reader can take apart its meanings at her own pace. Furthermore, it differs from verbal commentary in that it is not easily "taken back." Written statements—exemplified by formal charters, legal affidavits, and contracts—have a character that is both permanent and public. As might be imagined then, written principles and accounting systems were central to the development of capitalism, civil service, science, and jurisprudence. In the fashion of print-based writers, then, modern selves were fascinated by their newfound ability to make their mark on contemporary society—and, even more grandly, on people in other times and places—and to do this in a fashion that would memorialize their own qualities and contributions.

However inspiring this vision of an activist and firmly fashioned self may be, anyone reading this will be quick to note that cultural changes, including beliefs about what people should be and do, are not the same as social changes—that is, transformations in people's actual rights, responsibilities, and relationships. And it is worth repeating that even cultural changes do not come forward uniformly. Some persons and groups advocate the new styles of being, some cling to the old ways, and most are committed to combinations of old and new. At any rate, modernity did not play out simply as the extension of self-determination and citizenship that the Enlightenment thinkers envisioned. Some groups, especially the urban property holders who pushed forward these changes, experienced a dramatic expansion of their powers. The once-dominant rural landowners found that they now had to accommodate themselves to these new forms of wealth. And people at the lower end of the social scale often experienced conditions of economic insecurity, poverty, disease, and crime. As Marx (1964) himself emphasized, the modern predicament for many working people was unwanted subordination to the regimes of businesses and, by extension, governments.

In other words, subordination to the new (contract-based) organizations was different from subordination to the old, more communal forms. In the new world unsuccessful people might discover that they were also outsiders, with no secure standing in society. Just as changes occurred in the conditions and terms of "descending meaning" (by which people found direction from external forms), so too were there changes in the sense of personal agency and control (or "ascending meaning"). People were encouraged to accomplish all things and establish an identity that was a glittering symbol of what they had become. But many people lacked the resources to accomplish those ambitions. Because personal expression became focused on individual accomplishment—and success and failure was judged in those terms—I describe the modern period as the age of the *productive self*. People produced and maintained the social organizations of their societies. And in the same spirit, they produced and maintained themselves.

Selfhood in postmodern societies. Has the modern period, which has persisted for some centuries, now come to an end? To be sure, many themes of modernism still burn brightly (Giddens 1990, 1991). The policies and practices of nation-states and large businesses continue to shape public life. The age of machines has hardly ended; to the contrary, machine culture has increased its importance in daily affairs. Written contracts still anchor social relationships. Money relations, social classes, and occupational specialization persist as cultural touchstones. And many people remain committed to a mythology that tells them to take responsibility for their own movements through the world.

Still, the twentieth century witnessed some profound social and cultural changes that have altered the character of self-experience for vast numbers of people. By the end of that century many writers claimed that these changes were great enough to support the proposition that at least some societies—or some parts of those societies—had moved into a different era (Jameson 1984; Lyotard 1986; Bell 1989; Harvey 1990). One source of these changes is the continued development of capitalism, which now features *corporate* ownership and is global in its reach. Marx's modernist sociology was founded on the premise that the economic relations of industrial societies—and the social classes responsible for directing those relations—could be identified and changed. But in our contemporary era economic activity has become much more widely dispersed (with many companies having international operations), malleable in its organizational structures and principles, and diversified in its ownership patterns.

Moreover, for the wealthiest societies the problem of capitalist production is no longer how to manufacture enough cars or cheese to keep up with the demands of the people who are able to afford these products (see Ewen 1999). Rather, it is how to *increase* such people's demand for cars or cheese or, indeed, for any other good or service they were heretofore unaware they needed. In other words, capitalism has shifted its focus to consumption and to the discovery of additional "markets." In part, this means developing new customer bases in the economically developing countries, but it also means creating tastes for new *categories* of commodities. People who have garages filled with cars and refrigerators stuffed with cheese must be sold more subtle (indeed, social and psychological) products—essentially *experiences* that reward and decorate the self. Such products may include visits to experience-generating settings, such as malls, hotels, restaurants, museums, sports arenas, and the like. Other, more tangible commodities, such as automobiles, clothing, perfume, exercise equipment, and so forth, may be offered as opportunities to feel good about oneself. Even people's houses and furnishings may be re-envisioned as psychological enclaves, elaborately equipped—and privately controlled—settings where a distinctive range of satisfactions can be found. In every case the commodity being sold is "quality time," either alone or with others.

Many authors have noted this change to a more leisure-focused (and experience-based) society (see Riesman, Denney, and Glazer 1950; Dumazedier 1967). In the most obvious sense this means that large segments of the population no longer have to work the sixty-five to seventy hours a week that were common in 1900. It also means that the character of work is now different from the sustained, physically based labor of the past and that ideas of work, career, and "calling" are somehow less central to self-regard. People in postmodern societies are challenged to be interesting, appealing, or "cool." They are expected to have refined tastes with regard to eating, drinking, music, sports, movies, travel, television, and sex. They know that these matters are bases of activity (and of conversation) and that their current relationships—and the relationships they hope to develop—depend on this sort of knowledge. They know they will be judged in these terms. For such reasons leisure is not only a blessing for the socially advantaged but also a source of continuing anxiety.

It should also be noted that the spheres of work and leisure are now blending in a manner that recalls at least some aspects of the pre-industrial world. In contrast to the modernist emphasis on the productivity of individuals at their workstations, contemporary workplaces are more likely to stress worker morale, public relations, and satisfying customer experiences. Such themes are consistent with an economy that merges sociopsychological matters with tangible products and where the real product being sold is a style of life or even personhood.

The very success of machine culture effected these changes. In postindustrial societies, where there are highly developed technologies and many skilled labor jobs have been relocated to poorer countries, what are people to do? There is, of course, work for those who create, monitor, and service the machines, but many other jobs are now of the "service," "managerial," and "professional" types (Bell 1976; Cohen

2008). Occupations of those sorts develop informational resources—including technology—to establish organizational directives and manage relationships between workers and customers. However, it must also be said that many people are unable to find any stable jobs (meaningful and well paying or not) in these advanced societies.

In one regard, then, the increasing size, complexity, and fluidity of social organizations has undermined modernism's mythology of the assertive individual who can make her mark on the world. All of us now participate in global relationships. Goods are produced and sold abroad, once-local political conflicts threaten everyone, tourists and immigrants permeate country borders, infectious diseases can sweep across the world, and international students, who may or may not return to their countries of origin, populate universities. In this new context nations monitor each other's behaviors closely and develop principles to regulate their interrelationships. The largest corporations transcend national borders and allegiances; the soldiers of the most powerful countries go everywhere. When the operative social and cultural contexts involve millions or even billions of people, the influence of any one person is diminished. As a result, people narrow their attention to smaller circles—perhaps family and friends—where individual assertion and social regard continue to be felt concretely.

Once again, the special focus of this chapter is changes in technology—and especially in media—that abet these social processes. Although some of these inventions occurred during the middle and latter parts of the nineteenth century, they were more fully exploited during the twentieth. For instance, the automobile and the airplane were two notable developments in transportation. As trains had made possible the dense populations of the industrial cities, so cars, with their support systems of high-speed roads, both expanded and decentralized those environments. Automobiles and trucks could move individuals and small groups from one point to another at any time of their choosing. Airplanes extended that mobility. Because persons and goods could move so swiftly across the map, each town soon resembled any other (Kunstler 1993).

Even more important was the revolution in communications technology (see Briggs and Burke 2005). The development of photography during the mid-nineteenth century started what Walter Benjamin (1969) called an "age of mechanical reproduction," when images—presented as somehow "true" or accurate descriptions of people and events—could be produced endlessly and distributed everywhere. With one stroke photography challenged two established ideas about visual representation: that "originals" are different from "copies" (like the copies made from an original painting) and that "mastery" or "genius" is necessary to create important images. During the twentieth century all manner of people began taking photographs. Any print from a negative—and, increasingly, its graphic reproduction in a book or magazine—was seemingly as good as any other. At the press of a button, people could capture and preserve the moments of their lives. As they entered an era of "snapshots" and "pix," people circumvented some age-old constraints of space and time.

More curiously—and more profoundly—many people discovered that they preferred the image to the reality it was said to represent. A "best" high school photograph was selected from an array of possibilities for the senior annual; a beautiful postcard of a vacation destination was better than the noisy, litter-strewn spot that had been visited. As many writers have pointed out, this fascination with the visual stands at the center of the postmodern experience (Featherstone 1991; Ewen 1999; Durham and Kellner 2001). People wish to see attractive images of themselves comfortably stationed in beautiful or exciting environments. To exist as a cultural artifact—and to be able to revisit that wonderful image time after time—is one way to maintain a preferred vision of self in a complex, changing, and anxiety-ridden world.

In a related development, the technology of moving pictures made possible the distribution of scenes and story lines formerly reserved for plays and novels. Yet another invention, the phonograph, captured and spread sound, including speech and music. "Talking" pictures combined these senses. Important also was the development of technologies that transmitted sound and images through electromagnetic waves. Radio became popular during the 1920s and then television during the 1950s. During the twentieth century people understood themselves to be consumers of a range of shows, programs, and ads that were presented to them, seemingly free of charge, as interesting or edifying experiences. Having been exposed to such presentations, audiences considered themselves "informed." More than that, they became fans of selected programs, embraced some products more than others, and looked forward to their weekly encounters with on-air characters (Fiske 1991).

For the most part twentieth-century people functioned primarily as audiences for these presentations. However, the shows did reestablish at least some of the oral and visual emphases of premodern culture. In contrast to the contemplative, willful qualities of print-based culture, television viewing permitted an easier sociability, which keyed on being "in-the-know" about celebrities and celebrated events, and encouraged conversations based on *aesthetic* rather than moral themes.

The creation of a "viewing public" is one important theme of the transition from the modern to the postmodern period. However, media could be used for more than broadcasting; it could also facilitate person-to person discourse. In this regard the invention of the telegraph in the 1840s was critical. Now people could send and receive messages at the speed of electrical impulse. Information—albeit in quite abbreviated form—could come from anywhere. With the completion of the Atlantic Cable in the 1860s, Europe and the Americas were joined. One result of this process was the expectation that people should know something of societal and even international "news." The invention of the telephone in the 1870s likewise helped realize the opportunity for instantaneous, if still station-to-station, communication. In the twentieth century the practice of making and receiving "calls" opened new avenues for impromptu interaction as it also undermined modernist visions of home and office as formally guarded preserves.

The idea that people might be "users" of communications devices, rather than just audiences or recipients of information, became much more prominent with the development of computers at the end of the twentieth century. From their beginnings as calculators, word processors, and logic-driven simulators of real-world activities, those stand-alone machines have been linked to form the "information society" we know today. Older technologies, involving television, movies, phonographs, telephones, geographical positioning, and the like, are being integrated into devices featuring extreme miniaturization, increasingly fast and powerful computation, and satellite connection. If older technologies focused on people's abilities to receive information, then newer ones allow them to produce information and, in even more complicated ways, to interact with other users in acts of shared production.

An example of many of these themes is the making and dissemination of privately produced movies. Like photography, movie making was taken from the experts and handed to the amateurs. "Home movies" during the 1950s and 1960s were first replaced by videotapes, which could be copied and shared, and then by the digital formats that readers know well. Photographs allowed viewers to stop time, as it also encouraged detailed study of the visible qualities of persons and objects. Digital recording technologies allow them to capture sounds and movements, and as a result, people have a quite different sense of what it was like "to be there." In the twentieth-first century one can now "be there" while the event is occurring by watching or even participating from thousands of miles away on an electronic device. If photographs support the modernist credo that the elements of the world have stable, essential, and eternal qualities, then digital movies support the postmodern view that life is understood better as an immersion in ever-changing situations. In that latter vision, processes—including feelings about events—become more important than things.

As I discussed above, modern persons are *productive selves* who construct a tangible world and build their own character in the process. By contrast, postmodern persons can be described as *consuming selves*. To say that one is a consumer is not to imply passivity, for consumers are active selectors, interpreters, manipulators, and extenders of the worlds they inhabit (Fiske 1991). However, consuming and producing are different processes. Producers want to create things that have their own standing in the world. As makers, they are preoccupied with developing and applying skills. Consumers take satisfaction in encountering and appraising things that have already been produced, typically by other people. Consumers are not particularly interested in knowing how these forms were made; they are preoccupied with their experiences of them. To the extent that there is a productive focus in postmodern societies, that focus is on the creation of such experiences or—in an even more complicated sense—on the creation of the activities and settings that facilitate that consumption.

Just as postmodern people have lost some of the skills that stand behind tangible artifacts, such as repairing a car, building a house, using a sewing machine, and the like, so they have also become reconciled to the size, complexity, and fluidity of the social and cultural worlds that have been described above (Cantor 1997; Harvey 1990). Uniformity of belief and value—as in the cases of truth, morality, and standardized aesthetic experience—is not to be expected. If the modernist spirit is to tie down the world and make it submit to the schemes of the maker, postmodernism adopts a more receptive, flexible, and relativistic approach. Against the moralistic attitudes of the previous era, postmodern people are more likely to acknowledge as legitimate the positions and perspectives of differently situated groups. Old-style principles give way to softer attitudes, preferences, and feelings. Postmodern people understand that they live in situations—a theme that has been given some prominence in this book—and that those circumstances will soon change. They dream less of reforming society according to their own schemes and more of living inside that world, interacting with its cultural presentations, and sharing those experiences with treasured companions.

ELECTRONIC SELVES

The reader may think that I have paid entirely too much attention to changes in media. Surely, other kinds of changes—in the physical environment, the size and movement of human populations, health care, politics, economics, education, family life, recreation, and the like—are just as important in determining how people experience themselves. Each of these themes could be developed at length. However, I do agree with the general emphasis of postmodern scholars—that changes in media have created special opportunities for people to present themselves publicly and that new patterns of communication have arisen between formerly disconnected groups (see Strate, Jacobson, and Gibson 1996). If self-awareness arises from the process of putting oneself forward in situations and receiving feedback from others who regard those presentations, then electronic media are important settings for these patterns of acknowledgment.

The following discusses some of these possibilities. To make the argument clear, I'll return to Goffman's dramaturgical metaphor, in which people are said to present themselves as performers on the various stages of society. In our contemporary world electronic media have created some new settings for personal expression. In Goffman's spirit, then, I'll discuss people's involvement as *audiences* of electronic selves, as *producers* of electronic selves, and as *actors* who participate with one another in those settings.

Audiences of electronic selves. Photographic reproduction, movies, and television offered unprecedented opportunities to see people, places, and activities from around the world. For such reasons, Guy Debord (1977) argues that current times are the era of the "spectacle." Advanced societies are now populated by watchers who are fascinated by cultural productions of every sort. People want to see and possess these presentations and products: they organize their lives to gather them and discuss their latest acquisitions with their friends. In Debord's view many aspects of social life now depend on the consumption of such commodities. Increasingly, it is the glittering appearance of the product—and the vision of the person as possessor—that is valued. Indeed, who of us demands that such products be accurate "representations" or "reflections" of reality?

This general idea—that cultural presentations have become detached from their underlying bases or realities—is associated especially with the writing of Jean Baudrillard. In Baudrillard's (1983) view, media presentations are "virtual" realities, objects and events occupying new kinds of spaces and operating with new meanings of time (see also Castells 2000). Each of these dramatic presentations—a magazine advertisement, situation comedy, movie, cartoon, product package, and the like—is effectively a little world filled with its own (intracultural) references. Once again, those products and presentations are not stand-ins for some underlying or original object; instead, they are what he calls "simulacra"—copies for which there is no original. When we watch a funny commercial on television at home, our experience of that event is as good as anybody else's. And we do not require that the producers of that presentation explain to us why a cartoon lizard should be selling us automobile insurance, why that lizard should have an Australian accent, or why a rather aggressive species should now be presented as lovable. Instead, we permit the commercial to develop its own patterns of meaning.

Even if we don't demand that cultural presentations be tied to external realities, don't we at least require them to follow their own internal logics? That is, isn't there some relatively clear "message" that the producers of the presentation intend for us to "get"? Jacques Derrida (1981) answered this question in the negative. Contemporary cultural presentations, or so he argues, do not feature unitary or even tightly linked meanings. Quite the opposite: they open up ranges of meaning for us to consider. This is particularly the case for presentations that feature sights and sounds. When we watch a show or ad, the signs in play—such as our animated lizard in the above example—may well direct us to a range of cultural meanings for the objects and behaviors in question. But these meanings—such as the multiple meanings associated with the image of a lizard—are not sharply restricted or fixed. Instead, we are encouraged to follow our own trails of interpretation of what is presented to us. Signs may direct us to think and feel in certain ways, but those signs are mostly just claims that one object or experience is "different" from another. When we try to nail down just what those differences are, we find that our understanding of what is occurring is only—and endlessly—"deferred" to other experiences and understandings we've had. To combine these ideas in Derrida's invented concept, our search for cultural meanings becomes an exploration in *différance*.

To summarize, postmodern viewers are encouraged to participate in cultural meanings that are realities of their own sort, but those presentations do not dictate the precise meanings viewers take from that participation. Our animated lizard does not demand that we buy his company's insurance; instead, he merely presents himself to us in ways that lead us to decide that he is shrewd, jaunty, and unassuming. However, any conclusions we draw about his character are "up to us," as is our choice to purchase the insurance.

As the reader might note, how audiences are involved with media forms—including those audiences' understandings of what is occurring there—is an empirical question. Presumably, people's experiences vary with the kinds of media being viewed and with the ways in which society supports their acts of watching (see Livingstone 1991). Most of us, I think, would acknowledge that we are "into" certain shows and not others. Our enthusiasm for a favorite show may be linked to watching that show with a circle of friends or at least the prospect that we can talk to those friends about its themes. Furthermore, the degree of our interest in any show is a variable that may be exhibited by time spent watching, purchases of show paraphernalia, looking at magazine articles and websites devoted to this theme, membership in fan clubs, displays of knowledge, and other commitments of time and resources. Because this chapter concerns the visions of *persons* who are presented in contemporary media, let us focus on that theme.

What are we to make of the "selves" that are paraded before us in shows, ads, newscasts, press conferences, and the like? Should we think of them merely as "actors" who are playing a role—a role that may have no correspondence to the ways these people present themselves in the other portions of their lives? Or do we try to establish some connection between the on-screen and off-screen versions of these people? To be sure, if we have no prior knowledge about an actor who is playing an on-screen character, immersing ourselves in the fiction that he is who he now claims himself to be is easy enough. But what if we have seen him in other dramatic performances, such as commercials, movies, and shows, or in different public settings, like interviews and "talk shows," where he is presented as being more truly "himself"?

Although postmodern authors emphasize the relative separation of dramatic spectacles from social settings, audiences do seem to have some interest in connecting the actor (as person) to his or her on-screen role. Indeed, Hollywood manipulated that interest by developing its "star" system (see Boorstin 1987). Stars were claimed to be persons possessed of extraordinary gifts—beauty, allure, dynamism, strength of character, and the like—that they could bring to any role. Movies were sometimes "star turns"—that is, vehicles for such displays. For many stars it was important that their roles be consistent with public understandings of their wider social identity. For such reasons, a famous actor might find himself obligated to play heroes rather than villains; similarly, he should always have a more prominent role over a less famous actor.

Consistency of this sort was a way of honoring the expectations of fans. It was also a way of sustaining public interest in individual actors so that any movie they appeared in might have a following. By other practices as well—magazine articles, public appearances, fan clubs, and so forth—a cult of celebrity was established. Viewers were encouraged to learn more about the private lives of their idols and to gain behind-the-scenes glimpses of movie production. This model was also adopted in early radio and television, when celebrities might be the hosts of "variety shows" or the central actors in scripted shows bearing their names.

Slightly different is the circumstance in which an actor performs a particular role so well that the vision of her in that role dominates the rest of her career. One outcome of this situation is that she must henceforth always play roles of that "type," such as the kooky best friend or sultry temptress. As might be imagined, this is a special problem for those who have been child stars or whose popularity depends on youthful vigor and beauty. And if she has been established as a "smaller" star, changing her place in that hierarchy without switching to a less prestigious medium—for example, from films to television, theatre, night clubs, and the like—may be very difficult for her. However, the successful role may also spill over into her other, more "private" domains. That is, viewers encountering the star in a store or hotel may expect her to be like the character they know, such as daffy and lovable. They may express anger at the soap opera villain for the things she's done on screen.

At one level the claims of the postmodern writers seem true enough. As viewers, most of us want to be immersed in the fictional world before us. We do not want to be distracted by thoughts of the performers' acting techniques, though seeing those flourishes has a certain appeal in stage productions. We do not want to think about the triumphs and tragedies of their personal lives. And because we are now flooded with these spectacles—commercials lasting fifteen seconds, magazine ads that receive only a glance—considering all these matters and keeping pace with what is occurring becomes impossible. However, it also seems clear that viewers are interested in some of these spectacles more than others. For shows that pique our curiosity, we want to know who is appearing before us, how they achieved that prominence, and what is happening now to them, both in their acting careers and in the other moments of their lives.

As Daniel Boorstin (1987) develops his classic book *The Image*, there was a time when the public looked up to its heroes, persons understood to be great (and famous) because of their leadership and support for the human community. More common now, or so he argues, is the adoration of celebrities, persons famous for being famous. Stripped of its moral content, fame centers now on being well known. Any kind of success—in music, sports, comedy, crime, and so forth—will do. Because fame is synonymous with widespread recognition, people in contemporary societies are intrigued by their own ability to "make" these celebrities—sometimes seemingly overnight—and then to destroy them by withdrawing that recognition. When the fall of a public figure is truly spectacular, millions are entranced. For, in the end, societies with democratic mythologies celebrate only themselves (see also McGuigan 1992).

In that light, it should be noted that for some years "reality television" has been popular. The premise of these shows is that unscripted performances by ordinary people may be as interesting as the tightly controlled productions of expert writers, directors, and actors. In game shows, sports events, talk shows, person-on-the-street interviews, and candid camera formats, we purportedly catch people—albeit in highly contrived settings—in the act of being themselves. A current crop of shows, where contestants participate in timed competitions of cooking, fashion design, interior decorating, travel, survival, and so forth, combine many of the previously mentioned elements. Contestants compete in tests of physical or intellectual skill, are judged by experts, form social relationships under shared living conditions, get "voted off" by their peers or a national audience, and are videotaped expressing their seemingly most private thoughts to the camera. Pointedly, participants are introduced as being from different regions, social classes, ethnicities, genders, ages, and occupations. To see such people interact with one another and then to hear them describe later what they were "really" thinking and feeling at these moments is to be struck by the tension that I have developed in this book. How people treat one another in public (matters of social identity) and how they feel about those involvements (matters of self) are related but not identical issues. And how they present themselves to one person is often quite different from how they present themselves to another.

Both in their fictional and (more) reality-based forms, television shows provide spectacles of self. Audiences wish to see people in challenging or incongruous "situations." Spirited action and strong emotion are prized. Verbal reports should make clear the private reflections of participants. The people should form and dissolve relationships. Animosity should be on display fully, as should affection. We judge those on-screen characters according to their trustworthiness, loyalty, and other socially relevant qualities. We watch them manage success and failure, including their own banishment from the group. Performers who address these issues in compelling ways—either as heroes or villains—emerge as "fan favorites" and attain status as celebrities during and after the show's run. We follow these people so closely because they are presented as being versions of ourselves. When we criticize their behaviors, we express the standards we think others should apply to people like us.

Furthermore, computers have increased dramatically people's viewing possibilities. No longer are viewers restricted to a limited set of channels, programs from their host societies, or the times when these programs are initially broadcast. The channel-surfing of television audiences, amidst dozens of stations, not infrequently results in the complaint that there is "nothing on." Surfing the Web or Net is a different proposition. There is seemingly no end to the sights; the only limitations are the ingenuity and energy of the surfer. People from around the world can be observed doing almost everything. Newer technologies allow viewers to "walk through" virtual environments; people prefer videos to still photography. They hunt for displays that are comic, absurd, disgusting, perverse, and sublime (see Poster 2001).

Under such circumstances the role of the spectator or voyeur becomes highly refined. Personal tastes or interests are cultivated, and favorite visiting spots get "bookmarked." Unlike the scenes and passages of physical books, electronic images can be shared at no cost or inconvenience to the possessor. When an especially clever or apt presentation is discovered, it may circulate quickly through friendship networks and, by an extension of those processes, "go viral." Much like a physical epidemic, what is at stake here is the communication of private experience.

Producers of electronic selves. The second half of the twentieth century established a role for people as viewers of electronically mediated spectacles. Movies and TV shows were settings where we could observe constructions of selfhood. Audiences not only watched characters acting and interacting with varieties of others; they also heard them make accountings of that behavior. Still, audience participation was mostly a pattern of watching and then expressing approval and disapproval for scenes those viewers could not change.

The development of linked computers, digital recording, and satellite communications has made it possible for people to play a quite different role in the dramatization of self. Now people can inhabit on-screen roles in electronic dramas. More extremely, they can present themselves as the "stars" of their own productions.

The first theme—that people can inhabit on-screen roles and then watch their own actions as those characters—has become highly developed in video games (see Wolf 2008; Wright, Embrick, and Lukács 2010). Many of these are now what are called "role-playing" games, in which participants take on the identity, appearance, and capabilities of an on-screen character. In a fashion that is familiar to most readers, players move their characters though seemingly three-dimensional and increasingly sophisticated virtual worlds. During its journey the character is confronted by environmental constraints, puzzles requiring logical solutions, and the (typically) hostile activity of other characters. Whether that character succeeds or not depends on the way in which the player "controls" it. Participants may keep scores of the character's success; failures commonly result in "death." In such ways video games extend the social and psychological implications of board games. Players move their "pieces" or "men." They watch—and experience vicariously—what occurs to those pieces.

Recalling James's remarks from the preceding chapter, determining the difference between what is "me" and "mine" is difficult. Many of us are fascinated by the quasi-independent lives of those we control and feel some responsibility for. This interest has been exploited recently by the production of toys—dolls, pets, and the like—that include not only the physical artifact but also the opportunity to participate in the activities of that possession in an online or virtual world. The activities of a real "Barbie" or "web pet" are limited by the imagination of the child, whereas the imaginations of the adults who produce and control those settings enable the online adventures of that toy (see Henricks 2010).

More recent video games allow one to choose a name for and then construct—usually from a preestablished list of traits—the self that will appear on screen. Moreover, new controllers correlate the movements of the player's body with the movements of the on-screen character. Players swing imaginary golf clubs and tennis rackets, dance, kick box, and the like as they watch their on-screen selves achieve success or failure. If Boorstin's thesis that contemporary people wish only to see and celebrate themselves is pertinent, postmodern people do seem to desire visions of themselves in evermore exotic settings. In its origin, the term *avatar* referred to the various incarnations of Hindu deities, especially Vishnu; modern video gamers now enjoy these privileges of the gods. Players inhabit heroic—or villainous—versions of themselves, prepare them for battle, see them fall, and cause them to be reborn. If idealized identity is denied to us in ordinary life, perhaps our avatars can achieve it for us (Featherstone 1994; Wallace 2001).

Closer still to the postmodern spirit is the presentation of oneself—or at least a version of that self—in a virtual environment (see Turkle 1995, 2005). Many electronic formats are essentially opportunities for self-publishing, chances to display one's physical appearance, activities, social connections, interests, and even private thoughts to on-lookers from across the world. The idea that one's personal characteristics and reflections may be of general interest is the premise behind personal "homepages" and "blogs" (see Miller 2010). The modernist predecessors of these forms—albums, scrapbooks, and diaries—were occasions for private reflection or sharing with intimate companions. Electronic media, however, now allow people to publish those formerly private matters. Of course, many blogs address important public issues and, in that sense, contribute to the freedom of discourse in societies. However high or low its goals may be, then, blogging implements the view that private expression is a commerce that established social organizations should not control.

Similar issues surround the production and distribution of on-line videos. With the rise of twenty-four-hour surveillance equipment and cell phone cameras, behaviors of every type can be caught on film. People can upload many of these videos to commonly known websites or watch other videos in "real time," or as the event is occurring. Once again, the subject matter of such digital recording varies dramatically, from crimes in convenience stores, to traffic accidents, to political figures' supposedly off-the-record comments, to funny home videos, to "sexting" (the transmission of sexually explicit text and pictures). Some of this is produced for sale; much of the rest is offered for free. All this feeds our culture of voyeurism, but it also makes real the possibility that any individual can be the star of her own show. Indeed, this possibility has been pursued directly by what are called "camgirls" (see Senft 2008), who are women who set up cameras throughout their homes and then charge viewers to observe their behaviors.

Many of these themes are brought together in the creation of personal "pages" in what are called "social networking" sites (see Cheung 2006; Papacharissi 2010). Participants in these sites establish a "profile" that typically includes pictures of self, family, and friends. They may list certain "basic information," such as sex, relationship status, hometown, and a favorite quotation. Other categories may include details of education and occupation as well as a range of "interests," especially music, movies, books, and television preferences. Even more generally, people are encouraged to present themselves in terms of their "likes," especially commitments to activities and associations. Published also on these pages is the number of people who have been granted formal status as "friends" of the profile's possessor. Friends—as opposed to other members of the networking site—can move past the opening page to see the "wall," a more detailed record of the person's activities and comments. Indeed, friends can "post" their own responses to the materials they find there.

To be sure, "social utilities" of this sort have become important ways to maintain relationships with people one no longer sees on a day-to-day basis or, indeed, to learn more about the (publicly declared) interests of people one knows well. They are also opportunities to learn about significant events and life changes, such as parties, weddings, trips, and so forth; in fact, on some sites people receive such information about listed friends automatically in the form of "news feeds." Whatever functions they fulfill for spectators, these formats are also ways for people to establish and refine a public persona. The picture that emerges is typically that of a jaunty social self, someone who has a sizable number of "friends" and wide-ranging leisure interests. Such a person, or at least the cultural version that is presented here, merits universal regard.

Actors in electronic environments. To this point, I've emphasized how visions of self are produced and consumed in contemporary media. For the most part understandings of self in these settings have been described as psycho-cultural matters, interactions between publicly displayed information and the sensibilities of an interpreting public. However, the electronic world is also a social setting, a place where flesh-and-blood people communicate and establish ties with one another (see Jones 1995; Amichai-Hamburger 2005; Papacharissi 2010).

To return to Fine's (1983) analysis of role-playing games from the previous chapter, people interact with one another at different levels. They participate as role inhabitants—or "characters" in the most usual sense of that term. They also emerge as "players" of the game in question and as "persons" who have much wider spheres of interaction and knowledge, such as friends. The first two levels of self-expression seem directly related to the game; the third reflects the purportedly more "real" world that surrounds that setting. These differences become accentuated in electronic games, in which players can watch their characters perform on screen.

In the early days of stand-alone computers and video game consoles, players attempted to recognize and respond to the logic governing the game in question. Examples of this—in which people essentially play against the machine—are solitaire, Tetris, and Super Mario Brothers. Although familiarity with computer hardware and software remains necessary to game success, contemporary players have greater control over the behaviors of their characters and the scenes that appear before them. More significantly, the focus of play in many games has shifted to social relationships—both confrontations and alliances—between characters the players control (Turkle 1995). In the early days of video games those players were typically a group of friends sitting in a room. Since the advent of Internet games, however, one can play against people from different continents.

In the most obvious sense video games offer scenes of characters competing and cooperating. In such ways, they dramatize social life, or at least some of social life's more extreme and exciting possibilities. However, social behavior (in the more usual meaning of that term) is also going on in front of the on-screen action. Players in the same room watch one another's characters succeed and fail. They applaud and tease. They discuss equipment, game strategy, and controller techniques. Moreover, they acknowledge who is really good at this activity—perhaps a "power gamer"—and who is farther down that hierarchy of skill.

When people play in front of one another, Fine's three levels of self-involvement are conflated. That is, one's on-screen character may be described as "me." The player who controls that character is also "me," and so is the real-life person who is at this moment playing. When a character "dies" in a game, the player controlling that character usually has to quit playing for awhile, and this is visible to all. In addition, other players get to see how she handles that failure as a *person*, revealed by her facial expressions and comments. And they get to watch what she will do now that she is no longer playing—for example, whether she will remain interested in the game, choose to talk about the game with others who have also lost, talk about unrelated matters, wander out of the room, and so forth. To summarize, face-to-face settings display people's attempts to integrate the different dimensions of self-experience (see Stromberg 2009; Wright, Embrick, and Lukács 2010).

Because online play features unseen and often anonymous players, these aspects of self become disconnected. To be sure, there are still the on-screen dramas of success and failure. But we cannot see the players themselves. There is a presumption that such people exist, for everyone needs to identify themselves to log into the game, and often they must provide names—real or assumed—to be part of alliances and teams. The system may keep and publicize records of player accomplishments. Finally, those players may also provide in-game commentary to other participants—sometimes in blatantly aggressive language—through online comments.

There is also a wide range of activity going on outside the game itself as participants try to accumulate various kinds of "gaming capital," like special privileges, equipment, game knowledge, and skills, by such methods as receiving bonuses from the system for successful play, trading with other players, or purchasing game advantages with real money (see Consalvo 2007). By such means, the makers of the game reward and celebrate loyal participants and motivate new players to reach higher skill levels. Still, the interaction that occurs—between participants themselves and between participants and the producers of the system—centers on people's status as players rather than as persons.

Who are the people who play? For the most part, a person logged in from ten thousand miles away is unknown to her playmates. Or, rather, she is known only through the stylized version of herself that she presents to the online community (Turkle 2005; Donath 1999). As a player, she can be rewarded and punished, but as a person, she is not so easily sanctioned. For example, players who misbehave or abuse others in the game by use of "hacks," "macros," "bots," and other devices that rewrite the codes of games or create unfair advantages can only be punished as players—that is, by being denied admittance to game settings by the game's controllers. This is also the case for online "forums," in which people discuss game-related matters. People are expected to participate there in their player personas and should focus their discussions in this way. Remarks that are pointedly disruptive or discriminatory, such as racist, sexist, and so forth, can lead to banishment—temporary or permanent—from that setting. Notable among those improprieties is the revelation of names, addresses, or other identifying information about the game's makers, other players, or themselves. In other words, this is a world in which broader personal identity is discouraged.

The tension between these three aspects of self (as on-screen characters, as participants in the system that presents and regulates these characters, and as persons who choose to participate in these systems) is a persistent feature of Internet activity. For their part, the commercial sponsors of websites want to obtain the e-mail addresses (and, ideally, the credit card numbers) of their "visitors" so that they can sell those visitors their wares. Less reputable are practices like "data mining" that try to gain this information covertly during Internet connections. Still, these organizations are interested primarily in their viewers as customers or as financial contributors to their causes.

Rather different is the "stalking" or "lurking" done by viewers who wish to learn about the persons behind the on-screen images (see Rafaeli, Raban, and Kalman 2005). Persons admitted to "friend" status on social network sites—a privilege that may be extended to several hundred persons—can learn quite a bit about the current interests and activities, social connections, relationship status, and so forth of people they know only casually. Sometimes, they can obtain information by going to the profiles of the social connections that have been listed. Indeed, anyone who is a member of the broader system can see some of those interests and connections. Less cautious people find that their self-image—or rather the image they choose to present here—is available for inspection by current and potential employers, family members, enterprising acquaintances, and others who were once but are not now "friends." Currently, some of these issues are being addressed by system filters or by the development of networking sites that feature smaller—and presumably more trustworthy—circles of people.

"Social relationship" sites address this same tension, using online systems to collect and process information about people as potential dates, companions, and life partners. These sites provide profiles of candidates that the system or its users then "match" (for social compatibility). That personal information may include photos of the prospective candidates and lead to more direct—but still anonymous—online interactions. The purpose of these sites is to move participants beyond online connections to face-to-face meetings. That is, relationships ultimately must be moved forward in old-fashioned ways.

To what extent does the term "community" apply to gatherings of online players, members of social relationship sites, participants in forums, support groups like fans or political advocates, or even "friends"—in the newly expanded meaning of that term? Recalling Toennies's themes from earlier in the chapter, communities were once geographically based. People saw each other frequently and knew many details about one another's lives. Relationships might develop slowly and last a lifetime. Furthermore, a sense of public obligation dominated Toennies's village communities. Membership in those settings—often, based on being born there— entailed acceptance of shared values, routines, and interaction patterns. Identity was centered on social standing. Fundamental to all these patterns was the acceptance of limitation.

Contemporary people may still advocate and pursue long-term relationships; indeed, the Internet allows people to stay "in touch" with friends who were important in earlier stages of their lives. It permits people to stay connected to others in ways that have heretofore been impossible. However, the patterning of rights and responsibilities is different in an electronically mediated world (see Freie 1998; Watson 1998). Some of these changes Toennies foretold with this concept of *gesellschaft*. Relationships now tend toward the contractual or associational type; people make agreements to commit themselves to certain actions—and to certain people—in quite specified—and sometimes legally stipulated—ways. These contracts, like rental or licensing agreements, may be limited to times and places. The interested parties try to meet the prescribed terms of their various contracts, and then they move on to new contracts. In Toennies's modernist vision, people were encouraged to recognize their obligations to one another and to the social "relationship" that was the product of that agreement.

The Internet age has offered people the opportunity to possess without obligation, to take without giving. To be sure, many Internet sites secure payments from customers—such as the six-month contracts associated with social relationship sites—but many users support a rival ethos that information of this sort should be provided for free. That is, products and services like commercially produced music, art, movies, television shows, and so forth should be made available to all—or at least to those who are most skilled in the garnering of that information—and then shared. After all, "cultural" products of this sort are examples of Baudrillard's simulacra— images and sounds that can be reproduced endlessly.

In much the same spirit, people distribute themselves as publicly consumable images. To exist as a cultural artifact is to inhabit the world in a new way. A profile having been established, the provider submits to the gaze of millions. Little effort—and sometimes no money—is needed to maintain the profile; indeed, it may persist after its provider has died. Viewers are able to download these collections of information and image—and to possess them in that way—but there is no requirement that the provider respond to their overtures. Of course, the viewers themselves have even fewer obligations. They may desire to know what is happening at their sites or feel the need to "check" their other forms of electronic correspondence, but this can be done on their own terms and timing. In such ways, cyberspace functions as an "on-demand" world, in which neither rights (as public recognitions of people's entitlements) nor responsibilities (as equivalent recognitions of people's duties) are well developed. Instead, people are users who enter sites and take what they can. They do not wish the organizers of those sites or the inclinations of other users to burden them.

Such dispositions support new ideas about "relationship" and "community." Communities of users (as discussed above) are little more than aggregations of people who share a common interest and enter a site (temporarily) to gain the satisfactions pertinent to that interest. Having made their contribution to an online forum, played a game, viewed a profile, downloaded some information, and so forth, they retreat from that setting. And they do this typically without having to reveal their personal identity to the other users they encounter there. To that degree, Internet communities are like sporting crowds or tourists on holiday: People enter those settings intent on discovering certain pleasures. They take in the local sights, savor some brief experiences, and go home. They do not wish to clean up any messes they have made or to be required to stay when the event has ceased to be enjoyable. And it is not expected—or desired—that these vacationing selves should be consistent with the persons they must be in the other portions of their lives.

CHAPTER 5

EMOTIONS AS FORMS
OF SELF-AWARENESS

To this point, I've considered how people construct their awareness of situations by placing those situations into publicly communicable forms. I have given emphasis to three different aspects of situations—the activity that seems to be "going on" (chapter 2), the version of the self that is presented (chapter 3), and the setting in which such people and activities occur (chapter 4). In this chapter I address directly the subjective processes people follow when they try to make sense of situations. My special interest is the type of experience called "emotions." I argue that emotions are forms of self-awareness that help people recognize what is going on in situations and then guide their responses to what they've identified.

To develop that thesis, I've divided the chapter into four parts. The first of these sections provides an overview of emotions as distinctive forms of "affect." The second section describes what is sometimes called the "dual nature" of the emotions, the fact that both physical and symbolic processes are critical elements of those experiences. The third section develops my view that emotions are not intrapsychic processes of just any sort but instead are comprehensions of *self*. Fourth and finally, I examine emotions as plural forms. What people call emotions, or so I argue, is the result of a series of five "framing judgments" by which accounts of experience are created. I present and analyze a model of this process, positioning some commonly recognized emotions.

EMOTIONS AS FORMS OF AFFECT

As discussed in chapter 2, people are sense-making creatures. We think about the world by matching its occurrences to the ideas and images we hold in our minds.

But we do not ponder that world from afar; instead, we live inside it. In other words, sense making is not only a process of conceiving but also involves *perceiving*. We "sense" what is going on around us and have "sensations" of what is occurring inside our bodies. Experience is the point of convergence between these subjectively managed processes and the world's occurrences.

To illustrate this, imagine yourself in the presence of a beautiful rose. Initially, this means perceiving the rose through your organs of sight, touch, and smell. However, when you "take in" the rose, it is a not a static or passive affair; quite the opposite, you feel yourself bending down to touch and smell it. Moreover, as you take the rose in, you sense that the qualities of the rose are somehow affecting you. There is a sensation of being changed or even "intoxicated" by the event. Something within your body has been stirred; you are not quite the same as you were in the moments before this encounter. Many other encounters—eating, drinking, romantic interludes, meeting an old friend, and so forth—could be described in a similar way. People sense the world, but they also sense themselves in the act of sensing. And to make matters even more complicated, the *ideas* we hold about a rose or a friend or a romantic partner surely influence those sensations as well.

Social scientists commonly describe the bodily stirrings that influence behavior as "affects." Some of those bodily stirrings can be seen as clear reactions to what is happening around us, such as when we feel ourselves stopped, stunned, or otherwise shifted by some fast-moving object or loud noise. However, we also sense when we seem to be moving forward under our own steam, that some characteristic set of bodily processes is propelling us forward or, alternately, is causing us to pause.

As the reader might anticipate, scholars offer different conceptions of affect and of its relationship to thought and behavior (see Forgas 2000). My own interest here is not to explore those differences at length but only to show that bodily feelings can be attached to different kinds of contexts. To begin with Cooley's (1964) point from chapter 3, some kinds of affect seem to be rather uncivilized or "basic." Feelings of this sort are experienced as a variety of urges and surges, some of which seem centered in certain parts of the body. Most of these are attributed to "human nature."

Certainly, many older views of human feeling saw those matters as passions or stirrings, internal movements that disrupt the orderly, rationally directed states that are sometimes thought to represent the best forms of human possibility (see Frijda 2000). Indeed, for many centuries feelings of this sort were connected to the classical world's ideas of the bodily humors (Radden 2000). Blood, phlegm, yellow bile, and black bile were said to be present in the body in greater or lesser quantities, and the different allocations could mark patterns of mood and temperament. Even today, we imagine feelings in such terms: our "blood boils" or "runs cold";

we become "green with envy" or "swell with pride"; our heart "sinks," "skips a beat," or "is in our throats"; when we are terrified, we may "feel shivers down our spine"; and we can be so surprised as to "jump out of our skins." When we experience feelings of this sort, we discover ourselves in altered circumstances and feel our bodies move in correspondence with that awareness.

Other feelings seem to be more socially channeled or principled. "Sentiments" is the name Cooley gave to feelings of this type. Unlike urges, which seem to be expressions of physical functioning, sentiments are attached to ideas and understandings—that is, to patterns of cognition. When people think certain thoughts they (sometimes) find themselves becoming excited or even moved to action. To repeat Cooley's line of thought, although people are capable of thinking in fairly abstract ways or even of reflecting about themselves dispassionately—in the fashion of Mead's actors—they are also attached affectively to their own ideas and principles. In that light, moral principles are frequently also powerful sentiments. That is, morals are not simply dry ideas that we are free to inspect at our leisure; rather, they are commitments that incite us or even obligate us to act (see Durkheim 1965).

Sentiments themselves can be categorized according to the different kinds of patterns that are their objects. In contrast to ideas or *beliefs*, which are essentially cognitive matters, *values*—standards for how one should think, feel, and act—are affect-laden principles. To "have" a value or standard is to feel some impulse to impose or defend that standard against rival forms. Different from these general commitments are *attitudes*, which are affect-laden valuations of specific objects or categories of objects. All of us have our likes and dislikes about particular political parties, sports teams, foods, leisure activities, types of people, and so forth. When we encounter particular objects that (we feel) represent those categories, we often "tag" those objects with our patterns of preference. In that sense, attitudes are orientations that are both persistent and targeted.

The self can be included among those targets of feeling (see Laird 2007). Although we can regard ourselves as objects in fairly dispassionate ways—the emphasis in discussions of reflexive consciousness—those self-feelings are often tinged with affect. We may like or dislike specific qualities we believe we possess. We can have high or low self-esteem, a pattern of broader self-regard that makes us feel good or bad.

Moreover, feelings usually accompany our self-guided actions in the world. Some of those self-feelings are intensely particular—that is, they are reactions to specific situations we are in. However, I also believe that James is correct when he says we have an "average tone of self-feeling" that characterizes our behaviors over time. At any rate, most of us probably would acknowledge that people have *moods*, affect-laden personal dispositions that transcend situations. And it is also commonly observed that people have a *temperament*, an even broader quality of personality that marks their characteristic way of behaving.

Emotions differ from these other patterns of affect in that emotions are responses to occurrences in moments or situations (see Lewis, Haviland-Jones, and Barrett 2008; Mayne and Bonanno 2001; Harré and Parrott 1996). More precisely, emotions are registrations of one's standing in the particular moments of life. When we have an emotion, we "feel" ourselves moving into situations, interacting with the elements there, finding comfortable or uncomfortable locations, residing in those moments, and then moving away. We anticipate—and often feel keenly—the prospect of more desirable locations. We remember with pleasure or displeasure experiences we have had in the past. As we turn from one set of circumstances to another—and from thoughts of the present to those of past and future—we find ourselves excited, confused, angered, and bored. If sentiments are the affect-laden *principles* through which we comprehend the world, emotions are the affect-laden *recognitions and responses* we make to the particular conditions we encounter. Said differently (and recalling themes from chapter 2), emotions are constructions of subjective *meaning*.

Are we always aware of our emotions? If emotion is defined as a pattern of self-awareness involving changes in personal functioning, how cognizant must a person be of these changes for the word "emotion" to be applied? Many commentaries on the emotions restrict their subject matter to "feelings"—psychic stirrings that have come to conscious awareness. However, there is no widespread agreement on this issue.

To cite one of these counterviews, psychologists in the Freudian tradition (see Glick and Bone 1990) have emphasized the extent to which we are often unaware of our feelings. As I discussed in chapter 2, that tradition views the psyche as a kind of battle zone in which physiologically based drives and desires—especially sexual and aggressive urges—seek expression against the restraining and guiding influences of the superego and ego. Some of these wishes we have "repressed" or otherwise banished from consciousness; others work their way to the surface in socially acceptable or "sublimated" forms. Others yet may be preconscious formations that stand beyond our reckoning. The task of the ego, as the manager of consciousness, is to integrate these internal directives with the demands of external reality and to produce reasonable lines of action. Many of the so-called negative emotions—guilt, shame, anxiety, and the like—are said to be residues of failed coordination, which continue to smolder and sometimes burst into flame until those psychic conflicts are resolved.

Although other psychological traditions sometimes dismiss the Freudian contribution by claiming that the latter emphasizes psychic forces, drives, and desires more than emotions, it does seem apparent that the appraisal or interpretive process—so central to cognitive psychology—is sometimes ineffective or incomplete. To that extent, we commonly have the experience of being emotionally "mixed up" or "unsure of our true feelings." Indeed, some emotions, such as anxiety or surprise, are founded precisely on the inability of people to comprehend what is happening to them.

The Freudian tradition's emphasis on psychic "instincts" and "energies" helps it sustain a fragile alliance with physiological and behaviorist approaches. Those latter approaches have tended to see bodily commitments as unconscious psychophysical processes that facilitate the responses and orientations of the person (see Damasio 1999; Harré and Parrott 1996). The effectiveness of these processes does not require a conscious awareness of "feeling." At any rate, in both the Freudian and physiological traditions, people are often seen as being pushed forward or carried along by patterns that they do not entirely comprehend.

Can we control our feelings? As noted above, older philosophical traditions tend to describe emotions as passionate forces that sometimes "sweep us away" or at least distract us from our more rationally controlled ambitions (see Solomon 2000). Outside of socially approved settings and apart from certain artistic or romantic sensibilities, becoming "overly emotional" is something that people in modern societies usually guard themselves against. In my opinion, emotion is sometimes still seen as something that "comes over" or "overcomes" people, often "catching them unawares." And because emotion is composed of internal physical stirrings—and typically exhibits external physical mannerisms—as well as cognitive appraisals, it frequently happens that physical processes become the dominant influences on our behavior and we find ourselves "out of control."

Nevertheless, it is also clear that people have some control over their emotions. Adults are thought to exercise more control over their feelings than do children (or perhaps only with regard to certain emotions). Men and women are encouraged to organize their emotional lives differently, a process that facilitates their expressing certain emotions and withholding others. Those who cannot manage their emotions appropriately—in terms of level of intensity, duration, attending behaviors, justification, pertinent situations, acceptable "targets," and so forth—are criticized or otherwise sanctioned sharply for those failures. Even if we cannot prevent our feelings from occurring, it is thought that we should at least control the external mannerisms that reveal those feelings to others. In all these ways, emotional regulation is sometimes understood to be a form of management or even "work" (see Hochschild 1983).

In a different sense, people can effectively control their emotions by trying to create the conditions under which certain emotions are most likely to appear. With varying success, most of us have tried to "act happy" (with the hope that the appropriate emotion would soon follow) or have "picked a fight" (with every expectation of raising the level of hostility). Indeed, among psychological theories that describe emotion as an outcome of already existing behaviors and sensations is the so-called "facial feedback hypothesis" (see Strack, Martin, and Stepper 1988). That hypothesis suggests that producing the facial expressions pertinent to an emotion—for example, forcing a smile by clenching a pencil between the lips and across the back of the jaw—actually promotes the rise of happy feelings. To that degree, emotion is not simply a cognitive "reading" of feelings and behavior but also an extension of muscular-skeletal movements. In these circumstances, emotion is not interpreted but "caused"; five minutes of pretend laughter leads to the real thing. At any rate, people frequently undertake activities or enter social situations—go to a party, movie, amusement park, and so forth—with the clearly understood goal of reaching certain "emotional destinations." In that sense, we selectively inhabit situations and then allow those situations to do their work upon us.

Do emotions always feature arousal? In contrast to purely cognitive patterns like beliefs, emotions are thought to engage our bodies and ready them for action. Moreover, there are degrees of feeling (see Watson and Tellegen 1985). At times, we can appraise a situation with relative dispassion; at other times, we feel impelled to spring forward or jump away. To be sure, powerful feelings that make us respond quickly and involuntarily may attend some emotions—such as anger or fear. Other emotions—such as hope or contentment—are milder in tone. And even the above-mentioned emotions of anger and fear have their calmer, less aroused variants.

Much more problematically, feelings of emptiness and listlessness, such as boredom, resignation, and depression, are sometimes said to be emotions. In such cases, it is the *absence* of normal arousal levels that is noticed and felt deeply. Perhaps it is safe to say—once again following James—that human beings go through the day with a certain feeling-tone for their experiences that is, to them, normal and therefore unremarkable. The emotions *we recognize* are the moments of feeling that spike above or below this baseline. Thus we notice sadness and despair just as we notice excitement and joy. However, in every case we notice them because they somehow enhance or detract from our usual patterns of self-control and personal functioning. At times, we are able to make our own assessments of these changes; at other times, we depend on other people to tell us that we are "not ourselves."

Are emotions confined to the present? Because emotions are responses to specific situations and entail physiological stirrings and mannerisms, to think of those feelings as existing only in the present is natural. In the strictest sense, this is true.

Emotions are experiences, forms of participative awareness that reflect the concrete, sensuous, and ever-changing aspects of existence. Nevertheless, feelings can also focus on mental images of past, present, or future. To that degree, they are commentaries on the (psychological) meanings of time. Many emotions, then, are forms of remembrance. To ponder the past is sometimes to be seized by feelings of melancholy, regret, pride, sadness, and so forth. Alternately, people can turn their attention to images of the future and can experience feelings of hopefulness, confidence, despair, and dread. In both cases, such assessments tend to entail comparisons between understandings of a current situation and imagined visions of what that situation has been or can be. As situations change—and as the frameworks used to interpret those situations change—so the assessment of what is occurring will also change. For example, an embarrassing incident from the past may at some point in life produce chuckles instead of grimaces—or the reverse may occur. Visions of one's own death may shift from feelings of jaunty defiance to terror or resignation or relief.

This distinction—between what I call *emotions of remembrance* and *emotions of anticipation*—will be developed further in another chapter. At this point I want to emphasize only that emotions focusing on current situations—that is, *emotions of the present*—are typically more volatile than feelings centering on past or future events. As noted above, anticipatory feelings focus on interior or psychic occurrences, visions of what our standing might be in imagined settings. Feelings of remembrance are similarly mental affairs, ruminations on acts completed. Emotions of the present, by contrast, are ever-changing phenomena that are subject to forces beyond our control. As new people, objects, and ideas enter settings, our standing in those settings shifts accordingly. Our pleasure in telling a joke is suddenly derailed by a listener who blurts out that he's "heard it." A good stroke in tennis is followed an instant later by a poor one, or by a better one from our opponent. A happy occasion is ended by the revelations of a phone call; a run of good luck turns bad. The present is a precarious moment filled with personal ups and downs, slips and errors, understandings that shift or collapse, disruptions and distractions of every type. At each of those moments, unfolding events either confirm or disconfirm our vision for what that situation might be.

EMOTION'S DUAL NATURE

Perhaps the fundamental issue dividing theories of the emotions is whether to see those feelings primarily as physical or as symbolic realities (see Lewis, Haviland-Jones, and Barrett 2008; Harré and Parrott 1996). Some scholars see the emotions primarily as psychophysical patterns that become labeled as distinctive forms of consciousness and behavior. Others see the same phenomena—and their physical manifestations—as being generated by cognitive perceptions and recognitions, which are themselves the proper locus of study. In this section I'll describe these two viewpoints and offer my own integration of them.

Emotions as physical realities. Although social scientists tend to emphasize the cognitive and moral aspects of human experience, the emotions are striking examples of the physicality of life. At one level, this means that emotions are expressions of brains and bodies. The physical structure of the brain makes thought, sensation, and movement possible. Brains receive, store, and process "messages" of many different types from both the external world and the body and then coordinate the movements of that body through neural and chemical directives. Moreover, as neuroscience has made clear, the brain itself has different parts performing distinctive functions (see Damasio 1994; LeDoux 1996).

Of special importance for the study of emotions are certain structures within the older parts of the brain—the thalamus and hypothalamus—which process many kinds of physical sensation and regulate such bodily conditions as hunger, thirst, and temperature. The hypothalamus is also thought to play a major role in the sensation of physical pleasure, and another subcortical region, the amygdale, is thought to influence fear and anger. However, more than three-quarters of the brain is made up of the cerebral cortex—those outer, more evolutionarily recent portions devoted especially to the processing of sensory data, coordination of complex behavior, language, and analytical thought. Human emotion is a product of the complicated relationships between these elements.

Furthermore, emotions involve not only mental phenomena but also muscular-skeletal movements and even changes in body organs. Of special interest in this regard are processes of the sympathetic and parasympathetic nervous systems, which carry impulses from the spinal cord to the internal organs of the body (see Plutchik 2003). Activation of the sympathetic nerves alerts and energizes these organs. Heart rate increases; people show excitement and expend energy. Parasympathetic nerves have the opposite effect of inhibiting bodily activity or gathering energy. The more demonstrative emotions are thought to be expressions involving sympathetic nerves.

Furthermore, the body's chemical transmission channel, the endocrine system, is connected intimately with our feelings. A number of glands, coordinated by the pituitary, secrete a wide range of hormones—some of the best known being estrogen, androgen, adrenaline, serotonin, and dopamine—that facilitate the work of the body's organs and influence moods and feelings. In summary, the brain is connected to the body through a wide range of neural and chemical processes—and through that body to the wider physical environment.

Not surprisingly, scholars emphasizing the physicality of the emotions tend to see these processes as links to our animal heritage. One of the first to demonstrate that connection was Charles Darwin. In his *The Expression of the Emotions in Man and Animals*, Darwin (1872) compared the musculature supporting the facial expressions of related species. His conclusion was that humans have not *learned* to show rage, fear, surprise, and so forth but instead have inherited these expressive capabilities from their ancestors.

Perhaps the best-known examination of this thesis is the research of psychologist Paul Ekman (1973), who showed pictures of human faces expressing emotion to people in different societies. Those subjects were asked to identify the particular emotion displayed and explain potential reasons why the person in the photo might be feeling this way. At least six emotions—anger, surprise, happiness, sadness, fear, and disgust—seem to be recognized universally. Ekman's findings suggest that these six "basic" emotions, including their physical manifestations, precede and transcend cultural differentiation. However compelling this argument, the reader should note that Ekman's research centers on the ability of people to recognize emotions on the basis of facial expressions. It is possible that other emotions are just as "basic" but not as visible.

For his part, James (1884) offered a modified version of this viewpoint. James argued that emotion is a person's awareness that some external event has aroused the body internally (see Laird 2007). In other words, emotions are essentially recognitions of changes resulting from the activation of the sympathetic nerves. Thus, when we are walking down a dark passageway and suddenly hear footsteps behind us, we may sense an increase in heart rate or a tingling of the flesh. Emotion is an after-the-fact reading of these physical sensations.

In addition to describing the physiological underpinnings of experience, researchers taking this line of approach sometimes speculate on the possible functions or consequences of emotions for human evolution. In that light, Levenson (1994) argues that emotions help organisms survive by focusing attention, coordinating and mobilizing specific behaviors in response systems, recruiting broad-based physiological energy and support, and short-circuiting normal cognitive processing. This position has been stated in a broader way by Lazarus (1994, 163): "All complex creatures capable of learning—especially mammals—are characterized by the fundamental biological property of constantly evaluating what is happening with respect to their well-being." Emotions, in that sense, are devices that signal to ourselves and to others our sense of well-being or danger. As he continues, emotions are "the main evolutionary adaptational system in intelligent creatures."

Sociologist Jonathan Turner (2000) describes the importance of emotions to humans, arguing that people are not less emotional than modern apes but rather more so. A comparison of brain regions thought to play a role in emotions as well as the variety and extent of emotional expression that different species exhibit support this thesis. Scholars taking this general line of approach suggest that human ancestors living in a grasslands environment where they had few natural offensive or defensive weapons—sharp teeth, claws, thick skin, foot speed, and so forth— needed a complicated call system that would alert one another to danger and facilitate a more intensely "social" pattern of life. Thus, increasing emotional differentiation attended neocortical development, language, and tool use. In other words, because of their physical limitations and the complexity of their environments, early humans needed an extremely flexible behavioral repertoire. Today as then, emotions allow people to communicate quickly—in both qualitative and quantitative terms—their behavioral intentions.

Emotions as symbolic realities. However important the physical structures and processes described above, emotion is not reducible to them. That is, human awareness and the "contents" of that awareness are different from the vehicles that carry these thoughts and sensations. Said more simply, people are preoccupied with the conceptualized versions of their experiences. Even sensory data—from sight, sound, smell, taste, and touch—is evaluated less for its effects on our internal organs (processes we can hardly perceive or control in any case) than for its connections to our thoughts and actions. For such reasons, psychologist Jerome Kagan (2007, 76–87) argues that biological "features" or "profiles" are only one part of emotionality. Emotions also involve interpretations of context.

Emotion then is a matter of mind as well as brain. To speak of mind is to talk about the ways in which humans consciously manage informational resources, not only in general terms, such as learning, memory, moral reasoning, and the like, but also as sets of *specific* ideas and images that are gathered, stored, and applied in highly skilled thinking. In other words, although people have general mental abilities, they operate with quite specific cognitions—a belief in the existence of a certain God, a commitment to their own family, an understanding of what happened to them yesterday, and so forth. Moreover, just as our bodies and the physical environment intersect to produce our specific sensory experiences, so our minds are given specificity by the intersections of society and culture. As the discussion of Mead's work emphasized, this latter connection (of psyche/society/culture) is achieved through the creation, maintenance, and internalization of symbols, the publicly established reference system of names and conceptual meanings for the elements of the world.

The extent to which ideas help us interpret physical sensations—and even "cause" emotions—was demonstrated in a classic experiment by psychologists Stanley Schachter and Jerome Singer (1962), in which they administered epinephrine to cause physiological arousal to three groups of subjects. One group was informed correctly about the usual effects of the drug, one group was given incorrect information, and a third was given no information at all about its effects. Each subject was then placed in a room with another "subject" (a member of the research team) who modeled either happy or angry behaviors. How the various groups of subjects described their own emotions depended on the effects of the drug they had been told to expect and on the model the other "subject" provided. In the view of Schachter and Singer, emotion involves *both* physiological arousal and cognitive interpretation. Thus, people who hear footsteps behind them in a dark passageway will experience those sensations differently if they have been fore-warned or if that passageway is in a commercial haunted house. The arousal may be interpreted as excitement, amusement, or surprise instead of fear—or the people may not be aroused at all.

Other theories place even greater emphasis on patterns of conceptual expec-tation and interpretation. For example, cultural psychologist Richard Shweder (1994) argues that declaring any bodily movement or feeling to be an "emotion" or even allowing oneself to be "emotional" is an act that is influenced profoundly by cultural understandings of situations and selves. For example, how people react to a cut finger or a missed bus is the product of many things—their experiences with such matters, general self-assurance, expectations of support from other people, societal ideas about injury and treatment, and so forth. For Shweder, emo-tions feature complex narratives that include visions of the nature of the situation and our proper roles within it. To use an example, bumping into someone on a street may produce surprise (if the collision is deemed to be inconsequential), em-barrassment (if we conclude that the bumping was consequential but no one's fault), guilt (if we judge ourselves to be responsible), anxiety (if we cannot deter-mine what exactly occurred), anger (if we feel confident enough to focus our dis-content on an inattentive or intentional offender), or fear (if we feel we cannot handle the situation). On such occasions, the mind races to produce an interpre-tation of the event, and assessments of cause, blame, likely outcome, and so forth to channel the emotion we experience effectively.

Anthropological studies of the emotions have emphasized the ways in which cul-ture frames the outlook of a society and establishes what experiences are permissible or appropriate. In that sense, culture not only establishes the narratives—or chains of reasoning—that people use to guide their feelings but also identifies the set of distinctive psychological "conditions" that we recognize to be emotions. For such reasons, emotions should be studied not only as a set of universal experiences—the tendency of many psychologists and sociologists—but also as particular, historically situated agreements about "human nature" (see Stearns 2008). Perhaps the anthro-pologist who has done the most to advance this position is Catherine Lutz (see Lutz and White 1986; Lutz 1988). She argues that modern psychological theories of the emotions tend to be unwittingly ethnocentric and that other societies give credence to—and encourage—various kinds of experience that we Westerners ignore, dis-courage, or otherwise view as unnatural and perverse.

The tendency of particular cultures to emphasize some emotions while discouraging others has been termed "hyper/hypo-cognition" (see Heelas 1986). To use a familiar example, many Western societies celebrate a certain style of romantic love and move this experience to the center of public discourse; other types of societies talk about love—and connect it to marriage—in quite different ways. To take a different example from Lutz's research in Micronesia, certain expressions of fear in the society she studied were seen as entirely acceptable for men. In Western societies public displays of male fear tend to be seen differently—as failures of resolve or confidence that detract from manliness.

Preexisting interpretive structures also are pertinent to situations where people expect to find happiness and pleasure. We enter the pleasure-domes of modern society—amusement parks, casinos, restaurants, shopping malls, and so forth—with every expectation of finding certain kinds of satisfaction therein. Our subsequent experiences are evaluated in those terms. To repeat the general point, cognitive interpretations are as much a source of physiological arousal as they are a rationalization of what has already occurred.

Integrating the two approaches. As I've tried to show above, physiologically based and symbolically based theories focus on quite different aspects of emotions. For their part, physiologically based theories tend to see behavior as being pressed forward or "caused" by distinctive internal processes. Such forces, energies, and urges carry people through their lives. These processes are often seen as equilibrating mechanisms within a body conceptualized as a self-adjusting, interdependent, bounded system. Many of these responses are said to be involuntary reactions and escape our awareness. Nor can they easily be changed, for they are grounded in the long evolution of our species. To be human is to operate within a distinctive physical framework that determines our array of possibilities. Human ideation is only a little boat on that vast ocean, an attempt to name the features and survey the depths of what can never be changed. For such reasons, much attention is given in this tradition to the discovery of basic or "primary" emotions.

Symbolically based theories, though recognizing the physical aspects of our nature, have tended to see such urges, energies, and sensations as rather more distant and unfocused sources of behavior. This tradition argues that other animals are captured in scenarios of action and reaction, stimulus and response. Humans, by contrast, are able to extend the distance between or even to "decouple" entirely the relationship between stimulus and response (Scherer 1994a). We are able to delay or suspend behavior and ponder alternative courses of action. To be human is to participate in a more halting, reflective style of life that is dominated by our ideas of things. These ideas—and the language we use to express them—are not inventions of our own but instead are public conveyances that connect us to the minds of other people. We experience the world—and even the physical stirrings inside our bodies—in these public terms. The naming and management of experience and behavior are, for the most part, patterns people *learn*. For such reasons, the symbolic world is thought to be as "real" as the structures of our bodies and the broader physical environment. In that light, emotion is seen as an interpretive encounter, an entry into a jungle of cognitions that are themselves the causes of comfort and discomfort. Thought does not serve feeling but rather shapes and manages it into the recognizable, complex forms we call emotions.

In my view, committing oneself unreservedly to one or the other of these viewpoints is not especially productive if the goal is to gain a general understanding of the emotions (see Kagan 2007; Harré and Parrott 1996; Wiley 1994). Recalling my ascending-descending meaning framework from chapter 2, I emphasize that both symbolic and physical "meanings" inform human experience. Emotion is a meeting ground of sensation and conception, when forms of ideation and physical logics move in and out of alignment. Anyone who has felt his own lip curl upward in an involuntary snarl or otherwise found himself "losing it" knows that we are physical, passionate creatures who have at our readiness certain (unlearned) mechanisms of response. However, it is just as clear to anyone who has seen two animals fight that we do not possess their directness, rapidity of reaction, and deadly physical resolve. We humans are a brooding, gleeful, shouting crew who are fascinated by the ideas of things and preoccupied with the reactions of our companions. We beam and mutter, not only about present, past, and future but also about that which has never happened and never will.

In my view emotion is a judgment-making process that takes into account the elements of situations and their potential relationship to the person. Those situations are produced by the intersection of social, cultural, physiological, psychological, and environmental patterns that effectively "frame" the moment and intrude upon consciousness. When we have emotions, we are engaged in an attempt to make sense or "meaning" out of that intersection of possibilities. However, those meanings are not simply conceptual conclusions; instead, they are integrative forms of awareness that recognize and respond not only to the physical logics of our bodies and their environments but also to the more symbolically based challenges society and culture represent. In such ways, we "read" situations, and those readings lead us to subsequent thoughts, feelings, and actions.

EMOTION AS AWARENESS OF THE SITUATED SELF

There's a popular saying in which the teller claims not to know who first discovered water, but it surely wasn't a fish. Like that hypothetical fish, people have difficulty noticing and analyzing matters that are fundamental to their existence.

This is especially the case with physical phenomena that are too large or small for us to sense or for the internal processes of objects—including our own bodies—that are normally invisible to us. However, it is also difficult for humans to step outside their own conceptual frameworks, to analyze the world in terms that are entirely foreign to them. Such difficulties are especially apparent in the analysis of the emotions, for we are deeply embedded in the very appraisal systems we wish to describe.

How do people acquire a sense of their own location in the world? And what role do emotions play in that recognition? In this section, I present the case that emotions are fundamental modes of personal recognizance in situations, processes that help us know the qualities of the "water" in which we are swimming and whether we are doing well in that setting or drowning. Much more pointedly, I argue that emotions are not equivalent to all forms of personal awareness but instead are always recognitions of "self."

The view that emotions are processes of recognition and response has been well developed in psychology (see Frijda 1986; Ekman and Davidson 1994; Strongman 1996; Plutchik 2003; Laird 2007). In psychology, emotion is usually held to be something that goes on *within* the bodies and minds of organisms; that is, emotions are internal processes of noticing, appraising, and readying responses to external events—sometimes described as "stimuli"—that present themselves to consciousness. A list of definitions from just one volume (Ekman and Davidson 1994) displays this general theme as well as its variations. For Frijda (1994, 60), emotions are "object-related affective states of mind." For Scherer (1994b, 26), they are "stimulus evaluation checks." For Ekman (1994, 16), they are "appraisal mechanisms" that allow organisms to "selectively attend to stimuli." For Levenson (1994, 123), they are "short-lived psychological-physiological processes that represent efficient modes of adaptation to changing environmental demands." Although the above definitions focus on somewhat different aspects of emotions, the general refrain is this: emotions help organisms organize behavior.

In my view, emotions are not patterns of recognition and response of all types but only those more complicated systems that address the standing of the person as a whole. In other words, emotions are matters of self. Restricting the concept of emotion to self-based feeling may be a departure from general psychological usage, but it is not a shift from the way ordinary people use this term. For example, people routinely have "sensations" of bodily stirrings and urgencies—hunger, thirst, palpitations of the heart, sexual desires, urges to eliminate bodily wastes, light-headedness, warmth, fatigue, and so forth. Those signals set off complicated responses, but the resulting pattern of awareness is not usually described as an emotion. Likewise, our "sensory" experiences of the external world—provided by sight, taste, touch, smell, and hearing—are not normally labeled as emotions. This is the case even though those sensations may be appraised as being pleasant or unpleasant. Thus, smelling a rose, as in my previous example, is usually thought to be pleasant, smelling a cesspool is deemed unpleasant, and smelling a newly mown lawn falls somewhere in between. However pleasant it may be, few people would claim that the experience of smelling a rose is an emotion, nor are the experiences of pleasure and pain by themselves usually described in this way. The discomfort that comes from a stomachache or a sprained ankle and the comfort that comes from a caress or sexual release are not emotions but rather localized physical sensations.

All the examples given above are things that happen to or within the *body*; emotions are things that happen to the self. For example, a dull pain in the chest is perhaps only an irritation. However, if a person thinks that this pain may be a sign of a heart attack, he will surely experience the emotions of being "anxious" or "frightened." To return again to the example of the rose, that pleasant smell may produce emotional feelings if the person feels *herself* elevated or changed by the experience. In other words, an emotion is a quality of awareness in which the person has integrated a sensation into understandings of self. Emotions move or change the self; one's ability to act in the world is suddenly reconceived.

The reader may interject at this point that emotions are still basically psychological matters, patterns of subjective awareness that influence the way we behave. I do not disagree, but my point is that there are many psychological dispositions— such as "being in a mood"—that are not usually described as emotions. Instead, emotions are thought to be ways in which the subject reacts to specific situations. Being a "happy person" (a matter of temperament) is different from "being happy" (a mood), which is different again from "being happy at seeing an old friend" (emotion). My point is that emotion is not a self-sustaining psychological orientation but instead a process of recognition and response that depends on specific occurrences to "set it off." As I've argued in previous chapters, those occurrences can be cultural, social, bodily, environmental, or psychological in character.

Furthermore, although I'm saying that emotions involve the self, emotions are not the same thing as that more enduring quality that James described as self-esteem. I agree with James that the self exists as a subjectively monitored pattern of traits and commitments that we carry with us across time and space. However, we also experience selfhood in more immediate and transitory ways as we move from one situation to another, or even from one moment to the next in the same situation. As those situations change, our visions of who we are—and how we should act— may change as well. Emotions are the integrative responses of our bodies and minds to those changing circumstances.

Perhaps a more serious objection is the following. Surely, emotions are readings of the "external" aspects of situations as much or more than they are self-focused feelings. That is, all of us are moved by events that do not concern us directly.

When we hear of an accident or fire we feel sorrow for the families involved. We are thrilled by the victory of our favorite sports team; we watch movies and feel ourselves reacting to the plight of the characters. Human beings are not so egocentric that they cry only for themselves; they cry for others.

One can argue, of course, following Cooley (and, long before him, Aristotle), that people are moved emotionally when they identify with others. When an "I" becomes a "we," self-involvement takes on expanded meanings. Still, this does not explain our emotions toward people or events we do not identify with—or whom we identify with in a negative manner. People can read the news of the day with anger and frustration, or they can receive that information with boredom and indifference. In such cases, isn't the focus of the emotions the object, event, or situation instead of the person making this judgment?

To rescue my claim that emotions are always self-focused, it's necessary to return to the distinction both James and Mead offer between those two forms of selfhood—the "I" and "me." On the basis of that distinction, it must be acknowledged that only *some* emotions, such as shame and guilt, seem to be focused on the self as an object or "me." Others, like anger and disgust, are usually directed at others though they can also be directed at the self. Others yet, such as boredom and surprise, tend to be focused on external, situational matters. That is, we are bored "with" or surprised "at" something. To continue the claim that emotions are patterns of self-awareness, then, one must emphasize the ways in which emotions always involve the self in its "I" forms—that is, as a pattern of orientation or agency.

In sociology perhaps the most prominent scholar emphasizing this view of emotions as self-agency is Norman Denzin (1984). Following Sartre (1948) and Heidegger (1962), Denzin declares that emotions are critical elements in the "lived experience" of being human. For Denzin, emotions are not "objective" mechanisms or conditions, nor are they separable portions of experience. Instead, people *are* their emotions. That is, emotions are disclosures of people's ever-changing placements in the world, manifestations of who they are at any particular point in place and time.

Against other theories that tend to see the emotions as unusual or unanticipated states, Denzin follows the approach of James (and of Heidegger) that views experience as always emotionally toned. The emotional forms that we recognize in ourselves and express to others are essentially symptoms of our *attunement* to ever-varying situations. This attunement is not just a process of recognizing and accepting cognitively one's place in the world but also involves behaviors. Consistently, Denzin argues that the self is not some conceptual edifice that every person constructs and then carries about with him; instead, he follows James in claiming that the self is "all that I call mine" at any particular moment (Denzin 1984, 49).

These extensions of the person may include feelings, actions, material possessions, and body relations. Such possessions and commitments may involve conscious assessments of who we are, but they are also more fundamental forms of location or "being." In that sense, the self is a pattern of participation. Those patterns rise to consciousness as people interact with others and reflect on the significance of those interactions to their more stable forms of being. However, emotions are much more profoundly a sense of orientation and movement in the world and, as such, provide glimpses of the human predicament.

My own view is that self-awareness is a dialectical process in which people not only notice the qualities of situations but also their own standings in those situations (the "me"), and their action possibilities (the "I"). To recall the example I used above, the observer of a fire at a neighbor's house does not focus her attention on herself (the "me"); she is concerned about the fire. However, she is deeply engaged as an "I." That is, she is oriented toward the event in a highly excited, distressed way. At some point, she may become aware of that excited state and what she is doing—or not doing—to help. At that moment, her experience of selfhood takes a "me" focus, and her judgment about what she is doing or not doing may lead her to new forms of action.

Although I've distanced myself somewhat from many psychological accounts of emotions, I should note that some psychologists (see Goldsmith 1994; Laird 2007) take the self-focused approach I've developed here. Also, I should emphasize that the views presented above are consistent with the approach of the neuroscientist Damasio, whose work I discussed in chapter 2.

According to Damasio (1999, 168–94), it is useful to think of three different levels of the self, each of which involves a distinct pattern of awareness—a reactive "proto-self," a "core self" (that reflects the organism's awareness of itself in the momentary situations of life), and an "autobiographical self" (that exists as the organization of memories that guide our orientations through life).

To address the first of these levels, Damasio argues that many creatures are able to "map" their standings in situations—for example, whether they are safe or in danger—and such abilities are essential for survival. That "first-order" form of awareness is represented by the proto-self. Other creatures have an additional or "second-order" level awareness, which is represented by the core self. Those more advanced organisms are able to understand—and have feelings about—the character of those situations or even see them in terms of projected patterns of cause and effect. In other words, they are able to not only change their bodies in response to circumstances—as in the proto-self—but also comprehend how those circumstances are changing their bodies. That more complicated view of subjective involvement—and the attendant *feeling* that one is being changed by that involvement—is the foundation of selfhood. The final level, represented by the autobiographical self, is the feelings of personhood that transcend situations. This even more abstract level of analysis includes the qualities of self-esteem and self-improvement that James discussed.

In Damasio's view, *emotions* are more basic than *feelings*. That is, we are moved by patterns of appraisal that antedate, in an evolutionary sense, our conscious awareness of what is happening to us. My own emphasis is to show how both consciously and unconsciously directed processes combine in a series of judgments. This process is discussed below.

EMOTIONS AS FRAMING JUDGMENTS

I've argued to this point that "being emotional" means expressing our judgment that a current situation is somehow relevant to the self. Figure 2 is my attempt to display the process of how we become aware of something and then determine to respond to what we've identified.

The model displays three different kinds of occurrences central to this process of recognition and response. The first of these—termed "Occurrences in the World"—is displayed at the top of the figure. Things happen, and people try to make sense of those happenings. The second set of occurrences concerns the subject's perception and evaluation of these external conditions. This is titled "Appraisal Processes." At the bottom of the figure is the set of personal responses and movements termed "Behavior." Behavior includes both conscious, willful actions as well as other expressions that are less consciously controlled.

The focus of the model is the middle, or "appraisal," section. That emphasis makes this approach appear to be an example of what is sometimes called an S-O-R (Stimulus-Organism-Response) perspective in psychology. In models of that type, complicated interior processing by the organism is said to occur, and this processing helps organize behavior. Although I have placed external conditions or occurrences—effectively stimuli—first in the model, I should emphasize that people do not simply "respond" or "react" to what goes on in front of them. That adaptive or reactive posture, which I described as "descending meaning" in chapter 2, may well be a dominant theme of our lives, but subjects do not just accommodate themselves to external occurrences. Quite the opposite, people impose themselves on situations, disrupt the affairs of the world, and cause trouble. That attempt to manage action and experience on one's own terms is the project I described as "ascending meaning."

To illustrate the role of appraisal systems, imagine that you were just stung by a bee. Because you were stung, you may become afraid that this unpleasant experience will occur again. Will you be afraid of the next bee that comes toward you? After all, it is not the same bee. Will you be afraid only of honey bees—the culprit

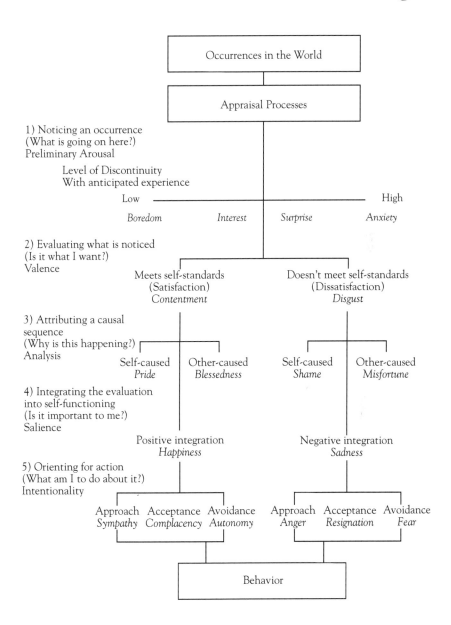

FIGURE 2. Emotions as Framing Judgments

in this particular case—or will your enemies list include other kinds of bees? What about wasps or, indeed, other kinds of flying insects? What about being outdoors again in that portion of the yard where the attack occurred? What about the rest of the yard, other yards, or outdoors in general? Should you keep from repeating your behavior at the time of the sting, perhaps never again walking barefoot or bending down to smell flowers?

Enough has been said to indicate my general point: humans exhibit a categorical intelligence. We put the world's phenomena into types and then operate on the basis of those typologies. And even behaviorist philosophers and psychologists, who try not to over-build the "black box" of mind, must employ ideas about "stimulus generalization" to show how we connect one experience to another.

The reader may recall that deciding what categories are appropriate to what occurrences is the theme of Goffman's *Frame Analysis*, and it is the theme that I follow here. Much like our victim of the bee sting, people make their way through events by making a series of judgments that rely on expectations they have developed for circumstances of that *type*. Those expectations are applied to not only the more or less external objects that we confront—other people, their behaviors, the physical items and settings of events, and so forth—but also ourselves and our own actions, thoughts, and feelings (see Heise 1979). However open-minded we imagine ourselves to be in our appraisals of situations, we inevitably rely on prior knowledge that takes the form of values, attitudes, habits, and other kinds of commitment. Those firmly established patterns are our internal guidelines for action.

To return to the model, the reader can see that I've identified five fundamental issues that I believe are involved in the construction of emotions. "Making sense" of occurrences, in my view, means reaching conclusions about these matters. Although I'm not claiming that the five issues should be seen as some lock-step or invariant sequence, I do believe that the issues display a logical progression—that is, each judgment builds off prior conclusions. In that light, the first three issues—noticing what is going on, evaluating that condition, and, if time and disposition permit, analyzing the possible causes and consequences of that occurrence—have a shared focus. All are essentially external or "situational" analyses. The fourth issue, however, is different. What I call "integration into self-functioning" is a focusing of concern more directly on the self. Essentially, we ask ourselves: is this occurrence important to me? Determining that a situation is important frequently leads to a fifth issue, a judgment about an action orientation. At this point, people turn their attention back to the (newly interpreted) situation that confronts them.

Why these five issues? One answer to this question comes from the research tradition of psychology (see Lewis, Haviland-Jones, and Barrett 2008). In that discipline emotions are said to feature certain "dimensions" or "aspects." In the model these five dimensions are called "arousal," "valence," "analysis," "salience," and "intentionality." Although psychologists usually emphasize only two or three of these aspects in their theories, my approach is to bundle all five together in the fashion shown above. With that beginning, I'll describe each issue.

1) Noticing an occurrence. The first dimension of emotion entails the idea that there is some level of affect or "arousal" that people feel and exhibit when they confront an occurrence (see Watson and Tellegen 1985). All of us can become quite agitated by something that happens; we can also be mildly surprised or even bored by it. In the model this theme, described as "preliminary arousal," is identified with acts of "noticing."

For an occurrence to occasion a response by the subject, it must be noticed and identified. If Goffman's "What is it that's going on here?" is the starting point of every social inquiry, so that puzzle is the beginning of emotional experience. Although the great majority of the world's events—including bodily events—escape our conscious attention, others are comprehensible to us. In my view, emotions are responses to phenomena we *notice*. As emphasized in Lutz's research, culture guides our acts of noticing. We may be encouraged to notice a banging screen door at night, a pain in our stomachs, or a curiously behaving stranger as "something" or, alternately, to disregard these matters as "nothing" and turn our attentions elsewhere. Whether or not there are cultural supports for our acts of noticing, emotion begins with the awareness of discontinuity/continuity that stems from our use of perceptual frameworks. In that sense, noticing is framing activity.

Although we tend to think of personal expectations as internalized ideas or images, we also have *physical expectancies*. That is, our actions in the world move forward with a certain momentum or sense of assurance to which we become accustomed. When these continuities or "habits" are stopped suddenly, we become aware of them in a new way. Many times we perceive that something is going on even if we cannot "put our finger on it." Sudden, radical departures from our expectancies startle, surprise, or stun us. Others are just different enough to pique our curiosity or "interest." Others yet are so extremely different as to disorient us and cause us "anxiety." At the opposite extreme, events can be so continuous with what we expect as to be hardly noticeable or, if noticed, to be deemed understimulating or "boring." The relationship of these four judgments is shown in the figure. In each case emotion of this most basic sort is an assessment of whether things are going as we anticipate.

2) Evaluating that condition. A second dimension is what psychologists call "valence," the idea that people commonly mark situations as being positive or negative, good or bad. Usually, valence refers not only to the *direction* of our judgment (that something is good or bad) but also to the *degree* of feeling that we possess

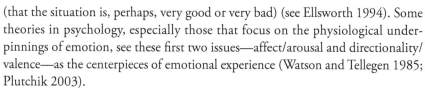

(that the situation is, perhaps, very good or very bad) (see Ellsworth 1994). Some theories in psychology, especially those that focus on the physiological under-pinnings of emotion, see these first two issues—affect/arousal and directionality/valence—as the centerpieces of emotional experience (Watson and Tellegen 1985; Plutchik 2003).

Although some emotions—such as surprise or boredom—are indicators of in-terest or alertness, most emotions feature these more complicated forms of ap-praisal. As noted above, surprise and boredom are reactions to what we *anticipate*. However, people do not just anticipate; they have *preferences* about what should happen in situations. Commonly, then, our emotional tone changes when we ex-perience a *discrepancy between our idealized standards for a situation and the actual character of the events that occur*. The term "idealized" is critical here. People are committed to having events unfold in a certain way. They have hopes, dreams, and desires that differ from simple anticipation. For such reasons, emotion is usu-ally a judgment that reconciles two or more forms of awareness. Emotions cen-tering on this second issue (evaluation) reflect the various patterns and degrees of alignment and misalignment between wishes and actuality. Of particular impor-tance in this regard is the tension between "satisfaction" and "dissatisfaction" that is displayed in the model.

Of course, the terms satisfaction and dissatisfaction do not do justice to the com-plicated range of feelings we experience in response to this issue—or to the many terms we use to describe that response. Partly, this is because there are different kinds of standards or expectancies that people impose on experience. When events corre-spond to essentially *cognitive* standards, that experience of consonance reassures us that we are able to describe the world well or even to know the "truth" of the matter. When those same events seem to defy our attempts to understand—and commu-nicate about—them, we are displeased. In that sense, feelings of being "betrayed," "baffled," and "disgruntled" are in play. Quite differently, when events match our expectations for idealized *feeling*, we attain a sense of aesthetic completion, pleasure, or even "beauty." The opposite of such contented feelings is revulsion or "disgust." Different again is consonance between events and *moral* standards. Consistency of this sort leads to assessments of propriety, equity, and justice. Feelings of moral "out-rage" parallel aesthetic judgments of disgust. Fourth and finally, events may be matched to our standards of effectiveness/efficiency and, by that process, result in assessments of competence, consequence, and *utility*. This last concern, which is a cornerstone of pragmatist and utilitarian philosophies, features the assessment that something is right/wrong or good/bad to the extent that it serves the "interests" of some element of the scene that we value.

Whatever pertinence these four standards have in the history of philosophy, I would claim that ordinary people routinely judge the world in the same ways. Our emotions, expressed as disgust, contentment, moral outrage, incredulity, bafflement, frustration, and the like, are the psycho-physical manifestations of such inquiry.

3) Attributing a causal sequence. The third (situational) issue is what I call "analysis." Processes of noticing (issue 1) and approving/disapproving (issue 2) invite ideas about causes and consequences of events. People who pick up a hot pan or otherwise find themselves in pain will very rapidly produce an assessment of the "cause" of that sensation. The immediate circumstances—that is, the holding of the pan—are placed in a wider scenario. Because the pan is clearly the source of our discontent, we may drop it—or we may not if it is filled with hot liquid that will spill on us! Visions of the likely course of events in the next instant are soon replaced by assessments of damage and attributions of blame. Although all of us are fully capable of blaming inanimate objects—including that hapless pan—for their imputed failings, a more satisfying course is surely the identification of some human agent who may have left the burner on under the pan. At any rate, the general point is this: people try to place events in plausible scenarios (filled with present, past, and future occurrences) and organize their responses in those terms.

In those attribution processes, ideas about the *self*, the *other*, and the *situation* itself play prominent roles. Praise and blame are doled out. Sometimes we recognize (and judge) ourselves as causal agents; sometimes we emphasize the role of "otherness"—that is, other persons and objects or even the situation as a whole. As indicated in the model, "pride" (self-caused) and "blessedness" (other-caused) are feelings associated with positively evaluated situations. Feelings of "shame" and "misfortune" are their counterparts for negatively evaluated situations. Retargeting attention toward the presumed causes of events can lead to new ventures in noticing (seeing aspects of the causal agent that we had not picked up on before) and then evaluating (deciding how praiseworthy or irritating some of those newly noticed traits are).

4) Integrating the evaluation into self-functioning. The fourth issue is commonly called "salience." Frequently we judge conditions to be pleasing/displeasing, just/unjust, correct/incorrect, useful/useless, and so forth. Still, those judgments may not arouse us emotionally or cause us to respond. Many occurrences that we observe—such as the scenes of a television show—are mildly diverting and sustain our interest, but they do not cause us to laugh out loud or otherwise feel engaged. Similarly, we can read the daily newspaper and sometimes be unmoved by the litany of death and destruction recorded there. However, we can also be touched deeply by participation of the above types or by more direct human encounters.

Arguably, the latter cases have been judged to be more important or *salient* to our understandings of self. That is, they are seen as situations that challenge or "touch" our sphere of personal commitment. What I'm saying is that there is a difference between events that are simply diverting, dissonant, or pleasant and those that make us *happy* or *sad* in a more self-focused way. For people to respond to an event in a considered way, they must decide that the event is important enough *to them* to merit that response. Many emotions are ways both of registering that sense of importance and then of helping us—through well-established internal processes—to act. Indeed, without those "encouragements," we might have trouble getting our bodies to respond quickly enough to confront the situations at hand.

5) Orienting for action. Finally, some emotions include dispositions to act toward some element of the scene. Such "intentionality" commonly relies on ready-made rationales that justify certain response patterns. Some of these response patterns are perhaps psycho-evolutionary formations (see Plutchik 2003; Turner 2000); others are products of instruction and habit. To illustrate this latter point, many families have values that tolerate certain kinds and levels of violence. Brought up under these terms, their members are disposed to yell and hit. Those publicly supported rationales serve as "cultural permissions" to harbor some kinds of emotions and put those emotions into action.

In the figure I've distinguished three *styles of relating* to the targeted element. Each of these styles can be applied both to positively and negatively evaluated situations. I've identified three responses to negatively evaluated situations as "anger" (the "approach" style of expressing animosity), "fear" (the quest for "avoidance" or withdrawal), and "resignation" (the passive acceptance of hostility). Although some of these styles feature more active resistance than others, all can be said to be forms of rejection or "disaffirmation." Within the animal kingdom these postures are sometimes described as "fight," "flight," and "playing dead."

I have also identified three positive action-orientations. The approach style is termed "sympathy." That feeling "for" the targeted element reached its highest expression in the sentiments and commitments found in love. The avoidance style is described as "autonomy," the feeling of self-containment or independence. Finally, the acceptance style is termed "complacency," the feeling of comfortable involvement that demands no special action on the subject's part. All of these are more or less active affirmations of the targeted element. Because action-orientations are central to the "social life" of the emotions, the feelings listed here will be discussed further in another chapter.

Refinements and reservations. Now that the five issues have been described, I offer some final comments on the model. As the reader may have observed, emotions beyond the act of "noticing" are presented as belonging to one of two columns, or "emotion-streams." Emotions generally held to be negative are presented on the right side of the model; positive emotions are on the left. Although some of this is done simply to separate the two categories of emotions, I believe there is a logical progression that connects the emotions on each side. To take positive emotions first, situational satisfaction (contentment) typically leads to causal attributions that are similarly positive (pride or blessedness) and to estimations of self-location that may also be positive (happiness). To continue this line of thought, happy people tend to produce "positive" action-orientations (sympathy, complacency, and autonomy). The negative stream has a similar coherence. Dissatisfying situations encourage patterns of blaming (and feeling of shame and misfortune). Negative assessments of self-in-circumstance (unhappiness or sadness) commonly lead to negative action-orientations (anger, resignation, and fear).

Having made my case, I must admit that logical coherence is not always identical to the ways that feelings play out in "real" settings. We can be at a party where things seem to be going wonderfully well and still feel "out of it" ourselves. We can take a certain ironic or bitter satisfaction in an unfortunate turn of events, such as the end of a friendship or the loss of a job. Although commonly we are angry at people who make our lives miserable; we can also respond by trying to love them more. That is, the feelings we possess and the behaviors we produce do not neatly coincide. Emotions—and emotional expressions—often exhibit mixes of positive and negative feeling, a theme that I develop in a later chapter. For now, I will simply say that human beings are too subtle and too ingenious to be captured by any diagram. However, I do argue that examples of the above sort are exceptions or inconsistencies rather than prevalent responses.

My other point concerns the list of emotion words that I've provided. In English there are a few hundred terms that serve as labels for emotions (see Shaver et al. 1987). Clearly my model does not include all those words, and I make no claims that the terms I've included are the best choices from that multitude. However, I do insist that a manageable set of terms exists and is circulated among a society's members. To that extent, I embrace Goffman's theme that situations—in this case, the "situation" of personal recognizance called emotion—are placed into publicly communicable formats. Once feelings are recognized and named, they take on a new role in human affairs. In other words, emotions may be the *results* of framing activity—the theme that I've emphasized in this chapter—but they are also *frames* in themselves. That view—that people do not simply recognize and respond to situations but instead shape them by their interpretations and actions—is considered in the chapters that follow.

CHAPTER 6

EMOTIONS AND
SOCIAL ORDER

The previous chapter emphasized the extremely wide range of occurrences that can trigger emotions in people—hot pans left on stoves, stories in newspapers, pains in the stomach, odors of flowers, and so forth. This chapter takes a much narrower focus. My interest now is the place of emotion in people's social relationships. To be sure, human beings have a special interest in one another. We live in circles of mutual dependency, develop shared symbol systems to communicate, collectively indoctrinate newcomers, administer a public round of life, and estimate the social standings of the other persons we encounter. Those who do not conform to those regimens may be punished or ostracized. Few people live outside this web of public regard; indeed, most of us find ourselves preoccupied with what others think and feel about us.

Because we sense that other people are watching us—and forming judgments about us—our responses to people are somewhat different from our responses to pains in the stomach or the odors of flowers. People are not simply objects of our regard; rather, they are subjects who can reciprocate our thoughts and actions. In that light, socially generated emotions exhibit a *double reflexivity*. On the one hand, we are concerned with what *we* think and feel about ourselves—that is, with issues of "self." On the other, we are concerned with what *others* think and feel about us— that is, with issues of "identity." These two themes are closely intertwined, for how can we comprehend ourselves without the reactions of other people to confirm our self-assessments? And how can we assign identities to others without subjectively maintained standards that we can apply with confidence?

For such reasons I present the current chapter as a counterweight to the themes I developed in chapter 5. In that chapter I discussed the extent to which emotions are inevitably personal matters. Two hikers come across a snake; one of the hikers is frightened, the other is not. By the same token, individuals have dramatically different reactions to bright holiday sweaters, televised golf, and children under the age of six. People rely on their own standards to process information in ways that are largely invisible to others. No person can know with certainty the character and depth of feeling another possesses.

To be sure, personalized idea systems are critical elements of the emotions, but those idea systems are influenced strongly by public beliefs, values, skills, and norms that are made available to such persons by their host societies. To repeat the theme of Marx, Goffman, and indeed most sociologists, people produce their own behaviors and experiences, but they do not produce them just as they wish. Our acts of noticing, appraising, attributing causation, determining importance to self, and selecting action strategies—the themes of my framing decisions—are enabled by preestablished formats that the decision makers themselves neither create on their own terms nor control entirely. Even the choices of what we "wish" for are only partly our own.

In what follows, I discuss some specifically *social* contexts—identities, selves, groups, statuses, and so forth—that impinge on human feeling. I try to show how human relationships are not only causes of emotions but also consequences of the ways in which those emotions are held and expressed. As in previous chapters, I emphasize the contributions of some prominent scholars, though I make no attempt to display the sociological literature on this topic in its entirety (see Turner and Stets 2005; Williams 2001). Instead, I use selected theories to highlight aspects of sociality that pertain to emotions. At chapter's end, I integrate these approaches into a broader view of the relationship between emotion and social order.

WHAT IS A "SOCIAL" RELATIONSHIP?

At the initial class meeting of first-year sociology students at my graduate school, those budding scholars were asked to produce their own statements of the proper subject matter of that discipline. As might be expected, the students offered a variety of definitions. Sociology was said to be the study of "society," of "social organization," of "human interaction," of "social structure," of "group life," and so forth. The professor in charge proceeded to criticize and even ridicule many of the comments. If not particularly pleasant for the students, the point of his exercise was plain enough: social reality is a complicated affair. To focus on only one of its aspects is to disregard other features that many sociologists consider crucial.

My own view is that sociology studies the patterning of human relationship. However, the term "relationship" can be understood in different ways. If people are connected to one another through acts of mutual recognition and response, what are some of the contexts in which these connections can be said to occur?

A look at the answers of those long-ago students suggests some of those possible contexts. To begin, sociality is about interaction. People take account of one another as they act. As I argued in a previous chapter, those actions are intensely particular. That is, we produce specific words and behaviors that we direct to specific people. We do not want the people we've addressed to respond in some dreamy, generic way; we want them to respond with similarly specific words and behaviors that are directed to us and that reflect the particularities of the situations we're in. Social life is the never-ending stream of such actions and reactions.

It can also be argued that we are "interacting" with others even when we are alone. As noted above, people have both identities and selves. We harbor ideas—whether they are correct or not—of how others see us and how we see ourselves. We feel the eyes of the world—including our own eyes—watching us as we act. Many of our private behaviors follow the guidelines of those standards. We feel uncomfortable committing certain acts because they seem "wrong" for us. Freud's "superego" and Mead's "generalized other" are two versions of this idea that society has not only expectations for people in general but also expectations for *us*.

However, social life is much more than culturally guided *action*; it is also a set of relationships between *persons*. Pointedly, we feel attached to others in a way that transcends space and time. This is particularly the case for those we love. Arguably, we continue to have "relationships" with loved ones even after they have died, for we carry powerful images of them in our minds. Similarly, we may have relationships with our unborn children, as we try to earn extra money to support them or ready a room for their arrival. Indeed, we are as preoccupied with our *ideas* of people as we are with their concrete manifestations.

Just as we have relationships with other people, so we have relationships with social positions. All of us hold varieties of social statuses—friend, brother, teammate, and the like; attached to those statuses are socially recognized rights and responsibilities. Those distinctive standings in groups and organizations are commonly very important to us. Our behavior is social to the extent that we enact and defend those placements. To summarize, we behave toward one another as *actors* (who are intent on accomplishing certain ends in situations) and as *persons* (who recognize attachments that transcend time and place). And we also act—and interact—as *status holders* (who address their responsibilities to groups and organizations).

Though social relationships feature individuals, we should emphasize that individuals are not the only social actors. There are many kinds of social units—groups, organizations, communities, societies, and the like—that also pursue lines of action and exhibit relationships. Relationships occur within those collectivities (e.g., between the marketing and engineering departments of a business), between those smaller units and the collectivity as a whole (i.e., between the marketing department and the company itself), and between those collectivities/units and external collectivities/units (e.g., between a marketing department and an advertising agency that is vying for that company's account).

To conclude, there are many kinds of social units that recognize and respond to one another. The task of sociology is to portray those relationships at their various levels and, more precisely, to discern the logic that makes these relationships coherent. At one extreme, this means describing social forms as abstract patterns—encounters, events, groups, organizations, and the like. At the other, it means showing how persons bring these patterns to life through their concrete behaviors. All this raises the question of how the emotions we feel and express are related to these different forms of social order.

EMBARRASSMENT AND THE INTERACTION ORDER

Because Goffman's writing has figured so prominently in this book, beginning with his views of emotionality and social life seems appropriate. A summary of that general approach is provided in his final essay on the "interaction order." That essay is a statement of his career-long ambition to promote acceptance of the "face-to-face domain as an analytically viable one" (Goffman 1983, 2). All his books center on the issue of what happens when people are in one another's presence and, more pointedly, how those interactions are able to move forward coherently. As we've seen, his thesis is that our moment-to-moment interactions are given stability by their connection to clearly established cultural definitions for behaviors of that type, their placement in equally well-defined events, the support they receive from organizations and their agents, and the reality that the material elements of the world grants them. But interactions are also given direction in another way—through their connection to the *identities* of the individuals and collectivities whose purposes they realize.

This last theme is developed most clearly in Goffman's 1967 book, *Interaction Ritual*. That work focuses on people's attempts to sustain orderly lines of behavior with one another at the same time that they maintain socially reputable versions of themselves in those settings. Sometimes behavioral irregularities that the participants themselves cannot control disrupt those preferred definitions of situations—including people's identities in those situations. Such "slips and errors" include ill-advised comments, unfortunate bodily failings, introductions of damaging information, and so forth. At such moments, people find that they are "embarrassed"—that is, that they have "lost face" before others.

Those slips and errors bother us less—or perhaps not at all—when we are alone or when we are in the company of those whose good opinion we do not court. What *does* bother us profoundly is a display of errors and inconsistencies that not only spoils our momentary standing but also spills outward to stain our identity in groups of our concern. To behave foolishly but anonymously at a party or at some other social occasion is one thing; to be recognized and held accountable for those actions is another.

Most of us see embarrassment as an unfortunate condition that happens to all of us from time to time. On that basis we may—or may not—extend sympathy to persons so afflicted. However, Goffman's approach is quite different. To be sure, he does recognize that embarrassment can be a personal calamity, but he is interested less in the discomfort that person may be experiencing than in the purely technical issue that the individual's ability to maintain a preferred identity before others is now hampered. Even more curiously perhaps, Goffman (1967, 97–112) is interested in embarrassment as a feature of "social organization." Consistently with the rest of his work, he wishes us to understand how social encounters develop as unified, focused endeavors and, alternately, how they blow up or fail. Sometimes, events are "uneasy" from start to finish; people are unable to get a handle on what they are doing and how they should treat one another. Oppositely, a situation can be going quite well when suddenly something occurs—perhaps the revelation of some damaging information—and things fall apart.

Because embarrassment is a social as well as personal problem, participants in encounters typically are motivated to repair these failings and inconsistencies. At least that is the case if they want the occasion to move forward along lines that have already been established. Thus, a man who has an unseen (to him) hole in his pants or shaving cream in his ears may not be told of his failing. If he does become aware of it, he will probably become "flustered." At that point, sympathetic others may continue to feign ignorance of the matter or, if it is called to everyone's attention, to treat it as something that is entirely insignificant or beyond the flustered person's control. Those who can get the interaction back to its original focus and tone— and in the process restore the flustered person's rightful status—are said to have "tact." Those who restore their own standing—by smoothly erasing the error, offering a little joke, or otherwise compensating for it—are said to have "poise."

In such ways, Goffman focuses on embarrassment as a social deficiency. That failure is essentially the inability of the participants in an event to live up to the expectations that have been established for them and on which the credibility of the event depends. In that sense embarrassment is one outcome of people's failure to be who they claim to be before others. A common thief may be frustrated or upset but not embarrassed when apprehended at his craft because he is in fact being who he understands himself to be. Others of us—who do not present ourselves as thieves—may be acutely embarrassed to be caught in this way. And even our thief may be embarrassed if he wishes to be seen as a master crook and then does something "stupid" that leads to his arrest.

Because embarrassment is an issue of identity maintenance and smooth social functioning, organizations develop procedures to ensure that individuals will not be placed in situations that challenge or erode those identities (Goffman 1983). In that light, high- and low-status persons may be allocated their own (highly segregated) settings where more egalitarian and intimate styles of conduct are allowed—and expected—to occur. Thus, separate lounges, eating areas, and restrooms are established, and office walls, receptionists, and other "administrative assistants" cut off the powerful from view and sanitize their presentations of self. Indeed, the many layers of underlings in organizations can be seen as a supporting cast that collectively proclaims the specialness of the leading actors. However, those same processes create expectations that the leading actors should in reality be as special as they are claimed to be. Just as a working man or woman may feel flustered when they are called into the grand offices of the boss, so the boss may feel flustered when he or she walks through the company shops and displays an unsettling ignorance of those domains.

For his part, Goffman argues that embarrassment is a normal, even desirable aspect of social life. When people fail to live up to the identities they have been granted and then exhibit their reaction to that failure through signs of discomfort, what their stammering displays is their personal commitment to the "principle" of social life as a moral order. That principle is that all of us should be who we say we are and, if failing in that resolve, should offer apologies to others and to ourselves. Similarly, when people try to save the identities of potentially discredited others by tactful behaviors, they are both publicly acknowledging the importance of social honor itself and giving damaged people a chance to redeem themselves.

Of course, people are not always interested in rescuing socially damaged others, and some of Goffman's other books develop this theme. His (1961a) *Asylums*, a study of life in "total institutions," such as mental hospitals, convents, and prisons, describes the "mortification rituals" that are used to break down and then reshape current social identities. His (1963) book, *Stigma*, studies the ways in which people have their identities "spoiled" by actions or circumstances and the processes they follow in dealing with these labels. In both these instances, people are forced into statuses, identities, and behaviors that are not entirely of their choosing.

STANDINGS IN INTERACTION AS CAUSES OF EMOTIONS

As Goffman's work emphasizes, only sometimes do people reach and inhabit the positions they desire. Furthermore, our staying within a preferred position is always problematic, for "slips and errors" occur, and others can withdraw their support in an instant. Theodore Kemper (1978, 1987, 1990) has explored how standings, considered in their most abstract sense, produce emotions. Like Durkheim and Cooley, Kemper acknowledges that feelings are connected to our membership in enduring social forms. However, Kemper sees emotions not just as the experience of placement in social entities but also as a consequence of moment-to-moment relationships between position holders.

Kemper is interested particularly in emotions that occur in relationships between people who hold differing amounts of "power" and "status," two forms of social advantage in which people acknowledge the ascendancy of another. For Kemper, distinctive emotions are connected to the stable possession of these valued social standings, to the sudden movement into these standings, and even to the anticipation that one will move into such a standing. Emotions of satisfaction, security, and confidence are tied to stable and high social positions. Experiences of downward movement from these positions—or anticipations that this will occur—are associated with negative feelings, such as anxiety or fear.

Furthermore, Kemper understands "status"—as socially validated reputation or prestige—to be quite different from "power." Those who hold positions of power are able to secure the compliance of others even against their will. Power holders get their way through the use—or threatened use—of pain, disadvantage, and their symbolic equivalents. Status, however, is a more consensual arrangement. People voluntarily grant status to others because they recognize that those people embody valued principles of the group. Mutual recognition of this sort (what he calls "status accord") is said to be the foundation of stable societies. To that degree, Kemper stands within the Durkheimian tradition: people must willingly support their societies and one another. And emotions are the vehicles that communicate and reward those commitments.

The importance of these longer-term feelings having been acknowledged, we should emphasize that emotions also reflect the dynamic, tension-ridden qualities of interaction. For Kemper, a gain in power (relative to another person) commonly produces feelings of security; a loss of power typically leads to anxiety or fear. Relationships involving status are, in his view, much more complicated. Normally, a gain or confirmation of status, such as when one person treats another respectfully or follows directions cheerfully, produces feelings of happiness and security. However, a loss of status can lead to a variety of outcomes. For example, if another person is thought to be the cause of the loss—such as that person has treated you rudely—then "anger" at that person may be the result. If the person feels that she herself is to blame for her fall in status, then "shame" is more likely. If the situation is thought to be irremediable, she may feel "sad" or "depressed." In such ways emotions are wrapped into the culturally shared narratives that I described in chapter 5.

Kemper's research focuses on the feelings of the status holders themselves. What do they feel when they gain, lose, or maintain valued positions? A different question is how people in such positions feel about others who are trying to raise their own status, potentially at the expense of the power holders. Cecilia Ridgeway and Cathryn Johnson (1990) have shown that people in higher status positions are culturally permitted to feel anger or annoyance at lower-status people who disagree with them or otherwise threaten smooth social functioning. Higher-status people are presumed to be more socially competent than those beneath them; that competence extends to their ability to makes judgments about others. Lower-status people—and Ridgeway and Johnson are interested especially in gender relations—are expected to blame themselves for social disruptions. Normally, lower-status people doubt themselves or otherwise "back down" when there are disagreements with higher-status people; indeed, there are powerful social pressures for this to happen, for restoring positive emotions means restoring social stability, trust, and smooth information flow. When lower-status people do not back down or, worse, display a level of competence that is higher than the challenged person's, an interesting group procedure sometimes occurs. Other persons who share the identity of the lower-ranking person—such as other women—may counsel them to take a slower, less aggressive, more diplomatic approach. This purportedly more tactful style is contrasted to the "selfish" approach that the status seeker has taken to this point. Ridgeway and Johnson's point is that status seeking—and emotional expression—is not a solitary matter but rather part of a much more complicated social dynamic.

Work of this type shows how feelings about self are related to longer-term structural advantages/disadvantages. It also makes clear that social structure is not fixed or ritualistic but instead interactive. Social standings are tied to the support or recognition of (multiple) others; status is something that must be continually granted or conferred. In that context, people's gestures and expressions toward one another are continuing sources of emotions, and the give-and-take of good (and bad) feelings regulate relationships in general.

EMOTION AS IDENTITY ENACTMENT

The above research shows how people derive their feelings from socially recognized positions in interaction, positions of advantage that last for longer periods of time (as in *social structure*) or for a few moments (as in *interaction*). Different from these approaches is the social psychological perspective, which focuses on the ways in which individuals recognize and respond to their treatment by others. This perspective—which commonly links themes of self (the subjective sense of who we are) with those of identity (the more external or public understandings of who we are)—has been taken by Sheldon Stryker (1980, 2004).

For Stryker, the self is a relatively stable entity. It is not invented by the person but instead is established through our connection to publicly recognized identities in the social world. Each person holds multiple—and sometimes competing— identities. For example, a woman may hold identities as a mother, computer programmer, wife, fitness instructor, and so forth. Each of these statuses has numerous behavioral expectations. We internalize many of these expectations, and to that degree our social self develops as a composite of the roles that we embrace. However, some identities are much more important or "salient" to this overall identity structure than are others. To continue the above example, a woman's identity as a mother or computer programmer may be much more important to her than her identity as a fitness instructor.

In Stryker's view people operate in society from the vantage point of this organized identity system. We put different identities into play at different times, and we expect others (for the most part) to treat us according to established public guidelines for those identities. In that sense, our "mother" expects her young children to treat her differently from the circle of adults to whom she is instead a "friend" or "coworker."

However, identities also transcend the social settings that are their origin. That is, people recognize that their more important identities are not simply placements in social structure but also ongoing commitments or qualities of self. They use those personal commitments to help themselves decide how to enter, behave in, and withdraw from social situations. Such choice making does not occur in a random fashion; instead, it is based on the "salience hierarchy" of these identities. To continue the above example, mothers frequently choose—and frequently are expected to choose—to attend to the more pressing needs of their infant children before they address other interests and commitments. Likewise, they may refrain from behaviors in other contexts that they consider unsuitable for someone holding a "mother" identity. Finally, they may act as a "mother" to other children when the need arises—that is, to extend aspects of that identity into other settings.

Although people are inclined to put their more valued identities into play in social situations, their ability to do this depends on the nature of those situations and the responses of other people to them. For example, highly structured situations, such as a job on an assembly line, typically give people few choices about which identities to use. Similarly, a situation in which the person is a virtual stranger or has few social connections will offer very limited chances to display preferred identities, neither will a situation in which a person finds herself dominated by another.

For Stryker, then, emotions are products of interactions between significant identities and the treatments we receive in social situations. Stronger emotions are produced in interactions in which our more *salient* identities are involved and where we have extensive, deep connections to others. When identities are "verified"—that is, when others respond to us in desired ways or when we judge our own behavior to meet prevailing cultural standards for that identity—we experience positive emotions. Negative emotions, however, are attributable to discontinuities or failures in the verification process.

Stryker's approach emphasizes the extent to which emotions result from matches—and mismatches—of our understood identities and our treatment in social relations. Somewhat differently, the work of Peter Burke (1980, 1991; Tsushima and Burke 1999) has focused on the internal processes that people use to resolve or "control" identity. Like Stryker, Burke sees emotion in terms of identity verification. However, he emphasizes that people are not prisoners of their social experiences but instead agents who monitor the reactions of other people to them and then adjust their own behavior to those responses.

According to Burke, people employ a *perceptual control system* that is composed of four elements: (1) an "identity standard" (ideas we have about a certain identity and how one should behave in that capacity); (2) a "perceptual input" (how we see our behavior and others' reactions to it in any particular situation); (3) a "comparator" (Burke's term for the judgment we make about whether the identity standard and the perceptual input are congruent); and (4) a "behavioral output" (the resulting actions that we perform). These elements operate in a sort of cybernetic or feedback pattern.

For example, a mother usually has fairly clear ideas about how she should act toward her children and, in turn, be treated by them. However, her perception of her own behavior and that of her children may or may not meet that standard. In either case, she continually makes comparisons or judgments about the degree to which the identities pertinent to that situation are being verified. As for Stryker, failures to verify identities produce negative emotions: the more important the identity, the stronger the likelihood that there will be a powerful reaction. However, Burke's actors set about to change these discrepancies. Negative emotions are frequently the starting point for the mother's altered behaviors. If she decides that her children see her as weak, then she may decide to speak more loudly and directly. Any parent knows that such techniques still may not produce the desired effects. Burke calls such failures to restore verification "interruptions." There are many potential causes for these interruptions, but the general effect of all of them is to breed increasingly negative emotions. Such emotions and the behaviors that they stimulate are then reprocessed in the cybernetic fashion described above. To that extent, Burke's people prosecute their own public standings, and for that reason his approach is called "identity management" theory.

EMOTION AS SELF-MANAGEMENT

Burke's theory grants a fairly activist role to the self. When behavior does not conform to the identity standards that we anticipate, we try to transform those situations to restore or "verify" those standards. However, some situations, as Stryker's work also emphasizes, are more difficult to manage than others. And some roles are more complex and tension-filled than others. When fulfilling these difficult identities, sometimes we feel frustrated or disappointed with the way the situation is unfolding, even though we are doing what is expected of us. That is, although our behavior essentially "verifies" our identity, we experience what Goffman (1961b) describes as "alienation" or "role distance." When roles cannot be changed to meet self-standards—that is, when we cannot change a social situation in a way we would like—we have two options: we can either live with that sense of separation or we can try to change our approach to it.

Such themes have been central to the work of Arlie Hochschild (1979, 1983, 2003). Hochschild's best-known work, *The Managed Heart* (1983), is a study of the "management" of emotions by flight attendants and other workers in the burgeoning personal service industry. At one level her work is an extension of Marx's (1964) ideas about the conditions of alienated labor. In the new service industries that focus on customer satisfaction, the providers of those services face a double bind. Not only are they subject to the usual bureaucratic restrictions regarding job performance, they also must serve or even "please" their customers. In the case of flight attendants, the fact that airline passengers sometimes behave in petulant ways compounds this latter difficulty.

In Hochschild's view service jobs feature a new kind of work—emotion management. For flight attendants this means, at one level, controlling the emotions of the passengers, a difficult prospect given the vicissitudes of air travel. However, a different and perhaps even more strenuous aspect of the job entails the service providers' efforts to control their own emotions. For Hochschild, this latter form of emotion management features not only the regulation of external gestures and language—exemplified by the attendants' commitment to be calm, courteous, and pleasant at all times—but also a great deal of internal emotional "work." As she notes, most human beings do not wish to be alienated, upset, or "fake" in their relationships with others. Thus, the flight attendants in her study tried hard to control their own negative feelings toward their frequently irritating customers, and they even developed elaborate rationales to help themselves integrate the outer and inner dimensions of experience. In that light, they struggled to not only control their expressions of anger but also prevent this feeling from occurring. In Hochschild's vision, then, emotional management is a complicated process of internal integration that involves not only the emotions we permit ourselves to *express* but also the emotions we permit ourselves to *feel*.

A key concept for Hochschild is "feeling rules"—cultural codes that delineate which emotions are appropriate to certain roles, relationships, and situations. Although each flight attendant may have his or her own personal standards for how to behave and feel in situations, there are also clear public expectations for persons holding that role. Requirements to be courteous, responsive, and friendly are reinforced by the fact that most flight attendants are women, who confront a similar set of gender expectations. Managing on-the-job emotions, then, involves two different kinds of "acting." "Surface acting" is a public performance of cultural norms. When we are with others, we typically adopt the words and mannerisms expected of us. This is the theme emphasized in Goffman's writing. More problematic is "deep acting," the psychological work of integrating these expectations. In the first instance the flight attendant only has to adopt a set of pertinent behaviors, such as smiling at a passenger even though she dislikes him. In the second, she has to convince herself that she actually *likes* the recipient of her smile. Clearly, those who "sell themselves" as purveyors of pleasure and assurance face levels of alienation Marx did not imagine.

The manner in which cultural rules frame, direct, or otherwise control people has also been emphasized by symbolic interactionist Susan Shott (1979). In the symbolic interactionist tradition, the ability of people to "take the role" of others— that is, to envision how a person in that role is likely to experience and respond to an event—is a critical aspect of human affairs. In that light, Shott is especially interested in what she calls the "role-taking emotions"—guilt, shame, embarrassment, pride, and vanity. As the reader may have noticed, all of those emotions are self-focused, in the sense that they are preoccupied with personal standing, but they are also forms of social awareness, a reading of that person's standing before others.

To a large extent, role-taking emotions are referential or comparative matters. We feel pride because we have met or exceeded a public standard established for a person of our type; we feel shame when our action has violated standards for what a person like us should be or do. Even in the case of a more private feeling like guilt, we somehow feel the eyes of the group upon us. Most importantly, we know what people are likely to think about us because we understand the perspectives of the roles they play. At one level, then, "empathy" of this type helps us feel compassion for the plight of others (see Clark 1997); at another, it protects us from social awkwardness. In that light, few adults are foolish enough to challenge a police officer, interrupt a judge, or severely criticize another person's loved ones. The likely responses of the persons we challenge are already established in our minds.

Shott emphasizes the degree to which these shared understandings facilitate orderly social processes and our continued commitment to them. In other words, social control succeeds as well as it does because of self-monitoring. In her view, the emotions listed above tend to operate "homeostatically." That is, feelings of discomfort or pain attend shame, guilt, and embarrassment. We wish to remove those unpleasant feelings so we attempt to atone for, deny, or otherwise redress that imbalance. Similarly, pride and vanity, as trans-situational feelings about personal character and accomplishment, are inherently unstable forms and need to be reaffirmed by behaviors that elicit positive social recognition. Emotions, then, are a system of self-regulated rewards and punishments that help us to move through the world in socially approved ways.

Of course people do not always behave—or feel—as they should. These possibilities are developed by Peggy Thoits (1990) as "emotional deviance." Much like Hochschild and Shott, Thoits is interested in processes of emotion management. As part of our socialization, she argues, people learn to coordinate different aspects of emotional experience. Thoits focuses on four of these aspects: *situational cues* (i.e., objects or circumstances that trigger emotions); *expressive gestures* (a socially appropriate package of behaviors); *physiological changes* (the internal reactions of our bodies to what is going on); and *emotion labels* (a set of publicly recognized names and understandings for such experiences). When a change in one of these elements occurs—for example, the "situational cue" of being surprised with a birthday present—changes in the other elements are anticipated. At one level, these expectations are personal matters—for typically we *wish* to feel good and to express those feelings with a smile when good things happen to us; however, they are also social affairs. That is, people *expect* us to display the "right" kinds of responses. Ideally, these adjustments come almost automatically; that is, the recipient of the surprise feels pleasure and offers exclamations of delight and gratitude. However, experience is often more complicated than this.

Thoits describes the different emotion-management strategies people use to bring their own emotionality in line with the "feeling rules" that I have described above. Essentially that means adjusting one or more of the four aspects noted above to make it consistent with the others. For example, players getting ready in the locker room for a "big game" know well what is expected of them. That situation requires a wide set of physiological adjustments (an energetic readying of the body), expressive gestures (revealed in facial and physical expressions), and emotion labels (culturally approved statements of readiness and desire). Even if they are unlikely to play in the upcoming game or have more important matters on their mind, players are expected to get themselves "up" in this manner.

At times, of course, people are not able to align their emotions with public expectations. That condition is called "emotional deviance." At times that misalignment is visible to others, and those obviously misaligned may be defined as being "unmotivated," "distracted," or even mentally or emotionally "unbalanced." However, a person may also experience this sense of disconnection or alienation at a level that is not visible to others. Still, we may sense that our feelings are not "right" and that there is some work that needs to be done.

To summarize, Thoits argues that emotion management is a corrective process that involves both *behavioral* and *cognitive* manipulation. Recalling her four themes, we can do something actively to change the situation we are in, our physical feelings, our gestures, and the emotion labels that apply. Alternately, we can reinterpret the personal meanings of that situation and our reactions to it. If we cannot "cope" in these ways, we may need to turn to others for advice about how to withdraw from the troubling situation or how to re-engage with it more effectively. In any case, our failure to mesh with the social situation is perceived to be a problem, and we seek to reestablish consistency in what ways we can.

UNDERSTANDING EVENTS

The emotion theories I present above describe how people's perceptions of well-being or success in social roles and identities are fundamental sources of emotions. When our behaviors and self-understandings match the requirements of valued social identities, we tend to be satisfied. However, David Heise (1979, 1989, 2007) argues that we are also pleased—and upset and angered—by what *other people* do in situations, even when their behaviors do not concern us directly. For Heise and his colleagues (see Smith-Lovin and Heise 1988; MacKinnon 1994), feelings are elements not only of self-understandings but also of understandings of "events."

In symbolic interactionism, a major theme is the way in which individuals define situations. Like Goffman, Heise emphasizes that people do not build these definitions from scratch but instead rely on publicly shared understandings. However, Heise's approach differs from Goffman's in that Heise argues that these understandings are not simply beliefs but instead ideas that are loaded with judgments and feelings. In such ways his work recalls Cooley's concept of "sentiments." Furthermore, Goffman and Heise view the interpretive process in somewhat different ways. In *Frame Analysis* Goffman argues that people rely on elaborate cultural scenarios or "frames" that spell out many aspects of the situation at hand, including the responsibilities of everyone involved. For Heise, events do not fall into such neat types. Instead, understandings of events are constructed from the different feeling-laden ideas about the *elements* of those situations—that is, about people, settings, and behaviors. Said differently, Heise's actors assemble or construct knowledge of ambiguous situations as compilations of privately borne sentiments; Goffman's look for fully developed models of situations and then adjust their behavior and understandings to those models.

In a striking argument, Heise (2007) claims that people often cannot decide how to interpret an event if they rely on cognitive terms alone. For example, at an airport we may happen to see a woman turn and walk away angrily from a man. We are curious about the nature and causes of the encounter, but we have no further information to help us determine what occurred. In Heise's view, our feeling-laden ideas about the "types" of man and woman, their respective behaviors, the airport setting, and their actions encourage us to be sympathetic toward one party or the other. They also help us take—or refrain from taking—particular actions to address what we've seen. So understood, feelings are forms of commitment and motivation that push and pull us through a complex social world. Although feelings to some degree "control" our behavior in that fashion, we also try to regulate and control those feelings. For such reasons, this approach is called "affect control" theory.

Heise understands "events" to have four central elements: an actor (which he designates in his formulas by the letter A); a behavior performed by that actor (B); an object or recipient of that behavior (O); and the setting in which that behavior occurs (S). Pointedly, the actor in question may be the self, but it can also be an entirely unrelated person. People are able to focus on any of these elements in isolation, but they also combine their perceptions of these elements into an overall impression of what is occurring before them.

Making sense of events involves two different levels of psychological orientation. The first of these levels Heise calls "fundamentals." These are the currently held sentiments we use to comprehend events we observe and enter. As we have seen, human feelings can be attached to many different kinds of objects, not only to the particular elements we encounter as concrete physical presences but also to abstract ideas about these objects. For example, all of us have well-established ideas about the individual people who are our parents and friends. However, we also have ideas about "parents" and "friends" as more general categories. Indeed, we tend to evaluate our own parents and friends, such as whether they are "good" or "true," in terms of these feeling-laden models. When we interpret events, we consider the particular elements of those events to be instances of general categories.

Although there are many ways of thinking about these four aspects of social events, Heise narrows this issue dramatically by focusing on three kinds of judgments that people make. These considerations are: (1) whether the object of our attention is seen as being good or bad (denoted in his formulas as E for "evaluation"), (2) whether that object is seen as "potent," or strong, rather than weak (P), and (3) whether the object is anticipated to be "active" rather than passive in its behavior (A). Once again, these are not judgments that are made on the spot. Quite the opposite, Heise claims that people approach the objects of the world with preconceived notions about the worth or value of that object, whether that object can influence or control them, and whether that object is likely to act toward them or otherwise become active.

To use an example, most of us have been told to "let sleeping dogs lie." Although usually genial, dogs can bite, and a startled animal might become active in unpleasant ways. However, our sentiments about dogs in general are modified by more refined, though still categorical, knowledge about the dog's breed and size, whether it is chained, how it is behaving, the characteristics of its owner, and so forth. We build our impressions of situations—in this case, the dog before us—as composites based on preexisting ideas we hold about the elements of those situations. Such preconceptions focus our attention and help us operate confidently in the world. Without that simplifying framework, we would be overwhelmed (see Smith-Lovin and Heise 1988, 1–33).

Deciphering the logic behind this maze of judgments—or predicting how people will react to any particular event—seems impossibly complicated. However, Heise and his colleagues have attempted to do just this by studying empirically how people evaluate (in terms of the three EPA criteria) extensive lists of words for categories of persons, objects, behaviors, and settings. To do this, they follow a well-known research tradition in psychology (see Osgood, Suci, and Tannenbaum 1957) that asks subjects to mark their evaluation of a list of words/concepts along a gradient between opposite terms—for example, rating the word "father" by placing a mark on a scale between –3 for "weak" and +3 for "strong." The averaged ratings for these "semantic differentials" are understood to be the public culture of senti-ments. Affect-control researchers use these averages to develop "impression forma-tion equations," mathematical models that predict our reactions to events. To use an example once again, we anticipate a certain chain of behaviors to occur if we know that we will be seeing a "mom" in a "nursery" with a "baby."

Our readings of what is actually occurring before us Heise terms "transient" feelings. In general, his theory argues that people are reassured by events that con-form to their fundamental sentiments. As he (Heise 2007, 47) puts it, "people try to experience what they already know." Most of us would expect a positively rated identity (like a "mother") to behave positively (e.g., "stroking" or "cooing") toward a positively evaluated object (e.g., her "baby"). When her actions exceed our ex-pectations in a positive direction (e.g., she shows special tenderness), we often feel a heightened rush of positive feelings. Similarly, our feelings move in a positive direction when we do better than expected in a situation (e.g., when we win an unexpected prize).

However, we are not surprised when negatively rated elements produce nega-tively rated behaviors. For example, we expect a villain in a movie (or in real life) to behave in less than admirable ways. In psychology this tendency of people to desire behaviors and relationships that correspond to already established beliefs is called "consistency theory." By such lights people who see themselves negatively (i.e., who have low esteem) may actually desire companions who criticize them (see Robinson and Smith-Lovin 1992). In other words, there is a certain—if ar-guably grim—satisfaction that comes from having one's expectations confirmed. Human beings, at least according to Heise's research, have a preference for famil-iarity and continuity.

FEELINGS OF SOCIAL SOLIDARITY

Most of the scholars we've considered so far have emphasized how people's feelings—or at least their "transient" ones—are responses to the situations in which they find themselves. Emotions are ways in which we affirm or disaffirm other people, ourselves, the actions we see occurring before us, and various other ele-ments of that setting. Conversely, Emile Durkheim tried to discover how people establish and maintain feelings for the vast and magnificent abstraction that is so-ciety. More specifically, he wanted to remind people just how indebted they are to the societies that make most aspects of their lives—including their freedoms—possible. How do societies—and smaller groups within those societies—impress upon people the importance of these wider levels of social involvement?

That dependence is articulated most clearly in what is perhaps his masterwork, his 1912 *The Elementary Forms of the Religious Life* (see Durkheim 1965). Ostensibly a treatment of the origins of religious belief and organization in society, the book is better understood as an analysis of society's importance and of the vehicles by which this importance is kept afresh in the minds of its members. Within this work Durkheim makes plain his view that society is an emotional as well as moral order. That is, for society (or any smaller group) to maintain its authority over individuals, it must do more than publicize abstract ideas or commandments; instead, people must be made to enact and thereby "feel" those ideas.

The most significant portion of the work—at least for our purposes here—is his concluding analysis of ritual as a conduit of religious—and, for Durkheim, social—awareness. In Durkheim's view religious rituals are carefully regulated practices that make people feel the power of community, both in a private way and as public expressions that indicate to others the nature and depth of those private feelings. The rules, objects, settings, and officials of the ritual context are understood to be quite different from similar elements in the world of everyday affairs. In that light, religious rituals are the vehicles through which people enter the realm of the *sacred*, which is the socially administered repository of those matters that people respect without reservation. To enter this sacred realm, participants must be cleansed of that which is profane or polluting. Once they have gained admittance, they must conduct themselves in the most scrupulous ways.

Durkheim divides rituals into two types—negative and positive. Negative rites are practices that enforce the separation of the sacred sphere from profane matters (Durkheim 1965, 337–65). Although some of these practices apply to conduct · within the ritual ground itself—words and behaviors that must not occur—most negative rites focus on procedures to purify participants. For that reason, negative rituals are commonly exercises in asceticism or mortification. To become worthy of entering sacred territory, people must divest themselves of activities and objects that normally give them pleasure. The wearing of uncomfortable clothing, cutting of hair, fasting, denial of sleep, assumption of humble or even painful postures and tasks, monetary donations, confessions of personal failings, restrictions on speech and human companionship, and so forth are all ways of denying the desires of ordinary persons and (oppositely) of affirming the superiority of the spiritual realm. To participate in the ritual processes that follow, aspirants must declare their normal (profane) identity to be inadequate or defiled. If simple declarations of unworthiness are not enough, whipping or other forms of punishment—sometimes self-induced—may help people feel the error of their routine commitments. In that way, arrogance is replaced by reverence, selfishness by vows of public service, comfortable satisfaction by feelings of misery and fear.

Negative emotions—shame, fear, self-hatred, and the like—are tutors in these matters. People must feel—in their bones—the inferiority of their current, secular identities. However, the purpose of preparatory rites is not to break persons but rather to demonstrate that those same persons can (voluntarily) challenge and subordinate their mundane, sensuous qualities. So strengthened, initiates are ready for the more positive forms of ritual that lie ahead.

Positive rituals specify ways of entering the sacred realm and behaving within it. Some of these rites (which he terms "sacrificial") feature the public sharing and (frequently) eating of some sanctified substance. Other rites (what he calls "imitative") set forth images or models of sacred beings that people enact or imitate in public displays. A third category ("piacular" rites) involves public acts of mourning and atonement, and a fourth type ("representative" rites) focus on commemorations of heritage and communal identity. For now, the point to be made is that people feel their own powers grow tremendously in these settings (Durkheim 1965, 408). Profane individuals are distracted, foolish, self-regarding, and weak. Purely private suffering is a horrible affair, akin to madness. By contrast, people who have entered the sacred through positive rituals discover that they are no longer alone, and this newfound communion gives them startling insight and energy.

The general idea promoted here—that people are empowered through symbolic participation in human communities—reaches its full expression in the circumstances that he (427) calls collective "effervescence." In some public gatherings, he notes, the sense of common cause or mutual support overwhelms the commitment to mere ideas. People are seized by feelings of brotherhood and sisterhood. At "such moments of collective ferment," he (1972, 228–29) argues in another context, "are born the great ideals upon which civilizations rest." Anyone who has found himself within a rhythmically swaying crowd at a public rally, concert, or festival has some sense of what Durkheim is claiming here. To hear one's voice magnified by a thousand others is to understand the meaning of "personal" possibility in an entirely different way.

Although Durkheim was interested in how participation in public events like these helps individuals organize their own lives, this was not his principal concern; rather, he wanted to understand how worthy communities can be built. When people feel and express powerful emotions in public settings, they communicate their support for the social body as a whole. Rituals are occasions to show that one has chosen to follow a publicly approved path and will accept the status that she has been granted.

INTERACTION RITUAL CHAINS

As we've seen, Durkheim describes rituals as devices that remind people of the importance of society. Goffman's rituals remind people of the importance of the "interaction order," the world of daily encounters. In both cases, people are honored when they match themselves to the requirements of socially valued identities, and they are dishonored, embarrassed, and otherwise made to feel pain when they fall short of these requirements or seek out identities that the group does not prefer. But how are these two levels of involvement related to one another?

That issue has been central to the work of Randall Collins (1981, 2004). Although Collins is known as a conflict theorist who studies the significance of disadvantage and disorder in societies, he also follows Durkheim and Goffman in his desire to understand the sources of solidarity and continuity in societies. To rephrase the question above: how is it that (potentially adversarial) individuals are able to cooperate with one another as well as they do and then move into new social situations with confidence and resolve? And how do small-scale interactions of people reinforce—rather than pull apart—the overall structure of society?

In his noted book *Interaction Ritual Chains*, Collins (2004) explores these issues. For Collins, emotionality is a kind of socially articulated "energy" that rises and falls in human relationships. That is, although our experiences with the world are always emotionally "toned" to some degree, social situations help focus and regulate these levels of arousal and commitment. In that sense, social interaction is something like a game, dance, or sexual encounter, in which participants anticipate the mood that is appropriate to such an activity, try to recognize elements of that mood in other participants, and then affirm and sustain that mood through their own words and gestures. In this way, events develop a rhythm that becomes "synchronized." People have a good sense of what each social form requires and knowingly play their parts with the appropriate level of enthusiasm to move the action forward. All this sounds like a tremendous amount of work for the participants; however, Collins emphasizes that events tend to develop a certain momentum— what he terms "emotional entrainment"—that coherently gathers, channels, and spends the energies of the individuals involved.

The concept of entrainment—which suggests that people "board" social events that may already be in process—is unusual but productive. Like persons stepping into a crowded subway car, we usually have some prior knowledge of the mannerisms— including the levels and forms of emotional expression—that are pertinent to that setting. Matching our own mood to those perceived expectations reinforces similar behavior by others in the car. At the conclusion of the event, most of us get off at our stops, reaffirmed in our belief that this is how one should feel and act on a subway. As Collins emphasizes at one point (4), the situation—rather than the individual— is what explains this development and movement of energy. In that sense, individual behavior and experience can be seen "merely as a moving precipitate across situations." Stated more extremely, Collins's work is not about "persons and their passions" but about "passions and their persons."

In some ways, Collins's approach is reminiscent of Simmel's, especially the latter author's essay on "sociability" (Simmel 1971, 127–40). For Simmel, persons attending a dance or party orient themselves to the expectations of that form and subordinate their own feelings and behaviors to that model. However, Collins sees people as being much more energetic and passionate than Simmel's abstract human types. Moreover, most human encounters are not as highly organized (or as "hosted") as Simmel's dinners or parties. Quite the opposite, many meetings between people—such as that sexual encounter—may be quite problematic as to their occurrence and direction. In that sense, people do not merely get "on board" moving events, attune themselves appropriately, and then get off at the appointed stop; instead, they effectively move those events ahead through their own commitments. Thus, affect is the engine that drives human interaction from one station to the next.

The bulk of this emotional regeneration occurs in face-to-face interactions or encounters. An interaction "ritual" for Collins (7) is a "mechanism of mutually focused emotion and attention producing a momentarily shared reality, which thereby generates solidarity and symbols of group membership." The reader will note in this definition themes from both Goffman and Durkheim. From Goffman's portraits of encounters as games and rituals come ideas about how interactions effectively—if only momentarily—build and sustain the public "realities" within which people operate. Whether any particular encounter develops into a ritual is problematic. Like Goffman, then, Collins (2004, ch. 2) sees certain "ingredients"—group assembly (i.e., bodily copresence), a mutual focus of attention, shared mood, and barriers to outsiders—as helping along the process of "rhythmic entrainment." Said most plainly, when people are in one another's presence, jointly committed to a line of action, and cut off from distracting elements, a mutually reinforcing event is more likely to occur.

Goffman is interested primarily in the encounter itself. Collins, by contrast, is concerned with how people shore up their identities emotionally and then move on to *new* situations. As his book title reflects, interaction rituals exist as "chains." We move from one encounter to the next—or from one moment to the next within the same encounter—because of the confidence that we build up along the way. Critical to this process is the fact that our feelings become stabilized as sentiments, emotionally charged ideas about the nature of the world and our place in it (see Heise 2007). Furthermore, Collins is more concerned than Goffman with the ways in which larger social structures are constructed from small events. For Collins, interaction rituals not only build the enduring identities and operating procedures of individuals but also help establish these matters for groups, organizations, communities, and social institutions—the larger social units of society itself. That is, ritualized situations—such as the dozens of conversations or other exchanges that occur each day between coworkers in a modern office—are themselves linked together as elements of a larger social configuration.

Like Durkheim, Collins ponders issues of social stability and continuity, and his interest in rituals similarly derives from the Durkheimian tradition. However, Collins's use of that tradition is somewhat specialized. For Durkheim, rituals are fundamentally devices in public instruction that produce cognitive, moral, and emotional "lessons" for their participants. Disorderly individuals need to be impressed with the majesty and stabilizing transcendence of society; both positive and negative rituals are occasions when people subordinate their private impulses to publicly imposed formats. Although Durkheim opposes social tyranny in every case, he tends to see emotional life from a "top-down" or "descending meaning" viewpoint. The continuity of a society—or of a family, church, or work group—depends on cadres of freshly inspired participants. Those individuals must somehow be fitted to the necessities of the whole.

In contrast, Collins is drawn to Durkheim's theme of collective effervescence, when people turn their eyes from prescribed doctrines and practices and focus instead on their shared connections to one another. That moment of mutual recognition—when people sense the emotional impact of being supported by others is critical. Although Collins acknowledges that "natural rituals" depend on all manner of formalities—observances of language rules, social etiquette, group customs, and the like—he is interested in what people bring to these settings and what they get from them. Thus, his listing of "ritual outcomes" (48) includes group solidarity, emotional energy in individuals, symbols of social relationship, and standards of morality. These shared symbols and standards are especially important. Symbols—such as a banner or battle cry—exist as mementos of meaningful events from the past. We attach ourselves to these objects—and to the ideas associated with them—and we continue to be inspired when we see or contemplate those symbols in other settings. In such ways, successful experiences are carried with us and energize us for new encounters.

THE CONSEQUENCES OF EMOTIONS FOR PERSONS AND SOCIETIES

Many sociologists are content to see individuals as abstract human categories that operate in various kinds of social situations. Simmel's intellectualized human types and Goffman's actors are of this sort. In that (intentionally dispassionate) perspective, social forms are thought to be the critical subjects of scholarly analysis, the "things" that either need explaining or are themselves explanations of other—again, mostly social—matters. The approach of Thomas Scheff (1990, 1997, 2006) is different.

Although Scheff recognizes the value of Goffman's understandings of how individuals operate in the social world, Scheff argues that Goffman does not consider how problematic or embarrassing social experiences affect people as they move out of those situations and on to new ones. In Scheff's view, people are not simply self-interested negotiators who suffer strategic setbacks from time to time; instead, people frequently take to heart their successes and failures. Those occurrences sometimes sustain or cripple them all their days.

Scheff is interested in both the themes that have been discussed above—that is, in the ways in which social experiences generate emotions in individuals and in the consequences of these emotions for their subsequent behavior and self-regard. Human beings, in his view, are profoundly social creatures. Our awareness of our standing amidst others—what levels of approval and support they grant us—is a critical determinant of well-being. High, stable positions, at which we routinely receive the respect of others, help us operate with assurance and self-satisfaction. In Scheff's approach this preoccupation with respect is perhaps the fundamental concern of social life. That issue is not something that pops up from time to time but rather is an ongoing theme of self-monitoring, which persists even into the moments when we are alone. In his view, that anxiety is expressed as the tension between "pride" and "shame."

For all of us social experience is filled with successes and failures, moments of public approval and reproof. At times our social standings are attributable to our own behavior; at other times these positions derive from our unchosen membership in valued—or, alternately, devalued—groups. In either case, when people are made to feel responsible for their social standings, they may feel pride or shame. Sometimes, these feelings are low-level, transitory affairs that punctuate our relationships with others and require no major psychological readjustments. However, other situations and relationships speak directly to a person's sense of integrity or self-worth. If we cannot respond to those challenges through Goffman-like strategies and realignments, we will have to manage them internally.

In a manner that is unusual for a sociologist, Scheff turns to psychoanalysis for an account of these internal dynamics. A particular source of his ideas is the therapist Helen Lewis (1971), who describes the dangers of "unacknowledged" shame. At times our personal failings are clear both to ourselves and to others, and we acknowledge that inferiority or slippage. However, there are also times when we repress or deny those failings and our responsibility for them. We can accomplish this denial in crude *undifferentiated* ways, as when we stutter or cover our faces, or we can try to *bypass* that spoiled identity through forms of personal resistance or subterfuge.

In the Freudian tradition, emotionally traumatic events are not sloughed off easily; instead, they continue to be objects of subconscious concern and often build in intensity. This gathering storm Scheff (1990, x) calls a "feeling trap." In his view, repressed feelings come back to us in a reciprocating or spiraling process that frequently involves expressions of anger. All of us who have been hurt by others may withdraw psychologically to prevent further injury. Alternately, we may foolishly proclaim ourselves too powerful or well protected to be damaged again. Differently again, we may lash out at innocent people for what someone else has done to us.

In Scheff's "shame-anger cycle," deep-seated feelings of personal insecurity or self-abnegation grind away inside us and await their chances for expression. We will do unto others what they have done unto us—and do so before they have a chance to do it to us gain. Such internal dynamics may well be personal pathologies, but they may also be encouraged by the value-system of society itself. In that light, Scheff (1990, 12) sees certain modern versions of "individualism" as a "defensive myth for organizing experience in an anomic society," a denial and repression of emotions associated with social commitment.

Although Scheff is concerned especially with damaged selves and their effects on social order, he (1997) also focuses on the opposite matter: the significance of pride for the maintenance of the "social bond." In a fashion similar to many of the other writers discussed above, he explains that acts of positive recognition or respect inflate the self-esteem of individuals in specific social settings and thereby bolster their commitment to return to or reproduce those shared patterns or forms. In his view, those forms may be categorized as a series of levels: from the tiniest instances of shared recognition and support to the broadest patterns of human collectivity.

For example, when two people focus on one another in a face-to face setting, that interaction is informed by—and informs—widening circles of connection. As I noted earlier, Scheff's (1997, 54) "part/whole ladder" is a vision of social structure that moves from a shared focus on single words and gestures to sentences, to exchanges, to conversations, to the broader relationship of the two parties, and to the life histories of those two parties. More encompassing yet are his "macro" levels that include all relationships of this type, the social structure of the host society, the history and future of the host civilization, and ultimately the history and destiny of the human species. In that sense, one setting or frame is contextualized by another. Through acts of mutual support for these forms, people prop up the various edifices of the world and are in turn supported by them.

It might be imagined that Scheff wishes to maximize individual pride—and thereby strengthen social order; however, this is not his position. Instead, his view is reminiscent of Durkheim's (1951) view of social integration that that author presents in *Suicide*. Too much "individual" pride or shame, in Scheff's (1990) view, promotes feelings of self-consciousness and social isolation. Too little of either is termed "engulfment," when people are unable to manage creatively their social responsibilities. Between these extremes lies "optimal differentiation," that delicate balance of public and private commitment. To assist this process, groups develop a wide range of formal and informal sanctions. These sanctions hold in or enhance the commitment of people who would drift away from the common focus at the same time that they blunt the aggressive tactics of those who would take over the group to serve their own purposes. Again, emotions build social order, but emotions do so only within social frameworks that regulate the shape and intensity of those feelings. Because Scheff shows how emotions work in two directions at once—to strengthen or to erode both personal and social frameworks—his views bring together many of the themes that have been presented above.

CONCLUSION: FEELINGS AS SOCIAL FORMS

This chapter has discussed some of the ways that sociologists think about human feelings. I've argued that feelings can be attached to different kinds of social forms—to collectively shared beliefs, public identities, visions of self, actions before others, events, social positions, and groups and organizations. People locate themselves in the social world by committing themselves to these forms. Those commitments are not simply cognitive approvals and disapprovals but instead are embodied orientations or "leanings" that help people make decisions quickly and move forward with resolve.

Because feelings are attached to such different forms, that they should vary in their continuity and predictability is not surprising. To use Heise's terms, we have "fundamental" (or enduring) feelings as well as more "transient" ones. When our fundamental orientations about how an event *should* unfold collide with our interpretations of what is actually occurring, the resulting alignments and misalignments produce reactions in us. In that sense, emotions are the psycho-physical responses our judgments produce about the situations we are in.

In this conclusion I want to make two related sets of comments. First, I want to discuss (more than has been done so far) the *social*, rather than the *personal*, character of the emotions. Second, I want to integrate the diverse portraits of the emotions that I've displayed above into a more general view of how emotion is related to social order. As I indicated in the introduction to this chapter, I believe that patterns of interaction, personal relationships, and social structure are somewhat different matters and that feelings play different roles in these domains.

Emotions as symbols. Although produced by sociologists, most of the accounts I've discussed above focus on emotions as feelings that go on inside people. And my own account, presented in chapter 5, also emphasizes that emotions result from processes of personal judgment. Having matched their standards to a situation, people approve—or disapprove—what is occurring and how they are placed in that setting. With such judgments in hand, they then support that situation, try to revise or dismantle it, or hesitate and withdraw. Most of the sociological theories I've described focus on how individuals consolidate their feelings and then move ahead in these ways.

However, emotions are also public affairs. There are, as Hochschild emphasizes, "feeling rules" that shape our sometimes confused, even inchoate reactions and put them into socially approved forms. Those rules also tell us what kinds of emotions are appropriate to what kinds of situations; so instructed, we try to avoid Thoits's "emotional deviance." We manage our personal experiences to make them conform to these public standards. Some feelings make sense—cognitively, morally, aesthetically, and practically—and can be advanced on those terms. Others are "improper" or "unworthy" and should be banished from consciousness.

This understanding of how social learning intrudes into the deepest and most private parts of experience is important. But it is also important to note another theme—that emotional displays are "symbols" that tell other people what we are feeling. Whether our displays present our true feelings or not, that "surface acting," as Hochschild calls it, operates within a publicly understood language of intention. If we go around the house with a scowling face, we should expect our family members to ask us, "What's wrong?" If we stand aside impassively while other team members are whooping and chanting in preparation for the big game, we should anticipate that they will "get on our case." As Cooley, Shott, and others in that tradition make plain, social life only works as well as it does because people feel that they have some access to the interior states of others. We believe that we "know" what others are feeling.

To attain this knowledge, we rely on the verbal statements people make to us, but we also rely on their facial expressions and bodily movements. Just as we make sense of what they say to us in terms of a socially shared language, so we also read their gestures with a similarly public system. That is why we feel comfortable in "calling out" someone who has a frowning face or a big smile. Willingly or not, they are participating in a society in which these expressions are acknowledged to have certain meanings.

Goffman is famous for demonstrating the complexity of this gestural system. There are expressions that we "give" (intentionally) and expressions we "give off" (unintentionally). We are skilled at both emitting these gestures and at reading others' gestures. In other words—and to turn Hochschild's conception a bit, there is surface and deep *acting*, and there is surface and deep *regarding* of people. All of us are committed to knowing the (true) character of others so we can manage our relations with them assuredly. With that end in mind, we not only pay attention to the gestures people present to us openly; we also regard the gestures that slip out unintentionally, those that are expressed when they think we are not watching, and even those that are withheld. When we give someone a present and she is not as effusive as she normally is on such occasions, we sense she doesn't like it.

Although there may be universally recognized gestures—recall Ekman's happiness, sadness, disgust, surprise, anger, and fear—the language of gesture is also culturally specific. As we've seen, there are rules about the proper occasions to display particular emotions, how these should be expressed, how long they should last, what words and actions should accompany them, what rationales are acceptable explanations for them, and so forth. As in word-based language, there are limited emotion words and limited ranges of meaning for each emotion. Happy expressions, for example, imply that a person affirms an action, object, or situation. We use that language to tell others how we are processing occurrences and what we intend to do next.

Three types of social order. The other theme I want to discuss briefly is the way that feelings—as personal commitments—stabilize and sustain social relationships. As we've seen, this is an issue for most of the sociologists described above, so my comments will largely be an attempt to organize those views. Based on what I said at the beginning of the chapter, I believe that there are three primary types of "relationships" in which feelings play a key role. These are "interactions" (what people do to one another), "personal relationships" (how people connect or bond to one another), and patterns of "social structure" (how abstract social forms are organized).

As the preceding pages have shown, some sociologists, like Goffman, focus on what people do with one another in particular—and sometimes face-to-face—situations. To such sociologists, this is the "real" stuff of human relationships, the comings and goings of minded bodies in space. We appear before others, we signify our intentions to act before them in certain ways, we prepare ourselves for their counter-actions, and then we move ahead. Their responses cause us to develop new evaluations and actions. These little strips of behaviors are organized into more fully elaborated "encounters," "events," or "occasions."

This "interaction order," as Goffman calls it, is the setting that most people associate with the emotions. Many of our feelings are reactions to what is happening at this moment. Occurrences in the world present themselves to us—or we "bring them to mind." Then we evaluate those occurrences and experience emotions. However, those emotions are not just reactions; they are also signifiers of actions to come.

To use an analogy, emotions in the interaction order function as a set of "traffic signs." Some emotions indicate to other people that everything is "on go," that situational traffic is moving ahead in a coherent, proper way. Other emotions are signals of damage and disability. They say to others: "I cannot continue to move forward in the way you expect me to." Like a broken car, such a person sits and waits for repairs. Still other emotions are signs of an aggressive, willful driver who shouts, "Watch out for me, a change in my behavior is coming!" Understanding these signs thoroughly, most of us steer our way through human traffic by heeding the gestures of the other drivers. And special attention is paid when we come to intersections.

A second type of human connection is what I call the "relational order." If interactions feature "actors," relationships feature "persons." As I've argued, persons are individuals who are understood to have a sphere of specifically *social* worth and capability that transcends any situation they are in. All of us act from moment to moment, but we also exist apart from those situations and maintain ongoing qualities and connections that we bring to bear on those situations.

Emotions are pertinent to both kinds of social order, though the focus of those feelings shifts. The example of someone's "getting mad" can illustrate this. In the interaction order, we get mad at actions or, somewhat differently, at the actor who committed that act. In the relational order, our anger is directed more completely at the person. That is to say, "You have done something to make me mad at *you*, and I am likely to stay mad at you for some time." The implication of this shift is that our *commitment* to the other person is now altered.

Arguably, social order is built as a series of mutual commitments that become established in the minds of those who participate "in" the relationship and also in others who know "of" the relationship. Those commitments—"I like you," "I dislike you," "I am indifferent to you," and so forth—in many cases become matters of public record. People are understood to be participants in relationships and members of groups—families, voluntary associations, communities, and the like. Because these commitments are commentaries on relationships that transcend the moment, feelings of this sort tend to become stabilized as "attitudes."

Because we are committed to our own identities, occurrences hurt us more easily than would otherwise be the case. Just as our broader connections and interests make us vulnerable, so they also grant us the prospect of joy rather than pleasure. This, the reader may recall, is one of Scheff's themes. Shame is not simply momentary inconvenience—a case in which our cars become stalled; instead, that condition sometimes challenges who we "are" as persons and poisons all our behaviors and relationships.

Emotionality is also pertinent to the more abstract social frameworks called statuses, expectations, structures, and organizations. We routinely take these abstract matters—what sociologists call "social structure"—into our heads and develop feeling-tinged stances toward what we find there. Take the example of a loan officer who has denied a loan to a deserving person because of a new policy at her bank. That loan officer may dislike *what she just did* as a consequence of her job (the interactional focus). She may dislike *herself* as a consequence of that (the relational focus). Differently again, she may dislike her *job*. After all, her job is what has caused her to do what she just did. And although she should not be surprised if the person she denied is now angry at her, she should take some solace from the fact that they are probably mad at her more as a functionary of an organization than as a person.

If feelings in the interaction order are commentaries on specific *actions* and in the relational order on the nature and extent of our *commitments* to others, then in the realm of social structure, feelings focus on *expectations*. As in the two previous kinds of social order, these are often public declarations. Who of us is not fond of complaining about our job or "situation" and how we wish we could change it? When we do this, we are preoccupied with highly abstract understandings of the nature of things and of their causes and effects.

As noted, this sort of discontentment—or perhaps contentment, for we may love our jobs, schools, countries, and the like—involves a different sort of identity. We understand ourselves to be members of categories or frameworks that are essentially arrangements of directives. By the terms of those positions and organizations, some behaviors are permitted, others are not. Millions of other people may occupy those same positions—as a woman, telephone company worker, mother, and so forth—and face a similar set of constraints and opportunities. When we proclaim our approval or disapproval of those frameworks, we assume that other people know something about the expectations that surround the position we describe.

Because of its abstract, even categorical referent, feelings of this sort tend to become formalized as "sentiments" or "values." As Cooley and Heise have explained, these are not simply feelings that come and go but instead are more enduring commitments to categories of things. In that sense, it is not that we dislike "Karen" or "her family" (as in the relational order); rather we dislike "girls with red hair" or "families who let their kids behave like brats" or "people with that kind of politics." In such ways, we consider ourselves principled.

Once again, these general themes can be presented as a chart.

	Social structure (Arrangements of positions)	Relational order (Arrangements of persons)	Interaction Order (Arrangements of actions)
Form of collective identity	Organizations: (socially recognized frameworks composed of statuses)	Groups: (socially recognized bodies composed of persons)	Events: (socially recognized "situations" offering formats for interaction)
Form of "social" connection	Structures: (socially recognized articulations of statuses/roles)	Relationships: (socially recognized bindings of persons)	Interactions (socially recognized actions and reactions in "encounters")
How individual standing is expressed	Expectations: (socially recognized rights and responsibilities of status holders)	Commitments: (socially recognized attachments to other persons)	Actions: (socially recognized expressions to other actors)
Form of individual identity	Statuses: (socially recognized positions in a collectivity)	Persons: (socially recognized qualities seen as possessions of individuals)	Actors: (socially recognized capabilities of individuals to interpret and respond to situations)

FIGURE 3. Three Types of Social Order

Figure 3 merits no extensive analysis, for it simply brings together the issues I discussed above. People are shown to be involved with one another through their interactions, their commitments to persons, and their support of publicly maintained social structures. Emotions can be expressed through actions, in feelings toward others, and as respect for expectations. We can be satisfied or dissatisfied with people in their capacities as actors, persons, or status holders. And we can contemplate and direct our feelings toward more abstract arrangements, like events, groups, and organizations.

Once again, the point of producing such a chart is to identify the different levels of social awareness and then to invite analysis of *how* these levels combine in producing and communicating emotions. This I take to be the ambition of the sociologists who I have discussed in this chapter. But I would argue that it is also the quest of any person who wishes to analyze the causes and consequences of her own feelings. If emotions are the framings of both thought and sensation, then pondering the elements of their making is one path to self-consciousness and the freedom of expression that is founded on that awareness.

CHAPTER 7

DISSATISFACTION, DISORDER, AND DESIRE

If readers were to depend on the arguments presented in chapter 6 for their knowledge of human experience, they would conclude that people are essentially stability-seeking creatures with a taste for order and routine. To be sure, most of us want an orderly world in which today's people, places, and events will still be there tomorrow to greet us. But is security—or comfortable placement—all that we desire? This chapter will explore an opposite thesis: that people are restless creatures who want a world that is different from the one they know. Those yearnings sometimes cause us to resist our current social standings, fight with others, and become dissatisfied with prized positions once we've attained them. Such desires can lead to combative relationships, but they can also produce supportive, fulfilling connections to others. That restless energy—understood as a taste for stimulation, disorder, and change—shapes the character of personal behavior. It also produces a bustling style of society filled with all kinds of assertions and disputes—and feelings are crucial parts of those negotiations.

In what follows I discuss this robust, yearning quality of personal and social life. My special interests are the sources of instability and disorder as well as the relationship of these matters to feelings. The central portions of the chapter present a theory of satisfaction and dissatisfaction, pleasure and displeasure. My final comments connect the themes of the previous chapter to those developed here by showing how social processes construct or *frame* desire.

RESTLESS HUMANITY

If people are just order-seeking creatures, why do they pursue movement and change? Ideas about the centrality—and perhaps inevitability—of instability and disorder have been especially prominent in three scholarly traditions in the social sciences: Marxism, Freudianism, and postmodernism. Each of these traditions points to a distinctive source of disorder.

Marx's writings begin with his statements about the fundamental needs of human beings. People are material creatures who require food, clothing, and shelter, but to realize the fuller dimensions of their humanity, they also must experience creative expression and the supportive companionship of others (Marx 1999). Ideally, societies are organized in ways that allow all their members to satisfy these needs. Historically, societies have not been organized in those ways. In particular, economies have been structured so that only some categories of people control the productive apparatus that creates and distributes goods and services. Worse, those controlling groups direct economic processes in ways that benefit primarily themselves, and they attempt to stabilize their positions by developing political, religious, and educational institutions that legitimize and protect their interests.

In the Marxian tradition societies are divided into social classes that have unequal access to economic resources. Although later interpreters argue that power, prestige, and knowledge also are critical hierarchies that may be organized in distinctive ways (see Mannheim 1967; Gramsci 1971), their point is much the same: important human resources have been made scarce by self-interested elements of society. Although these dominant groups try hard to impose their schemes on others, in the end they cannot be successful. In part this is because their schemes founder on their own contradictions, but it is also because human needs are forces of their own sort. Disadvantaged people await their chances to change the social order and, at some point, put everything at risk in their attempts to do so.

Marx's writing is an analysis of the causes and cures of social conflict. Freud performs similar functions for the conflicts that occur within the individual. As I discussed in chapter 2, Freud recognized that people are confronted by quite different kinds of challenges. There are the challenges that external reality represents, including the claims of other people and society itself, but there are also the different imperatives that course through the body and the psyche. We feel psychobiological demands strongly and are attentive to the pleasures and pains of the body. But we also face internalized moral and cognitive strictures, principles that command our attention. Sometimes we are able to reconcile these different challenges in our thoughts and actions; frequently we cannot.

Moreover, we do not live only in the present—deciding what to do in one situation and then the next; we also live in the past and future. We are, by turns, tormented and comforted by remembrances of past occurrences; we look to the future with mixtures of confidence and dread. For the most part, we try to organize our personal lives by developing elaborate accounts of ourselves and of our circumstances and, in that fashion, focus our attachments and energy. But this project cannot be completed. Too many things have happened to us, too much is going on inside us, and too many possibilities lie waiting to destroy our carefully assembled visions.

The third tradition, postmodernism, emphasizes similar themes, but its focus is culture as a source of human instability (Harvey 1990; Rosenau 1992; Bertens 1995). In a previous chapter I emphasized the role of culture in organizing—and even unifying—people. Postmodernism, by contrast, stresses the vast diversity of cultural forms and the incompleteness of the meaning systems they entail. By such accounts, people are said to participate in culture much as they read a novel or poem. Always, there is so much more meaning in it than any person, even the creator of the form, can manage. Meanings are ambiguous and even contradictory. Many things are insinuated rather than said directly; indeed, things *not said* may be more important than things that are. In a world that has become saturated with cultural artifacts and displays, no unitary meaning system prevails. Just as we read culture in specialized ways, so we "write" it with personal meanings that seem suited to the circumstances of our lives. Alone or in company, individuals position themselves in social and cultural settings, take from them what self-styled meanings they can, and move on to the situations that follow.

If individuals are restless and uncertain for the reasons just described, what patterns of social life do such individuals create and sustain? In the above traditions, relationships are said to feature diversity, tension, and change. When people honor their personal feelings in more openly expressive—and less directly competitive—ways, multiple meanings and the pluralistic, antinomian spirit that is emphasized in postmodernism may mark social formations. When personal commitments are viewed as moral or psycho-biological compulsions—as in the Freudian tradition—society is seen as a struggle against public forms of instinctual repression and becomes marked by interpersonal conflict arising from the opposing wills of the participants. Much contemporary writing in the social sciences is an amalgam of these themes.

Some of these possibilities for social and personal expression have been described by Simon Williams in his book *Emotion and Social Theory* (2001). Because Williams's work is itself an integrative venture, I will not repeat its various points here. However, one of that book's primary contributions is to direct the reader to analyses that challenge the "rationality" of contemporary experience. Among those writings are Williams and Bendelow's (1998) studies of the body, not only as this is defined, directed, and experienced in terms of social processes but also as an agency of its own sort that challenges and transforms social order. Other noted works include Bakhtin's (1981) images of social order as dialogical imagination and carnival, Bataille's (1986) emphasis on sexual excess, and the critique of masculine styles of rationality presented by poststructural feminists like Cixous (1994) and Irigaray (1985). Such authors claim that the dominant models for person-hood in contemporary societies are representative only of the views of empowered groups—typically upper-class males—who wish to administer others on their own terms. In other words, the fascination with order, calculation, and control is his-torically and socially situated. That abstract, formal, and sometimes bureaucratic worldview is less pertinent to people in traditional societies, who may idealize communal identities, or to other categories of people in contemporary societies, who may be more receptive, exploratory, and relationship-focused in their life orientations.

The importance of the above issue—the role of untrammeled expression in personal and social affairs—is not to be denied. Arguably, social disorder is as im-portant a theme as the "miracle of social order" that I have emphasized in this book. Arguably also, one cannot understand one of these themes without ac-knowledging the other. Fluidity and change are made comprehensible by envi-sioning their opposites. In that context, my ambition in this chapter is to present a theory of human satisfaction and desire. Because that theory focuses on pre-existing sources—or underlying patterns—of our passing desires, I must acknowl-edge that this is a "structural" response to contemporary, poststructural emphases on transient, nonobjectified processes. Be that as it may, my approach emphasizes the sense of moving in and out of relationships that are framed by patterns that stand beyond those moments.

SYMBOLIC SOURCES OF DISSATISFACTION (AND SATISFACTION)

I've claimed that emotion is a "contrast concept," an awareness that develops when we compare a "model for" reality (what we think should occur) with an under-standing of what is actually occurring (in effect, a "model of" reality). Dissatisfac-tion, or so I argue, occurs when the latter model fails to live up to the former one. What this thesis suggests is that there are two primary sources of failed experience. One is the occurrence itself. To bring that occurrence into alignment with our stan-dards, we must either change what is going on or—in a more subtle way—change our interpretation of it. The other source of dissatisfaction is the standards—or "models for" reality—that we use to evaluate occurrences. Perhaps discontent comes from standards that are too high or are otherwise "wrong." This latter theme—the kinds of interpretive standards that people bring to situations—is the one I discuss in this section.

Whose standards should apply? Much of our emotional life turns on the double awareness of how others see us (our identity before them, particularly as this is reflected in their treatment of us) and how we see ourselves (the self, more strictly defined). Sometimes the standards of otherness is what rule the day (forcing the patterns of adjustment I called "descending meaning"); sometimes we make matters proceed according to our own terms (my "ascending meaning").

To illustrate this, consider a situation with which every child is familiar. As children we must often ask our parents' permission to do something or, failing to do this, must justify our actions to them after the fact. Commonly the conversation becomes a rivalry of standards. The child feels that the event—perhaps staying out late—is entirely appropriate for a person that age. The adult does not agree. To make her point, the child brings up examples of what her friends' parents allow them to do. Becoming a bit bolder, she argues that, indeed, *most* children her age are permitted to stay out until the hour in question. Her parents, or so she implies, are clearly out of touch with those societal standards. Not infrequently, the parents reply that the latter claim is not true (that most children are not allowed to do this), that the standards of the child's friends have been falsely reported, and that—even if either claim is true—these are *not* the standards that are going to prevail in the current situation. The application of one set of standards produces joy itself in the child, and the other, the bitterest disappointment.

However unreasonable parents may appear to their children (and vice versa), most people try to justify—and indeed ground—their standards by connecting them to what other people do. In the fashion of the child above, we claim that what we are asking for is appropriate for a person "like us." In an even more sophisticated way, we may argue—like a person requesting a salary increase—that we deserve this not only because of our qualifications and abilities but because of the contributions we have made to the group, because our level of responsibility recently has been increased, because the group itself has been doing well (with our help), because other groups would value our contribution highly, and so forth. However valid these claims may be, what is sometimes also driving our request is the knowledge that another person, who we feel to be equal or inferior to ourselves, is actually receiving more privileges and rewards than we are. That latter idea—that judgments of a person's worth should be based on what others are giving and getting—is described in a number of disciplines as "distributive justice" (see Homans 1958).

Sometimes one of the parties to a dispute gets to have her way; sometimes a compromise is reached. Whatever the settlement process, satisfaction occurs when actual events correspond to standards that the persons involved have *internalized*. At times this satisfaction is only vicarious; that is, we live up to someone else's standards and take some pride in that accomplishment and the idea that we have made them happy. For some children that means becoming the medical doctor their parents always wanted. However, deeper satisfaction surely comes from attaining standards that are fully our own.

Are there different kinds of standards? I noted in a previous chapter that there are different criteria people use to judge the worth or success of occurrences. I argued that things may be deemed "good" or "bad" by applying standards of truth, beauty, justice, and utility. Such matters should be discussed more fully here.

At one level occurrences can be considered satisfying because they meet our standards for truth or correctness. All of us have particular beliefs or "cognitions" about the world that are based on many factors, including our life experiences, and they include ideas about cause-effect sequences. The world, as we understand it, should operate in a certain way. When that world conforms to those cognitive anticipations, we feel a certain satisfaction. Our feeling is that we "knew" what was going to happen—and now it has happened. Although few people would claim that seeing their cognitive expectations confirmed affords the highest levels of satisfaction, the failure of those models can be deeply troubling. We expect to wake up in the same bed where we fell asleep, find the same family members in our house, have access to familiar possessions, and so forth. Randomness in such encounters is intolerable.

Moral standards are different. In this case, the meaning of "should" no longer centers on cognitive predictability or accuracy but instead on the propriety of behaviors in human communities. Events are said to be ethically "good" when they correspond to people's understandings of idealized human conduct. As Durkheim and many other sociologists have claimed, those moral standards are charged with feeling. They are not merely predictions of what will occur—that is, whether occurrences proceed as we expect them to; they are claims for what should happen if the people involved want to maintain their current levels of social respect and support. Moreover, we are able to apply those same standards to judge our own behavior. When other people fail to meet our *cognitive* standards, we feel disoriented or "baffled." When they fail to meet our *moral* standards, we are "outraged."

Different again are standards for satisfying aesthetic experience, models for what "feels" or "looks" good. In a particular society, for example, one may learn to avoid wearing brown shoes with black pants, to not display food in the mouth while chewing, and to stay in "tune" while singing. Requirements of this sort are neither cognitive nor moral commandments; rather, they are claims that (in any society) people are expected to behave in certain ways if they wish to produce satisfying feelings in others. Abject failures in this regard may cause other people to be "disgusted." However, it is not only other people we wish to please. Similar to moral and cognitive standards, aesthetic standards are necessary to our judgments that our experiences are consonant with what we *should* be feeling in the setting at hand.

Finally, there are standards of utility or practicality. We judge events in terms of their connection to the "interests" of the objects, persons, and groups involved.

We *should* water our houseplants because they will die without that attention; we *shouldn't* mouth off to our boss because that action will result in being fired. As I've argued, people understood themselves to have spheres of commitment that transcend the moments of their lives. One occurrence, or so we think, impacts another. The "right" or "best" move in a game of chess is the one that will lead to victory; parents should get up and go to work because they have a family that requires their care. Sometimes we define those consequences in advance as "goals" or "objectives" that must be met. We judge behaviors and events by their effectiveness in reaching these ends.

Again, these four standards are not the same. Many behaviors "feel" good but are immoral. Some are "correct"—in that they are intelligible responses to situations—but they do not serve our longer-term interests. Feeling satisfied or dissatisfied in situations depends on which standards we apply.

Are there levels of standards? The preceding discussion has focused on different kinds of "expectations." Expectations are our anticipations—cognitive, moral, aesthetic, and pragmatic—of what *should* occur in an event. For example, most of us expect the day after today to be of a certain character—perhaps another load of assignments dumped on our desk at work—and we may even feel that this is appropriate. After all, we're paid to do work of this sort, the pay supports our family, that work is part of the daily "feel" of our lives, and so forth.

Still, this is hardly the extent of our anticipations. Beyond expectations are "hopes," and beyond that "dreams" and even "wildest dreams." That is, we are able to envision many conditions that we have no right to expect, such as winning the lottery or becoming a famous athlete. However unrealistic these desires may be, such conditions—which we can imagine clearly in our minds—are also "models for" experience. At the other extreme we can anticipate negative conditions. Models of this sort include "concerns" or—more strongly—"worries." Darker scenarios include "fears" and even "nightmares." Most parents have sharply etched visions of the terrible things that *could* happen to their teenage child, who at this late hour is motoring about the highways in the company of friends. As the reader can see, my view is that there is a gradient between our highest hopes and darkest fears, and that "expectations" lie in the middle of these extremes.

Some psychologists have advanced a similar view. According to Campbell (1981), our perceptions of actual standings are compared routinely to what we *expect.* However, those standings may also be contrasted to our reasonable *aspirations* for those situations or—quite differently again—to what we think we *deserve.* Another proponent of this approach, Michalos (1985) argues that we interpret actual conditions in terms of six major criteria: wanted conditions, ideal conditions, expected conditions, best past conditions, what others have, and what role we played in producing those conditions. The implication of such arguments is that we create the possibilities for satisfaction and dissatisfaction with the standards we apply.

If satisfaction derives from the meeting of valued standards, it can be argued that most of our activities and experiences conform to these valued standards and therefore should be deemed satisfying. However, taking a few steps forward in a direction we choose is exhilarating only for toddlers or others who have been unable to walk because of accident or illness. Similarly, the great bulk of our daily activities—so many of them wonderful accomplishments—give us little pleasure. Performing routine duties is doing only what we—and people like us—are *expected* to do. Although the successful performance of those ordinary endeavors provides little pleasure, we must emphasize that an *inability* to perform them— such as a sudden incapacity to walk or talk—may fill us with extreme displeasure and worry.

To state the theory in general terms, people's level of satisfaction with regard to a condition is consistent with the "distance" between the real and the ideal that has been closed. In that context, satisfaction is an awareness of both movement and completion. We are pleased when we feel ourselves moving toward an ideal condition; we are displeased when we are moving away from that ideal or, by extension, toward a devalued condition. Thus, we feel no special pleasure when we receive only what we expect—or feel is our due—from life, for little "distance" has been crossed in that transaction. We are quite pleased when we realize our hopes; we are even more pleased when we realize those "wildest dreams."

To bring together most of the above points, consider the example of a woman who has just received a "B" grade in a college course. Though not the ideal grade, the student is pleased—though not ecstatic—because she did better than most other students in the course, she improved from her poor grade at midterm, and she did well enough to keep her scholarship. Adding to her satisfaction are the facts that the subject in question is not her strongest and her professor has a reputation as a tough grader. Further sources of comfort come from the knowledge that she worked hard to earn the grade and that the "B" effectively removes the "D" she received the first time she took the course. A difficult stretch of life has been completed successfully. She calls her parents and friends and, at each telling, relives the pleasure of receiving her grade. Their supportive responses confirm her satisfaction, and she feels the additional pleasure of meeting her parents' high standards. She maintains these feelings of contentment and pride until she learns that her roommate, whom she does not like, received an "A" in the same course with little expenditure of effort. At that instant, her pleasant feelings depart.

Although satisfaction can be diminished quickly in the manner shown above, restoring satisfaction with a new perspective or change of "attitude" is also possible. If present circumstances fail to meet our ideals, we can encourage ourselves by remembering proud moments from the past (thus indicating our promise) or shameful moments (thus suggesting our present state of improvement). Alternatively, we can keep our eyes focused on the future. Surely the dissatisfactions we endure now are preparations for satisfactions to come. If we cannot find comfort in some idealized vision of our own standing, we can employ negative or devalued visions of what others have. Compared to our sibling who is in jail, the homeless man we saw yesterday, or the billions of other humans suffering every type of infirmity, we conclude that—all things considered—our current circumstances are satisfying indeed.

Clearly, self-estimation is a multireferential process in which people look above, below, to past, to future, and seemingly to the ends of the earth to find images that stabilize and reassure them. Most people are able to sustain the fairly high levels of self-satisfaction that psychologists report because they can adjust their frames of reference. We are able to differentiate the standards that we "reasonably" expect to reach from those we know we will reach only in our dreams. Images of past and future as well as present-time happenings nourish us. Experiencing consonance with valued images and avoiding devalued images is the process of adjustment that fuels happiness.

THE PHYSIOLOGY OF SATISFACTION AND DISSATISFACTION

Does satisfaction depend only on an artful choice of perspective? Certainly, that is the position that I have advanced so far. But satisfaction—and its opposite—is more complicated than that. Even if people choose "realistic" standards for their behavior, there are reasons why they do not get to choose those standards just as they would like. That point will be developed later in the chapter. For now, the criticism of the above viewpoint is a different one. Does the body have its own "standards" that exist independently of—and potentially conflict with—symbolically organized understandings? Do bodies make "claims" on consciousness in ways that are not entirely dissimilar from what has been described above?

Just as emotions are not simply cognitive assessments but also bindings of thought and feeling, so it is clear that there is an important physiological component in judgments of the satisfying and unsatisfying. Admittedly, those bodily claims are not like the cognitive or moral standards that seem critical to our social relationships. Instead, they are profoundly pragmatic, in that they support the survival of the organism, and they are communicated through a language of sensation or feeling—and thus become formalized as aesthetic matters. To survive, humans must become aware of their "needs," which are made apparent to them through sensations of the pleasant and unpleasant, or even of pleasure and pain. Arguably, ideas of the good and bad are layered upon processes of physical recognition that have prior status from an evolutionary viewpoint. Some of those physical processes—as patterns of sensation and response—are fairly well understood (see LeDoux 1996).

I'll begin by noting that the concepts of "pleasure" and "pain" are sometimes distinguished from ideas of the pleasant and unpleasant. Pleasure and pain are often said to be forms of awareness that have significant physiological involvement. For example, psychologists Fredrickson and Branigan (2001) equate "pleasure" with patterns of physical satisfaction—that require little appraisal, correct an "internal trouble," depend on physical stimulation, and involve automatic responses to bodily needs. In much the same way "pain" can be defined—as it is by the International Association for the Study of Pain—as "an unpleasant sensory and emotional experience associated with actual or potential tissue damage or described in terms of such damage" (see Bonica 1979). In definitions of this sort, pleasure and pain are essentially the rumblings of the body that have causes, consequences, and remedial processes regarding which the subject has little conscious knowledge or control.

Damasio (1999, 72–76) emphasizes that pleasure and pain are not opposite ends of a continuum but rather separate and *asymmetric* processes. Pain, in his judgment, is an after-the-fact assessment that develops as an awareness of tissue damage. Typically, pain arises as a "local dysfunction." Special pain receptors relay awareness of the event up the spinal cord as a part of a broader "activation wave." Those signals are then processed in the brain stem and thalamus and in sectors of the cerebral cortex, where the event is "mapped" and responses are initiated. Some of those responses—such as wincing or jerking in response to a pinprick—can be elicited in patients who have diminished states of consciousness.

Stated more generally, pain is one element of a pattern of organisms' protective withdrawal. However, Damasio emphasizes that the "sensation" of pain is not the same as pain "affect." That is, sensation is not equivalent to the quality of self-recognition, in which a person "knows" she has pain and is prepared to do something about it. Furthermore, pain is distinguished from "suffering," the emotional state that comprehends pain as the awareness of ruined circumstances. At its physical basis, then, pain operates as an automatic response of organisms, but there are many links in the chain of pain awareness and management.

Physiological and psychological processes associated with pleasure are different. If pain is an after-the-fact protectionist pattern, pleasure is a reward system that recognizes and motivates behaviors beneficial to organisms. In that light, many accounts—including Damasio's—see pleasure as part of a set of autonomic responses that restore the body's natural balances. This "homeostatic" view goes back at least as far as Plato, who saw pleasure as a way of correcting a physical deficiency, a silencing of the body's clamor (see Solomon 2000). In accordance with ideas about our bodies as *systems* of interrelated elements, this approach to pleasure argues that bodies have physiologically based needs and that conditions of physical imbalance are communicated within those bodies as sensations of "un-pleasure" (mild or nagging discomfort). Feelings of hunger, thirst, and sexual agitation are signals that particular needs are not being met. Such signals are the starting points of motivational processes—drives, urges, and so forth—that lead to activities that address those needs. When an organism is full or satiated, these urges are no longer felt and consciousness turns to other matters.

Are there "centers" of pleasure within the body? In a classic experiment by Olds and Milner (1954), mild electrical stimulation was administered to certain portions of the brain in rats; that stimulation created (what appeared to be) intense feelings of pleasure. This interpretation was based on the rats' almost continuous efforts to press a lever to receive that stimulation. In humans as well, it is understood that previously described areas of the mid-brain—the hypothalamus, septum, and amygdala—are associated with pleasure. Among the brain's neurotransmitters is the chemical dopamine, which facilitates and rewards certain kinds of internal communication. Moreover, the brain is also able to produce its own opioids, the endorphins, whose release is related to various physical functions including eating, exercise, and sexual activity. In such ways, the brain directs and rewards a wide range of activity.

Although it is true that physical pleasure and pain are sometimes localized in bodily sense organs and give messages to which we respond without conscious deliberation, other feelings of physical comfort and discomfort are much more diffuse. For example, taking a warm bath or a brisk walk often produces generalized feelings of relaxation and wellness. Notably, the degree to which these activities are considered pleasurable depends on the state of our physical functioning at the time. A cool cloth on the forehead is no pleasure to the person who is cold, and a sumptuous meal has little appeal to the person who is full. Moreover, the intensity of pleasure may be related to the urgency of our discomfort. Thus, almost any meal tastes good when we are very hungry, and water is delicious to the thirsty. Such points are not really criticisms of this viewpoint, for they fit within a theory of pleasure as system restoration.

Concepts of physiologically influenced drives also have been central to Freudian analyses of pleasure (see Glick and Bone 1990; Brown 1966). The reader may remember that Freud's own thinking about the nature of human discomfort began with the more positivistic models of the medical doctor or natural scientist and moved during the course of his life toward more symbolic or cultural analyses. At any rate, Freud's models of the libido tend to emphasize ideas of nervous excitation, frequently localized in certain regions—or even orifices—of the body. This excitation builds up almost hydraulically, demands its release, and then spills as a sort of psychic energy that is directed toward various objects of the environment. Onto this patterning of psycho-organic drives, Freud added his complementary frameworks of ego and superego. However, he never relinquished entirely his view that there is some physical foundation to our processes of desire, and notions of drives and instincts always played prominent roles in his theories.

Modern psychoanalysis has maintained the view that physical experiences—which we layer with our own idiosyncratic interpretations—are important aspects of human development. The early years of life are perhaps more physically intimate than the symbolically preoccupied later years, and patterns of awareness about our bodies and their expressive capabilities become building blocks—or stumbling blocks—for later views of the world. Our experiences with the different regions of the body—and especially the various orifices—help us comprehend the meanings of pleasure and pain, providing us with opportunities to develop systems of motivation and self-control. Experiences of comfort and discomfort as well as anticipations of moving from one condition to the other dominate much of life. In a very concrete sense, our bodies are the little worlds out of which we operate. They are both the conduits and sounding boards of experience, and they provide the central metaphor by which we understand what it means to be a person.

How are pleasure and displeasure related to emotions? For the most part, I've portrayed pleasure and displeasure as accompaniments of thought and behavior. Some experiences seem to "feel good" whereas others do not. Even emotions, as complicated evaluations of the self's involvement in circumstances, can be described as being more or less "satisfying" or "pleasing" to their possessors. Positive emotions comfort and reassure us; negative emotions are discouragements. People who experience love, hope, and pride commonly wish to maintain or even increase those feelings; people experiencing sorrow, guilt, and shame wish to escape those conditions. "Good" feelings serve as psychic rewards for acts completed and motivations for acts undone; "bad" feelings punish and discourage us.

I should acknowledge that there are critics of this view. Some philosophers, including Gilbert Ryle (1951), have argued that pleasure/displeasure and emotion are entirely different matters. In his opinion, positive emotions like love and hope can be experienced as either pleasure or pain; negative feelings like melancholy and hatred can be sweet satisfactions or festering complaints. It is sometimes remarked—and always pejoratively—that a particular person "enjoys poor health." To be sure, people can be fascinated by and grow comfortable with infirmities of every description, including emotional maladies. People can find pleasure in being disgusted or "grossed out"; that is why we willingly listen to crude jokes. Fear can be fun, which is why we go to haunted houses and scary movies. Arguably, we enjoy anger and hatred. Some of us "pick fights" to indulge those emotions and look forward to rooting aggressively against our archrivals in sports. In other words, people's assessments of conditions not infrequently involve complicated mixes of feeling. When people express their scorn for the referee at a sports event, their outrage is mixed with their thrill at expressing themselves in such a voluble—and perhaps out-of-character—way. Under the right conditions, what we think of (typically) as positive and negative feelings can be felt as their opposites.

In her analysis of the "counter-pleasures," MacKendrick (1999) pushes this theme of contradictory feelings even further. Sadism, masochism, and asceticism (the last, the supposed denial of pleasure) may all be intensely pleasurable. Teenagers engage in "cutting" to feel the thrill of personal control; lovers bind and hurt themselves to make complicated their sexual pleasures; religious penitents endure the lash to better know God; suicide bombers envision that event as a moment of aesthetic and moral realization. Such practices—at least in the hands of their intellectual or literary advocates—are, in MacKendrick's view, an "eroticization" of the death drive, a preening and gorging of the self.

Perhaps the greatest statement of emotional contradiction is found in Aristotle's theory of tragedy, which he develops in his *Poetics* (1947, 624–67). On the face of it, dramatic tragedies—at least of the Greek sort—are spectacles of human dissolution and decline. Valiant—if flawed—characters are trapped in circumstances that they cannot comprehend or control. As audience members, we watch their struggles from a vantage point customarily reserved for the gods. We feel sad as we watch them twist and turn on the hook of fate, a predicament from which they can never escape. Oddly, however, our tears are mixed with feelings of pleasure. Unlike the protagonist, we know that we can spill our feelings and walk out of the theater unharmed to face another day. More curiously, we find that viewing the drama has somehow strengthened rather than weakened us. In part, that is because the "second sight" granted us by the dramatist has ennobled us. But it is also the case that an encounter with a great play means that we have had the aesthetic pleasure of watching a beautifully crafted work of art. In other words, spectacles of the fearful and pitiful are pleasing when they ultimately reassure us of people's ability to comprehend the forms and forces of otherness. Protagonists die so that we may live in clearer, stronger ways.

In my view, such combinations of the pleasant and unpleasant are not paradoxes but simply encouragements to think about the different *aspects* of experience. As I have emphasized throughout this writing, emotions are integrations of different kinds of meaning. Processes of symbolic appraisal (emphasized by cognitive psychology) may align themselves with physical logics (described by bio-psychology); however, contradictions sometimes occur, and the experience of such inconsistency may itself be fascinating. Acts that are considered "deviant" by some standards are wonderfully consonant by others, and people are capable of sustaining both kinds of judgments as they commit the act in question. Indeed, some particular emotions—such as greed, contempt, and haughtiness—seem to be combinations of pleasant and unpleasant feelings, and some unnamed feelings are surely combinations of the emotions we name. As in instances when parents watch their child go away to school or get married, experience may be bittersweet.

ORDER, DISORDER, AND FEELINGS

So far, the discussion of pleasure and displeasure has emphasized satisfaction as a feeling of comfortable completion. Physical pleasure has been presented as bodily restoration, symbolic pleasure as a feeling of consistency between the actual and the ideal. By extension, unpleasant feelings—of both the physical and symbolic sort—are registrations of damage and disorder, the sense that things are not going as they should. By the terms of this perspective, pleasure is akin to filling up one's tank at a gas station. As you are driving along, the dashboard indicator for low gas flashes. You can choose to ignore this warning, but if you persist in driving too much further, your car will start to sputter or even die. Fortunately, a service station is nearby. You pull in, fill your tank, and drive away—freshly energized for new ventures.

However, this view of pleasure—as satiation, replenishment, and the removal of distress—disregards other important elements of pleasure, at least as most people understand that concept. Isn't pleasure also about amusement, excitement, and fun? In other words, although pleasure may well take the form of a satisfied look backward at an event completed or a confident readiness for new pursuits, pleasure is also attached to feelings of uncertainty and to the experience of adventure itself. To ask the above question a little differently: don't people find pleasure in experiences of disorder and tension as readily as they find it in experiences of order and repose?

This distinction between these two styles of pleasure seeking was recognized by Epicurus more than two millennia ago (see Warren 2009). Some pleasures, Epicurus argued, are associated with stable conditions—periods of rest and recentering—whereas others stem from processes of confusion and change. He called his two types "catastemic" (based on restoration and stability) and "kinetic" (based on exploration and movement). His two types can be applied to both symbolically dominated and physically dominated activities. To take first an example of symbolic pleasure, a political debate or game of chess is enjoyable not only as a setting where people take pride in successfully completed actions (catastemic pleasure) but also as a tension-filled arena of move and countermove (kinetic pleasure). Dance, to use an example of physical activity, is an opportunity for satisfying bodily positions and accomplishments (catastemic), but it is also enjoyable as an experience of risky physical movements (kinetic). The following sections analyze these two kinds of feelings.

Feelings of order. Catastemic pleasures are experiences that counter or respond to some previous imbalance, tension, or "lack." For example, in the Freudian tradition the "pleasure principle" is the drive of the psyche to respond to "un-pleasure," the buildup of nervous excitation or tension (see Freud 1967, 22). In experiences of this kind, one finds release, fulfillment, and completion. Feelings like joy, contentment, and pride are recognitions that one has reached some kind of stable, valued condition.

An extreme example of such stability is serenity or "peace of mind." To feel one's spirits elevated in this way is akin to standing on top of a mountain. From that vantage point one can see the comings and goings of the world, but those struggles seem small and insignificant. There is a sense of being cut off from distant affairs but also of being attached to them in a new, more controlled way. Entirely without haste or urgency, the serene person can turn his gaze in different directions. He can see the path he took to get to his current location and the many paths that enter the lands below. This surer, steadier vision may derive from a firm relationship to the supernatural, to the loving embrace of family and friends, or to some transcendental vision of self. In any case, serenity is the sense of unshakeable connection to valued patterns that transcend life's occurrences.

Because catastemic pleasure often takes the form of controlled reflection, it is commonly associated with the *emotions of remembrance* described in chapter 5. Like the view from the mountaintop, "pride" is a satisfied reflection. We are satisfied because we have met previously envisioned standards. Typically, the proud person attributes that favored position to their own self-guided efforts; however, it may also stem from the efforts of another person or group with whom they share a strong "we" feeling. At such moments we feel "blessed" to be part of a something greater than ourselves.

In some ways this satisfaction with the past is even more comforting than satisfaction with the present. By definition, the past refers to events completed. However we embroider those events in our minds, there is a sense that those occurrences have taken their places in the history of our lives and cannot now be undone. In what is probably the most famous account of happiness, Aristotle (1947) argued that this condition is a proud reminiscence of the many dimensions of a life. The most important forms of happiness are not found in the present; they happen when we look back. For such reasons, Aristotle advanced the controversial view that people in the rush of life—such as children or young adults—cannot know happiness.

Orderly feelings can also be associated with the future. That is the case when we are pleased with our visions of what lies ahead. If the past is tucked away and cannot now be modified and the present is an entirely messy affair, the future can be seen in glorious perfection. For example, in activities in which no portion of the event is particularly pleasant—as in exercising on a treadmill—a person sometimes finds pleasure in being "almost done" or in "seeing the light at the end of the tunnel." We take comfort from that connection even as we endure the unpleasantness of the moment. In situations of that sort, orderly feelings result when we think only about the vision in our minds and do not concern ourselves with the difficulties of reaching that destination.

As I've described, many feelings of stability are pleasant. However, other feelings of stability are not pleasant. If heaven is sometimes envisioned as a secure and stately place, hell is equally well fortified. At least in Dante's (2003) visions, people's darkest fears are realized as entrapments from which they can never escape. Pain and suffering—as the physical and symbolic comprehensions of damage—are there made permanent. What makes that agony even more unbearable is the awareness that one has no control over the administration of the torment and that there is no hope for improvement. For such reasons, hell lies beneath purgatory in Dante's Christian scheme, and both are so much worse than the earthly predicament of the seeker, who—in the poem's famous opening scene—is lost in a "dark wood." That seeker may, with fortunate guidance, discover the spiral path up the mountain to obtain the serene views described above. Now, however, he knows only the unpleasant feeling of being lost and undirected.

Like pleasant feelings, unpleasant feelings are marked by psychological meanings of time. Sorrow is the catastemic recognition of ruined circumstances. Although happiness usually contains the sense that many things are possible and that the person has the energy to take them on (see Fredrickson 2003), sadness contains the double recognition that the current situation contains few possibilities for improvement and the person has little energy and resolution for making those changes. Situational despondency of this sort has its future-oriented manifestation: despair. Against hope, despair is the sense that one is trapped in an unsatisfying, futureless present. Like a solitary passenger in a long-forgotten lifeboat, there is nothing to do but wait for the end.

Another negative—and orderly—feeling about the future is "dread." Dread is not the same as worry or anxiety, in which many visions of the future are cast up and we are haunted by our suspicion that the worst of these may be realized. For the same reasons, the negative emotions of remembrance—guilt, shame, and regret—are in some ways the most painful of all. In many cases, there is no action we can perform to correct an unfortunate event. The world, for its part, has moved on; our portion is to live with the consequences of what we've done.

To summarize, feelings of stability may be pleasant or unpleasant. In either case, a sense of orderliness or even certainty anchors these feelings. One "knows" what is happening—or has happened or will happen—and feelings are marshaled to address that "reality." We feel very good indeed when our placement in the world mirrors our fondest ideals and very bad when we find ourselves in devalued conditions. Whether we live in dream houses or ruins, our awareness of the scope and permanence of those settings mark our experiences.

Feelings of disorder. If catastemic pleasure results from the awareness of stable connection to valued forms of order, then kinetic pleasure is the appreciation of disorder, novelty, and confusion. Rides at fairgrounds, sports and games, artistic activity, and many other forms of recreation provide kinetic feelings. Although these activities sometimes result in material products or other recognized endings, such as a finished painting or the final score in a game, the more essential pleasures of such events derive from being in these settings and moving amidst them. One does not play a game or hum a tune to finish it but rather to enjoy the process of engagement. In that sense, the frequently used examples of catastemic pleasure—eating, drinking, exercise, and sexuality—are much more than efforts to achieve system restoration; they are just as importantly dalliances, digressions, explorations, or other forms of foreplay. Said differently, kinetic pleasure is essentially an awareness of process, in which the self scrambles to establish and adjust its position.

Although kinetic pleasures are intimately related to concrete, sensuous experiences in the present, the *emotions of anticipation* may also be tinged with feelings of excitement. In that light, distinguishing between "self-confidence" and "hope" is useful. Self-confidence is a relatively catastemic look at the future. That is, the confident person expects and—on that basis—"feels" that the desired outcome will be achieved. To feel confidence is, effectively, to banish nervous excitation; anticipation is primarily an act of waiting. Hope also raises and focuses expectations. But the hopeful person is unsure how these anticipated events will play out. When we are hopeful, we know what we want, but we do not know that we will get it. And even if we do succeed in getting it, we are not entirely sure what will happen next. Every bride and groom has hopes for the future; what that future holds for them is unclear. In the same way, children have high hopes for holidays and birthdays; adults anticipate vacations and retirement. To have hope is to be at the same time optimistic and yet unsure that one will inhabit the visions she beholds.

Again, such examples raise the question of whether people take pleasure in uncertainty, surprise, and novelty. It can be argued that hopeful people take (catastemic) pleasure in the envisioned attachment to the object of their desires and only endure the anxiety attached to their efforts to reach that goal. However, if this were true, we would always keep the answer page beside us when we work the crossword puzzle, and we would prefer to hear the punch lines of jokes before we listen to the story that precedes them. A slightly different version of this argument is that events are always mixtures of pleasure and unpleasure: an activity is deemed pleasurable when moments of the first type predominate. For example, competitors playing a game of tennis take pleasure in the points they win and dislike the points they lose.

Although there is clearly some truth in that claim—that events are composed of smaller moments of satisfaction and dissatisfaction—it would follow that people desiring pleasure should always pick opponents they can trounce. Quite the opposite, tennis players—and the rest of us—seem to take pleasure in certain levels of tension and arousal.

Differently again, it can be argued that experiences of difficulty or risk are only "sweeteners" for the later—and more "real"—pleasures that accompany success. Gratification deferred during an event may lead to enhanced gratification at its end. The severe difficulty of a marathon contributes to the (catastemic) sense of accomplishment at the finish. Although this proposition can hardly be disputed, it evades the question of whether people actually enjoy difficulty. To answer this question in the affirmative is to suggest that our marathon runner finds pleasure in the running and not just in the moments of congratulation at the end. Certainly, people's visits to commercial haunted houses, amusement parks, sports arenas, and nightclubs are attempts to find disorder, confusion, and novelty. People who pursue "extreme" sports, abuse alcohol and other drugs, or engage in risky sex actively court danger.

This focus on movement and disorder has also been an important element in some radical reformulations of Freud's view of pleasure. Perhaps, such interpreters argue, people enjoy the experience of desiring as much as they do the attainment of the desired object. This is in fact the position taken by philosopher Gilles Deleuze and psychologist Felix Guattari (Deleuze and Guattari 1984). Opposing the standard Freudian view that desire is a response to a feeling of lack, they follow Nietzsche in arguing that people seek—and even exult in—change and transformation. In that light, people do not feel ashamed or guilty about their desires, nor do they indulge them so they can "get them over with." In a postmodern fashion, these authors conceive of desire in a way that attempts to move past Western divisions of self/other, action/experience, conception/feeling, and so forth. In that sense, desire is less an independent feeling—or even a separable portion of bodily experience—than it is a quality of awareness in which one is engaged proactively in the particularities of life. In that sense we become our desires, and our desires are effectively our modes of becoming.

Whether one appreciates this line of thought or not, it does seem that people orient themselves to and within fluid processes as much as they attach themselves to stable objects. We enjoy the "thrill of the hunt" perhaps more than the possession of the prey; we may be "in love with love" more than we are with our beloved. To alter Pavlov's great dictum, we do not salivate because we anticipate our bowl of food or even because we are alerted to the prospect of such food by that learned symbol of the dinner hour, the ringing bell; rather, we salivate because our own feelings of anticipation entrance us.

The above examples have emphasized the pleasures that attend movement and change. However, many people do not like haunted houses, carnival rides, taking drugs, or other forms of disorientation and risk. And many who do insist that the "real" dangers inherent to the activity should be controlled—through safety devices, training, equipment, regulatory procedures, and so forth—before they enter that setting. That is, we want the feeling of being in a dangerous situation without having to face its (usual) consequences.

The request for such protective devices makes clear the point that tension and uncertainty are also breeding grounds for negative feelings. To recall an example used above, we may be fearful because we *know* what is coming (catastemic displeasure), but we may also be terrified—that is, even more disturbed or disarmed—because we do *not* know what it is we face. The terrified person, whether he is being pursued down a lonely street or viewing the aftermath of a bomb, cannot quite grasp the mentality—or the capability—of otherness. Fear at least fixes the mind. Terror is psychological disorientation, an awareness that thought and behavior cannot fully anticipate what will happen next.

Integrating feelings of order and disorder. Although I've insisted that feelings of movement and of stasis are different things—and receive different names as emotions—I would argue that sensations of pleasure and displeasure are much the same in each case. As indicated above, catastemic pleasure is the sense of completion that results when one has moved into a condition that realizes a valued model for life. Catastemic displeasure is the feeling that one has moved into the opposite condition, far away from those valued models or, indeed, into clearly devalued ones. Satisfaction of that sort is usually found at the endings of action, in acts of remembrance, and even in connections to the future when people focus only the model that inspires them.

Kinetic feelings are deemed pleasant and unpleasant for the same reasons. This is the case even though kinetic feelings focus especially on the present. Disorderly feelings involve the sense that we moving through the world or, when we focus only on the future, that we are filled with excitement about what is to come. Such feelings are held to be pleasant when we sense that we are moving toward some valued model. However, movement itself—that is, movement that features no clear direction—can also be held to be pleasant. This occurs when those directionless movements meet our standards for processes of that sort.

What unifies a wild ride at an amusement park and a quiet moment on a park bench is the extent to which each of these experiences may be set against the subject's idealized or optimal standards for such experiences. My view is that people maintain ideas and images of "best-case scenarios" for activities—for example, remembrances of thrilling roller coaster rides—and then match current experiences to those models. To feel pleasure is to feel ourselves located within idealized standings or moving into such standings in ways that we approve. To feel displeasure is to feel ourselves moving away from those idealized standings or toward devalued conditions.

To take the case of kinetic or exploratory pleasure first, no one would claim that all exciting or confusing movements are pleasurable. Feeling yourself falling from a high building or your car skidding on ice is surely an exciting moment, but is it pleasurable? Pleasure is a judgment about the nature and direction of that process. Sometimes we "know what we are getting into" and can evaluate the occurrence based on standards we already possess. At other times we have no standards developed for this situation and must construct those standards as we go. More confident or adventurous people may decide that something is fun during the activity itself. Others may have to "get through it" safely—or do it several times—before they declare the matter a success.

Furthermore, the body also has its own parameters for what levels and kinds of stimulation it requires. All of us can only take so much buffeting before we are made to feel uncomfortable or "get hurt," but people have different pain thresholds and otherwise vary in the kinds of physical treatment they can tolerate. These physical capabilities may be connected to our (symbolic) standards of what is right for us. For persons with the proper "constitution"—both physical and mental—wild stirrings or confusions may be deemed wonderful instead of terrifying. Falling from high places is considered "fun" if you enjoy skydiving or bungee jumping. Being in a skidding car is not frightening but amusing if you are a teenager making "doughnuts" in the high school parking lot.

Similarly, people differ in their tolerance for order and stability. Lying in bed for long hours is a pleasure for some and a misery for others. Our bodies and minds tell us what real-life conditions we must accept, reject, defend, or pursue ardently. Experience is a sense of self-location, and we sometimes accept or see those locations as permanent. Whether we judge those locations to be pleasant depends on the standards we bring to them. Feelings of tranquility and repose are not, in themselves, ideals. A prisoner may well accept his fate and walk steadily to the gallows, but who would declare his acquiescence a pleasure?

THE SOCIAL ORGANIZATION OF DESIRE

When we produce visions of valued feeling-states and then try to realize those anticipations, we are said to have "desires." It may seem, from what has been said above, that individuals manage their own desires. We try to keep our visions in line with (what we consider to be) realistic expectations for experience; we distract ourselves from some of the urges of our bodies. Satisfaction and dissatisfaction are the results of self-direction. If people lived alone on desert islands, this calculation of pleasure and pain might be an adequate theory of behavior. However, we do not live alone. Instead, we live amidst communities of people and—more abstractly—amidst social and cultural forms that societies have created to administer those very

desires. For such reasons, this concluding section discusses the ways in which desires are publicly regulated.

Societal restrictions on desire. It is difficult to say what desires are fundamental
to human nature and whether those desires should be understood as needs, urges,
drives, wants, and so forth. Perhaps we have the "instincts" for sex and aggression—
or even for life and death—that Freud (1967) posited. What is not difficult to say
is that societies have long attempted to regulate these appetites. Indeed, Freud himself concluded in his 1937 classic, *Civilization and its Discontents*, that "repression"
is a necessary element of public life (1961).

In sociology some of the most important reflections on this question were offered by Max Weber. In a famous thesis Weber argued that Western societies have
been marked by a centuries-old process of "rationalization"—a cultural shift that
encouraged an abstract, calculating, emotionally reserved, and systematic approach
to life (see Sica 2000; Henricks 2006). This calculating mentality expressed itself in
economics as the growth of capitalism, in politics and law as the spread of constitu-
tional government and independent judiciaries, in administration as bureaucracy,
in knowledge making as science, in music as highly organized "symphonic" playing,
and even in religion as an individualistic, calculating style of Protestantism. In each
of these cultural realms people developed highly formalized, written "accounting
systems" to manage behavior and achieve goals. For the most part people accepted
such codes and formats, not because those formats had any emotional appeal but
because people felt them to be understandable frameworks created by understandable processes.

Other styles of behavior and expression, Weber explained, dominated earlier
stages of European history. In that light, he (1964, 115–57) discussed four different kinds of social action: traditional, affectual, value-rational, and instrumental-
rational. When people behave traditionally, they follow codes simply because they
have always followed those patterns. Similar to this unreflective or habitual pattern
is affectual action, in which people express themselves in terms of deeply established,
internal commitments they feel no need to "understand." More "meaningful"—at
least in the sense of being consciously understood and controlled—is value-rational
behavior. In this form, people orient themselves to recognized principles that they
hold with much conviction. Honoring these principles is one goal of action. Examples of this include the soldier who willingly endangers his life to serve his country
or the minister who sets aside her worldly goals to serve her parishioners.

In all of the above forms, people rely on internalized frameworks to guide their
lives. Instrumental rationality is different. In this instance, action is guided by considerations of "what works" or otherwise seems most effective in helping the actor
reach his own, rationally chosen ends. In the pattern of value rationality, firmly

held values sharply restrict the ends of action; in instrumental rationality, both means and ends are juggled. In other words, everything is now provisional; values become little more than transient attitudes. People shift their perspectives—and their commitments—as quickly as their changing "interests" in a situation demand.

To be sure, Weber was no champion of the older, unreflective styles of being, but the self-conscious, pragmatic, litigious, and otherwise scheming mentality that had arisen in economic and political life did trouble him deeply. Would that cold-blooded style also take over the "softer" enclaves of society represented by family life, sexuality, and religion? Even more generally, Weber worried that this new vision of the world—as a rationally crafted artifice—was undermining the quality of experience that earlier generations had known. In a bureaucratic, bourgeois, legalistic age, where does one find mystery, reverence, and ecstasy?

Some writers have noted that many of the themes described above—instrumental scheming, emotional regulation, cold-blooded resolve, and the like—are not new. Perhaps the best-known of these commentators is Norbert Elias, whose two-volume *The Civilizing Process* addresses the rise of bodily and emotional control in European history. Basing his account on a study of etiquette books from the early modern period, Elias (2000) argues that people—even those of high status—used to have much more relaxed or naturalistic attitudes toward the body and its functions. Practices related to eating, urinating, defecating, sexual expression, clearing one's throat, and the like were, by modern standards, crude. Such customs changed with the ascendancy of a "court" society, in which geographically scattered nobles were brought into restricted settings that emphasized competitive displays of personal quality or character. This new style was part of a general shift toward individualism, and social life itself became reconstrued as a collective, rather than communal, enterprise sustained and monitored by these newly situated persons.

Fertile soil for these changes—and thus the intended readers of the above-mentioned etiquette books—were bourgeois citizens who organized themselves in a variety of abstract collectivities, including business associations, congregational churches, sporting clubs, and parliaments. Because of the increasing scope and complexity of the new social arrangements, citizens of the new type had to calculate the consequences of their behavior in much more abstract and "distant" ways. Personal control, and especially the self-conscious awareness of one's standing before others, became a value to be maximized. Following William James, Barbalet (1998) explains how rationality itself became a "sentiment" and how other styles of relating became discouraged.

In a later work Elias (with Eric Dunning) modified this position. As Weber himself realized, modern societies express a countervailing theme. In contrast to their commitments to personal status striving and careful presentations of self, people also seek escapes into less rationally controlled, more emotionally charged settings. Elias and Dunning's (1986) *The Quest for Excitement* addresses this tension. In keeping with Elias's earlier theme, civilization is still associated with social configurations, in which dispersed individuals come together to agree on the principles that will oversee their often competitive relationships with one another. To use Elias and Dunning's terms, this "parliamentarization" of society is associated with the "sportization" of its pastimes. In the contemporary era sports and other forms of expressive association continue to be regulated formally; that is, they exhibit a "controlled de-controlling of emotions" (Elias and Dunning 1986, 44).

Such comments are consistent with the theme of the current book: that emotionality—and indeed all patterns of personal expression—is routinely framed in societies. I would add that self-regulation or "sportsmanship" of the above type is especially pertinent for the special categories of people whose play is publicly celebrated and who have something to gain by conducting themselves in an orderly way (see Henricks 1991). When settings are more anonymous, when people feel that they have been marginalized or otherwise separated from patterns of respect and reward, and when the groups they identify with are founded on different kinds of principles, then other less carefully regulated styles of festivity may occur. In that same spirit, *The Quest for Excitement* explores other styles of playful expression—including soccer hooliganism—that socially disadvantaged groups sometimes exhibit.

To what extent do rationally committed, bureaucratically administered organizations control human expression? In response to that question, George Ritzer (1994) has described what he calls the "McDonaldization" process, the extension of that company's organizing principles—calculability, efficiency, technological control, and predictability—into many other areas of contemporary life. Religion, sports, sexuality, art, and so forth may all be yielding to this commercial, standardizing ethic. Michel Foucault has advanced a much stronger claim about bureaucratic excess. In Foucault's (1977) view, many of society's institutions are organized on terms that resemble prisons. Organizations like factories, clinics, schools, and the military take on the character of Goffman's (1961a) "total institutions," in which people are reconceived in quasi-scientific language, subjected to all-seeing administrative control, and "disciplined" to ensure that they conform to this distinctive logic. By such processes, some people are marked off as deviants and quarantined so they will not contaminate others. However, all citizens are essentially "domesticated" or "pacified" so that they pose few threats to social order. In Foucault's view, we come to regulate ourselves in terms that our social regulators have provided to us. Facing threats of institutionalization and incarceration, we allow our bodily feelings to be moved along socially prescribed channels.

Societal encouragements of desire. Hochschild's writing, the reader may recall, emphasizes the tension that exists between society's rules for how we should feel and our own self-standards. All too often we adjust the latter to the former. That is, the flight attendant convinces herself that she does not hate her obnoxious passengers. But neutrality—the absence of dislike—is not enough. She must also convince herself that she likes those same passengers. Good feelings are the order of the day, and she should have them.

This general theme—that societies encourage certain feelings at the same time that they restrict and channel other feelings—is quite important. Arguably, an ideology that emphasizes good feelings and the cultivation of desire now dominates contemporary society. There are many causes for this. As Hochschild (2003) emphasizes, many of us now work in service professions that depend on pleasing clients. This process, she feels, has intruded into domestic life. Women in particular are encouraged to feel responsible for their family's feelings and for manufacturing "good times" and memories. Outside the domestic sphere people are encouraged to have the sorts of good times that can be found in recreational settings, travel destinations, bars, and clubs. If social relations are not enough to produce good feelings, then those desired ends can be obtained from the medical world, where pills and surgical procedures are on sale to make people feel better about who they are. A "therapeutic" culture that sustains legions of psychologists, counselors, nutritionists, and fitness instructors has also been well established (see Bellah et al. 1985).

Technological shifts have also encouraged personal satisfaction. As Williams (2001, 11) argues, we now live in a "mediascape" society focusing on emotionality. Electronic media—movies, television, computers, and the like—serve up images of people in highly emotional moments, scenes that range from wonderful serenity, joyful celebration, and unabashed lust to spectacles of distress, anger, and fear. The intent of such displays is to provoke emotion in viewers.

This may also be the rationale behind the many "interactive" forms of media, such as video games, social networking websites, and handheld communication devices that I described in chapter 4. Although machine culture has probably not replaced face-to-face communication as the fundamental setting for emotional generation and display, it has made possible new forms of personal participation and interaction that allow people to experience sociality "at a distance." Moreover, because machines themselves can simulate many aspects of social interaction, they allow people to preferentially "bowl alone" (Putnam 2001) or to otherwise pursue pleasure on their own terms and timing. No longer, it seems, do we have to rely on the support of familiar others. As in the cases of music, television, and movies, experience can be had "on demand."

Prominent also is the culture of advertising. Whatever importance advertising once placed on the transmission of information about products, that pattern has yielded to seemingly endless displays of pleasing visual images of the "good life." Viewers are encouraged to imagine themselves in these settings. In his aptly titled *All-Consuming Images*, Stuart Ewen (1999) argues that advertising no longer appeals to idea-based thinking, which requires logical or calculating skills, but instead to *imagaic* thinking that solicits evolutionarily older and less consciously controlled processes of response. If people once tolerated advertising as an irritating but commercially necessary interruption of programming, now these little scenarios and vignettes intrigue and amuse them. Increasingly, the ambition of the advertiser is to insert ads into programming as artfully or even seamlessly as possible. Economies that have addressed the basic material needs of their populations feel themselves impelled to develop new standards of the necessary. In that process of consumer re-education, ads are tutorials in expectation and desire (see Featherstone 1991; Schor and Holt 2000).

Unlike newscasts and prime-time programming, which feature accounts of the unpleasant or dangerous, ads provide counterbalancing "jolts" of the pleasant. Contrasting sharply with the unresolved public issues of contemporary society, the scenes of ads are presented as opportunities for privately controlled experience. In ads we picture ourselves in a well-appointed home, vacation spot, or luxurious automobile; we imagine ourselves alone or with our most intimate, self-chosen companions. Everyone is beautiful. Successful ads are those that enter into or even "colonize" our dream life. By viewing beautiful, amusing, or thrilling scenes, we find ourselves wanting to belong to them. We are encouraged to believe that the vision presented to us is a socially supported pathway to personal fulfillment and that we *deserve* to inhabit this world, whatever its financial, interpersonal, and societal costs.

One can argue that the desire for good feelings is a natural proclivity of human beings, and that social organizations only respond to preexisting concerns. Critical theory, a perspective that describes the social machinery behind private desire, opposes this argument (see Jay 1973). Weaving together Marxist ideas about capitalism, masses, false consciousness, and the commodification of experience with Freudian emphases on personal desire, repression, and moral regulation, writers like Marcuse, Benjamin, Lowenthal, Adorno, and Horkheimer argue that the greater danger of contemporary capitalism is the way in which it organizes the idea systems and aesthetic sensibilities of the public. Marxism proper focuses on the organization of *production*—and the possibilities for worker alienation—in capitalist societies; critical theory focuses on the organization of *consumption* and the alienated self-experience that derives from this activity. Horkheimer and Adorno (1972) depicted these issues in their classic account of the "culture industry." Large businesses, they argue, have taken control of many of the agencies by which visions of life are created and displayed to people. As in Hollywood movies, emphasis is given to individuals' spirited, romantic gestures and to the "interpersonal" relationships they develop with others. Few scenes question the propriety of the social order—or its economic system—as a whole. The result is a thoroughly private and "bourgeois" view of human possibility. People buy these visions and dream of greatness in such terms.

In the view of the above authors (and in my own view), private desire is connected intimately with themes of social structure. Those public forms and processes honor some of our dreams of the good life while stoutly opposing others. For such reasons we do not simply "flip through" a set of interpretive standards to find the ones that make us happy. Instead, society's groups and organizations broker our quest. We accept some of the visions held out to us, reject others, and adopt most without knowing we have a choice. Having formulated our desires and set off to fulfilling them, we meet society again—as a set of powerful repercussions to our choices. Like most of our experiences, pleasure is socially constructed.

CHAPTER 8

BEHAVIORAL PATHWAYS

Although opposite in their objectives, the arguments of chapter 6 and 7 are perhaps both true enough. That is, people desire an orderly, even ritualized world. But they also desire certain levels of disorder, especially if that disorder includes the prospect that they may move to standings that are better than the ones they currently occupy. The character of such movement is the subject of the current chapter. My special interest is a question that Goffman did not address directly in *Frame Analysis*: are there are some very basic forms of human behavior that have their own emotional implications?

My thesis is that there are recognized behavioral trajectories that help people make their way through situations. Those trajectories are essentially models that spell out the intentions of the persons involved, especially their desire to move from one standing to another in social relationships. To consider this issue, I offer first a view of social life as a seeking—and negotiating—of these standings. As part of that argument, I describe emotions not only as a "social currencies" that aid this status seeking but also as "destinations" for such activity. The next section describes four fundamental standings that people seek in their relationships with one another: "privilege," "subordination," "marginality," and "engagement." Each is said to offer distinctive opportunities for experience. My final comments describe four trajectories or "pathways" of human action—work, play, communitas, and ritual—as strategies for reaching those locations. My general point is that these standings and pathways hold out certain possibilities for satisfaction and deny or restrict others.

SEEKING STANDINGS

The idea that people seek what they do not have—and use recognized social currencies to obtain those ends—was a theme developed by Simmel (1971, 43–69). In Simmel's view human interaction can be viewed as a series of exchanges, the results of which are a change in the *personal condition* of the individuals involved. Although people commonly think of exchanges in terms of a Western economic model—in which people try to acquire valued goods and services at the least cost—exchanges are fundamentally shifts in social rather than economic condition, and they involve various kinds of trading at the same time. That is, benefits and costs can be of many different sorts. As Simmel (1971, 43) explains, the view of interaction as exchange "is true of every conversation, every kind of love (even when requited unfavorably), every game, every act of looking one another over." One may spend a compliment and receive a smile, exchange knowing glances, or perform a good deed for an elderly person and experience a rise in public approbation. Some exchanges involve great sacrifices on the part of the giver; some cost almost nothing. Some benefits are garnered and then saved, perhaps for later use or simply for the joy of possession. Some are spent immediately.

Simmel's ideas about the kinds of goods and services that are given and received are intentionally broad; however, the general point that unites his examples is important: relationships are organized around the respective contributions of the participants. In that light, the publicly recognized "value" of any social relationship is connected to ideas about the "worth" of the participants' contributions. To use an example, kisses that are given casually or indiscriminately mean little, kisses that are bestowed rarely and earnestly mean much more, and a kiss between two deeply committed persons is a matter of some public import. However, the value of the kiss—or any other gesture—also derives from the imputed social worth of the *person* making that gesture. Rightly or not, kisses from some people—such as the most attractive boy or girl at a high school—are held to be more valuable than kisses from other, less favored students. And, as he argues, an exchange of kisses is more than a process of giving and getting; it is a moment of mutual commitment that cements the social bond.

Pointedly, emotional expressions also function as media of exchange. Those expressions—such as a smile or a look of concern—are essentially forms of personal and social commitment, indicators of the seriousness or worth of a relationship to the expresser and receiver. We can evaluate those expressions in part because they have become culturally standardized. That is, we understand that a gentle gaze or the words "I love you" mean certain things. However, we also evaluate the context in which the expression occurs. A flirtatious remark (Simmel 1984, 134) made before a crowd at a fancy-dress party means one thing; the same words and gestures directed to someone in private are quite another matter.

Much like Randall Collins, whose work was discussed in chapter 6, Simmel emphasizes the ways in which people commit themselves to situations—and to one another—through ritualized exchanges. For Simmel, the strength of those ties is connected to judgments about the value of those gestures. As we've seen, determining that value depends on shared ideas about the "meaning" of the gesture as an abstract form, the social standing of the person making the gesture, the level of personal commitment or sacrifice involved in its expression, and the social context in which the gesture occurs.

Contemporary exchange theorists have moved beyond Simmel's loose formulations. Indeed, contemporary scholars using an exchange perspective to understand the emotions (see, for example, Lawler and Yoon 1996; Molm 1997) have, for the most part, turned from Simmel toward other social theorists, most notably George Homans and Peter Blau. In such approaches social life is seen as a goal-oriented activity in which individuals are motivated to attain certain valued resources, described as benefits, rewards, or pay-offs. Attaining these end-points typically involves costs, which are understood both as short-term expenditures and longer-term "investments." Stable social relationships feature settled agreements between the people involved. It is assumed that people who remain in such relationships have concluded that the balance of benefits and costs, if not ideal, is at least acceptable. Positive emotions occur when one's standards for this balance of benefits and costs has been achieved.

To be sure, interaction can be seen as a process of giving and getting, of surrendering some things that are valued in order to receive others that are valued more. In that sense, social life is a compromise between satisfaction and dissatisfaction. Two points should be added to this thesis. The first is that people are not free agents in their choice making. As many of the sociologists in chapter 6 emphasize, people depend on ritualized forms to guide their thoughts, behaviors, and feelings. We do not continually reinvent the social world with a series of clever compromises; we rely on culturally approved patterns that move us toward culturally approved goals. The second point is that people rarely conduct their exchanges on equal terms (see Molm 1997). Whether the trading is to be done in the currencies of wealth, power, prestige, or knowledge—or in their more tangible equivalents—it must be acknowledged that participants tend to possess differing amounts of these resources. A wager of a thousand dollars means nothing to a rich man and everything to a poor one. A woman who is securely positioned in a social group can take a few risks with her status; a woman without those solid connections may find herself abandoned after the smallest misstep. Like the parent and child in the preceding chapter who were discussing that girl's curfew, social actors may appear to be negotiating in equally earnest ways. But like that parent and child, their circumstances are often quite different, and one party usually has additional resources they can bring to bear when agreement cannot be reached.

Emotions as tokens of exchange. For the most part emotions are discussed in exchange theory as the feelings people have when negotiations either go their way or don't go their way. We buy a new car at a price cheaper than we expected and feel elated; we learn that our neighbor paid less than we did for the same vehicle and we feel miserable. A secondary theme is the way in which emotions function as trading cards or currencies. When people interact with one another, they let others know how they are feeling about that situation—and about those other people—by displaying culturally recognized emotions. These emotions are signs of approval and disapproval for what is occurring. In effect we say to others: "Because of what has just happened, I now feel differently about your actions, about you, or about the situation of which we are both a part. Having seen my reaction, you should be careful as you move ahead." Social relationships—and social structure itself—are built on such public displays (see Lawler, Thye, and Yoon 2009).

However, there is another way of thinking about the functions that emotions serve in exchanges. That approach is to consider emotions as the "ends" rather than the "means" of rational calculation. In other words, emotions are not simply the accompaniments of action or of standings. They can also be seen as that action's desired outcomes or "destinations." In our contemporary, media-saturated world, people are encouraged to attain certain kinds of feelings. Some of those feelings are the catastemic experiences of completion and repose described in the preceding chapter—the satisfaction of regarding one's newly purchased home or seeing one's beautifully composed visage in the mirror. Other feelings are of the kinetic type, feelings of pleasurable excitement. When we plan a vacation, get ready for a party, call our friends to go shopping or hiking, and so forth, we effectively prepare ourselves for a certain kind of "time" filled with a distinctive range of emotions. Arguably the object of our quest is not to go tromping through the woods or through the malls or even to be with our friends; instead, it is to achieve certain emotions.

To state this idea in the most general terms, people desire emotions as they desire other matters, and a great deal of "rational" activity is oriented toward achieving those ends. In that light, the impulse of an acquisitive, change-oriented, capitalist society is not simply to keep people in a condition of constant desiring but also to get such people—as consumers—to implement the decisions that will lead them successively closer to realizing their perceived emotional destinations. In the final analysis we do not want that new car or bottle of perfume. We want the distinctive feelings that we anticipate to be associated with the possession of such objects. Unfortunately—or fortunately, from the vantage point of the purveyors of these products—the completion of one quest leads almost immediately to the envisioning of another, for emotions are transient affairs.

My father, also a sociology professor, routinely depicted contemporary society as a "happiness cult." We want to live in a world constituted by an endless stream of "pleasing buzzes" and "jolts." To constantly dose ourselves in this fashion—in the manner of Olds and Milner's rats—is to possess a certain kind of happiness. In ways that our animal kindred cannot match, people hold images of pleasing sensations in their minds and exhibit the greatest ingenuity in reaching and then inhabiting those visions. In a post-Weberian world, emotion is not the antithesis of rationality; it is its culmination.

INTERACTION AS SELF-LOCATION

If interaction is a bartering process in which people try to acquire what they do not have, the result of this process is a society where relationships are in a state of continual tension and change. To use the terms of chapter 6, people try to accomplish certain ends as "actors," to move into and take on the expectations of certain preferred "statuses," and to sustain valued identities as "persons" in relationships. Only sometimes do the people in question achieve these ambitions: sometimes they try and fail. Differently again, they may find themselves trapped in behaviors, statuses, and personal identities they wish they could avoid. Some of these locations are long-standing affairs, such as our ethnic and gender assignments or membership in our birth families. Others, such as being the frontrunner in a race or the recipient of a compliment, are transitory. In any case, what people seek and experience can be called "standings," a sense of social predicament that contrasts the position of one person to that of another. Seen in that light, social life features not only endless interactions between people but also endless invidious comparisons. What we have and are is compared to what others have and are. And those presumed qualities and acquisitions are put to the test when we interact.

If human interaction can be seen as an attempt by subjects and objects—or, to use slightly different language, by selves and others—to impose their strategies of action and interpretation on one another, that process of self-location can be shown as four different patterns. Those standings are displayed in figure 4.

As the reader can see from the figure, I'm claiming that there are four principal patterns of self-location—privilege, subordination, engagement, and marginality. Two of these patterns—privilege and engagement—display conditions that I described in previous chapters as instances of "ascending meaning." That is, they describe circumstances in which the subject or self is able to control a relationship or otherwise claim the activity of the other in the subject's own terms. In more settled social conditions, these abilities to control tend to be recognized as "rights." In less settled conditions, they are said to be "powers."

Two of the patterns—subordination and (once again) engagement—represent locations characterized by "descending meaning." At such times, the subject accepts the directives of others and comprehends herself as an object in their terms. When people recognize their obligations to others as legitimate, those obligations are said to be "responsibilities"; in less settled conditions they are "duties." The remaining

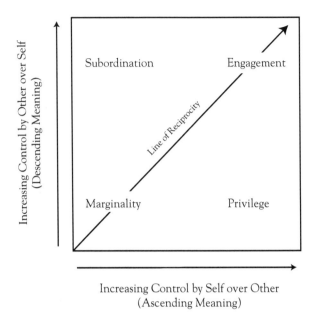

FIGURE 4. **Four Modes of Self Location**

condition—marginality—reflects a situation in which the interventions of both self and other are minimal.

The purpose of the model is to display human relationships as an interchange or dialectic between selves and others. That dialectic is ultimately a balancing and alternation of "claims." To illustrate this idea, consider the relationship between self and other as a sort of handshake. That bond is strongest when both people's hands are holding firmly, and it is weakest when the grip of each is soft or being withdrawn. However, a bond may also be established when one party holds tightly against the weak or absent pressure of the other. In this last instance the person who holds tightly is said to "control" or "claim" the other.

All of us are familiar with these experiences of controlling others and of being controlled by them. We also know the feeling of being embedded deeply in relationships of mutual control. And we are aware when we are marginalized and, in that double sense, are "out of control." To experience the world is to comprehend one's predicament within a wide range of settings, and issues of power or status, as Kemper (1978; Kemper and Collins 1990) emphasizes, are inevitable portions of that awareness. In that context, our emotions reflect our sense of moving into, residing within, and moving out of these standings. Finally, the four standings I've depicted are not only the *circumstances* within which we appraise ourselves as social objects; they are also the *vantage points* from which we draw conclusions about

what is possible for us in the moments ahead. The remainder of this section discusses briefly each of these standings.

Privilege. No standing in contemporary Western societies is exalted as much as
privilege. To be privileged is to possess special rights, immunities, and benefits.
What makes these rights special is that other people do not possess them. In the
figure, privilege is shown as a condition where the subject is able to control or claim
the activity of the other. A privileged person is able to summon or beckon others,
typically without fear of obligation or reprisal.

For sociologists privilege is understood to be an advantageous standing with regard to the valued resources of society—specifically wealth, power, prestige, and
knowledge. Although each of those four resources is in certain ways different from
the others, those who possess social advantages of these different sorts share a sense
that they can make their way through the world in a relatively unhindered fashion
and, when encountering others, can use those resources to secure their compliance.
Such persons find themselves being carried along as if on one of those moving walkways found in airports. Compared to other people outside that enclosed walkway,
our mechanically assisted pedestrians can either race past them or—with absolutely
no effort—simply ride along and keep pace as the outsiders scurry along. In either
case, the privileged person finds herself advantaged in ways that others are not.

Commonly, positions of advantage carry with them their fair share of obligations; however, many of the obligations of privileged people are to position holders who are even more advantaged than they are, and many others are taken on
voluntarily as acts of charity or "public service" rather than as real compulsions.
In any case, what is crucial to the idea of privilege is that one can set her own
agenda for relationships with others, can interfere without being interfered with.

In class-based societies, the theme of economic prerogative especially expresses
this ideal. One acquires and spends money so as to enter a setting where the customer is customarily right, where the resource holder does not serve but is instead
served. Like owners of publicly traded stocks—who possess no obligations to
those companies, to the clients of those companies, or even to the broader communities in which those companies operate—we wish to separate rights from responsibilities. The ideal life, or so we imagine, is distinguished by the extent of its
prerogatives. Belonging is seen as an opportunity to control others. "Membership," to adopt a slogan of a credit card company, "has its privileges."

Subordination. Entirely problematic—at least in the Western view—is the opposite circumstance, in which orders are taken rather than given and people find
their behavior constrained at every turn. In societies that prize independence, conditions of subordination and restriction are something to be escaped. The status
of underling is bad enough when it is judged to be temporary—as in the case of

a child in a family or a lower-level manager in a company—but much worse are those forms of continuing subordination based on factors such as gender, class, ethnicity, physical ability, and sexual orientation. At any rate, most of us aspire to manage our own destinies. At the very least we want to choose the standards that will be applied to our own lives.

Although Western religious traditions do explore ideas of "servanthood," typically that posture of humility is before a transcendent God and not before some more proximate, secular being. As Simmel (1950, 181–306) explained, subordination to an abstract principle is quite different from subordination to a person or to a group. Moreover, the religious person commonly undertakes this subservient position *voluntarily*, often through public rituals featuring acts of self-abnegation, formal vows, offerings, and other displays of penitence and obedience (see Durkheim 1965). Such pledges and commitments, when undertaken freely by adults, are understandable to the Western mind. However, a certain suspicion persists about what will happen to those earnest devotees who have surrendered themselves to the persons and organizations—monasteries, sects, military outfits, hospitals, gangs, radical political groups, and the like—that will henceforth manage their behavior.

In my view, this emphasis on the involuntary and permanent aspects of subordination blinds one to the importance of responsibility in human affairs. As noted in chapter 6, this was the abiding theme of Durkheim's sociology. People need clear directions for how to proceed, including limits or boundaries for their movements. These boundaries may well be self-imposed, but they also may come from socially recognized "others," especially those well-established groups and communities that articulate and encourage certain forms of human possibility. These directives should not be taken lightly or playfully but instead should be considered with utmost seriousness. People must learn to understand themselves not just as "subjects" (who discover what they can do to the world) but also as "objects" (who find out what can be done to them). Society, in Durkheim's view, is "real," and we need that transcendent, superordinate reality to display and coordinate our obligations to one another.

Marginality. I have discussed two quite different places to experience selfhood: privilege, where one learns the lessons of power and control, and subordination, where the teachings are about dependency and constraint. Marginality is the condition that minimizes both forms of awareness. The marginal person is someone who is—or at least who understands herself to be—disconnected from others. Neither ascending nor descending meaning guides such a person.

However, independence of this type is not equivalent to complete isolation or disaffiliation. Once again, Simmel (1971, 143–49) makes this clear in his essay on the "stranger," the marginal person who is both connected and disconnected at the same time, "in the world" but not "of it." Pointedly, the marginal person continues to be involved in the situation in question or at least oriented to it; that is why they are "on the margin" rather than fully apart. Those who feel themselves to be outsiders have not turned away from the group entirely but still look inside, sometimes with their noses pressed against the window. Rebels—both those who merely disavow the world and those who seek to recreate it—maintain their former object of reference. In that context, the independent person understands her freedom in terms of the forces that once held her captive.

It is customary in the social sciences to think of marginality as an unwanted or even mournful condition. The outsider is presented as someone who wishes to be more involved in a group that will not grant him full membership. Being in a minority group commonly means being both subordinated *and* kept at a distance at the same time. However, as the examples from the preceding paragraph suggest, *relative* separation can also be a valued condition that allows one to judge the group critically and creatively and that provides its own distinctive spheres of operation. As Simmel explains in his essay, the marginal person does not merely pass through society (as a traveler does) but remains to live (in a partially accepted way) among its members. "Foreign" merchants, professionals, and civil servants of this sort may be invited to formal social occasions or consulted for their advice by more established group members. Those foreigners are invited to do this just because they have no firm basis from which to threaten or control the recipients of that advice.

The ambiguous status of the marginal person is attributable to two different aspects of the idea of freedom. On the one hand, freedom means "freedom from" objects and persons, disconnection from the usual obligations and interferences that others impose on our sphere of thought and action. That aspect of freedom—the absence of *descending* meaning—is celebrated routinely in Western societies. People imagine themselves to be "free" when they do not have to listen to their parents, pay taxes, receive telephone solicitations, take the dog for a walk, and so forth. However, freedom also means the "freedom to" accomplish our ambitions and desires. Typically, meeting our goals is dependent on the cooperation and support of others; sometimes their acceptance of us is the very goal we seek. Without firm connections to others, as Durkheim emphasized, we can accomplish only the most limited, self-oriented tasks. In that sense, marginality also features the absence of *ascending* meaning. Because we are positioned on the edge of a situation, we cannot turn that situation to our purposes. We have all the "freedom from" we want—to do and go as we desire—but we do not have the social resources to realize those ambitions.

Engagement. The final condition is the opposite of the separation described above. "Engaged" persons are those who find themselves in the thick of interaction with the world. Difficult external demands frequently confront such persons. However, they do not seek to evade those demands but instead confront and respond to them. Moreover, engaged people play active roles in situations, claiming others as vigorously as those others are claiming them. Clearly, a relationship of this sort is a pattern of give and take, an effulgence of both ascending and descending meaning. Images of busy homemakers, striving businesspeople, and actively playing children apply.

The use of the term "engagement" (and the general appearance of figure 4) is intended to remind some readers of Csikszentmihalyi's (1975, 1991) depictions of focused involvement or "flow," which I described in a previous chapter. To say that we find ourselves most effectively when we participate voluntarily in worthy, intricate challenges is not a paradox. Said in the opposite way, we can know neither our selves nor the world around us by regarding those objects from a distance.

Sociological readers may recall that Durkheim's sociology confronts similar issues of personal immersion or participative involvement. In his *Suicide*, Durkheim (1951) displays four potentially dangerous modes of human relationships. Two of those patterns concern the absence of descending meaning. What Durkheim terms *anomie* and *egoism* are patterns in which the individual is inadequately attached to social settings, a detachment that is facilitated by the failure of those settings to draw him in and hold him (anomie) or by the relatively asocial character of guiding beliefs (egoism). Humans need to be involved with others and to hold beliefs that recognize those connections in order to live fully and well.

However, Durkheim also emphasizes the dangers of overinvolvement in situations that effectively extinguish the self. His criticisms of *altruism* (commitment to a set of beliefs that disregards selfish interests) and *fatalism* (surrender to dominating groups or persons) are essentially recognitions of the importance of ascending meaning. People need the demands and guidance of others, but they also need opportunities to express themselves and receive public acknowledgment for those expressions.

Like Csikszentmihalyi, Durkheim believed that the most productive human relationships feature a kind of reciprocity between the demands of the self and the demands of otherness. Assertion and compliance, rights and responsibilities, freedom and dependence must be balanced. That having been said, the question remains: how *deeply* involved should people be in their relationships with others? Is an extremely focused, even passionate embrace with the objects and contexts of our lives—whether those forms are other people, organizations, hobbies, pets, jobs, social causes, and the like—the preferred path for self-development? Or does deep engagement present its own set of difficulties?

To respond to my own question, I would recall here that "marginality" also is a balanced or reciprocal condition featuring (quite limited) claims from both parties in a relationship. Although marginality seems to be a rather disaffected and disengaged pattern of self-awareness, it does, at its best, provide a certain distance that allows a person to evaluate critically the object of her regard. In contrast, to be fully engaged is frequently to lose that sense of perspective. Like Plato's (1963) famous residents of the cave or Dante's (2003) pilgrim lost in a dark wood, we can be so captured in the give and take of a confining environment that we cannot comprehend our own predicament. We feel ourselves moving about—and experiencing the distinctive joys and sorrows associated with those movements. But we have no vantage point from which to glimpse the character of our lives.

FEELINGS OF ASCENDING AND DESCENDING MEANING

I've argued that each pattern of self-location opens up certain avenues of experience and restricts others. A more precise version of this is that each pattern holds out to its possessor a distinctive range of satisfactions and dissatisfactions. Still, the issue must be addressed: are the feelings associated with privilege, marginality, engagement, and subordination really any different from each other? After all, the author's own definition of satisfaction has emphasized that almost any condition can be declared satisfying as long it conforms to the optimal standards—physical and symbolic—of the interpreter. Isn't satisfaction or pleasure of one type the same as any other? In this section I argue that the positive feelings associated with ascending and descending meaning are somewhat different.

One of the best-known attempts to explain the differences between positive feelings is that of Csikszentmihalyi (1975, 1991), who contrasts pleasure and enjoyment. Csikszentmihalyi argues that enjoyment is a much more complicated—and more rewarding—experience than pleasure. Pleasure, at least as he sees it, is equivalent to feelings of contentment or satisfaction. Pleasure is homeostatic: it restores equilibrium. Pleasure occurs, as he (1991, 45) states, "when consciousness says that expectations set by biological programs or by social conditions have been met." In other words, pleasure is essentially a closing rather than an opening of possibilities, an act of restoration instead of exploration. It is a self-indulgent feeling that requires "no psychic investment" (46) and produces no psychic growth. In that sense, we take or receive pleasure from eating and drinking.

By contrast, enjoyment represents an awareness that goes beyond satisfaction, a kind of "forward movement" (46) in which the person achieves "something unexpected." Enjoyment is an active experience requiring an unusual investment of energy. It is psychically more complex, and it promotes personal growth. Compared to pleasure, enjoyment is a more full-fledged encounter with the world. Enjoyment causes us to change and does not necessarily satisfy us at the time of its making.

A listing of Csikszentmihalyi's (1991, 48–67) "elements of enjoyment" makes clear the relationship of that experience to flow. Enjoyment features a challenging activity that requires skills, a merging of activity and awareness, clear goals and feedback, concentration on the task at hand, a paradox of control, a loss of self-consciousness, and a transformation of time. Furthermore, enjoyment is understood to be an "autotelic" experience in which we create for ourselves a context that is intrinsically rewarding. When we enjoy ourselves, we focus only on the moment; we do not look about. The "paradox of control" he refers to is the sense that even though we are not in control, we feel as though we are.

Csikszentmihalyi claims that enjoyment is the mode of experience most appropriate to our best or optimal selves, when we energetically engage the world in focused and committed ways. Pleasure reflects our less heroic side, when we are merely "filling our tanks," to repeat my metaphor from an earlier chapter. To translate Csikszentmihalyi's conceptions into the terms developed in the current book, he seems to take the ideas of excitement (i.e., the sense of resistance, novelty, and disorder), self-direction (the attempt to comprehend and control the world), and even other-direction (the adjustment of the self to the world's forms and forces), granting all of these to "enjoyment." That latter experience is held aloft as the rightful satisfaction for those who dare to address the difficult challenges of life. Pleasure is merely its bloated, self-absorbed companion.

Csikszentmihalyi's view of enjoyment is well suited to his concept of flow and to the view of engagement that I have described above as a basic form of self-location. When people are in balanced or reciprocal relationships, they have to deal with many kinds of challenges. They make claims on otherness, otherness makes claims on them, and the resulting dialectic is much more complicated than anything the participants would produce on their own terms. My own interest in this matter is to describe the positive feelings that seem pertinent to the other three patterns of self-location.

If enjoyment is the positive feeling associated with the reciprocal give and take of engagement, then pleasure—or at least the kind of pleasure that Csikszentmihalyi emphasizes—is connected to the more withdrawn posture I've described as marginality. At any rate, the kind of pleasure he depicts is of the solipsistic, self-regarding type. To find that type of pleasure, we flee from the challenges of otherness. Instead, we desire to live inside a well-defended psychological domain, informed by pleasing images and biochemical secretions. That pattern of comfortable isolation seems particularly pertinent to the postmodern or "consumerist" self described in chapter 4.

As profoundly important as that withdrawn posture may be—if only as an occasion to rest, recuperate, and speculate on new possibilities—my own approach is to see the concept of pleasure in a broader—and less pejorative—way. In my view, pleasure embraces both contentment and excitement. That is, people desire both security and stimulation, and pleasure is our evaluation that these concerns have been met. Moreover, I maintain that pleasure, as the more self-contained experience, and enjoyment, as its participative equivalent, can be achieved in different ways: through self-direction, through other-direction, and through combinations of these extremes. In other words, I advocate a much more "activist" view of pleasure than Csikszentmihalyi does. In my view, people do not merely *receive* pleasure; they actively *manipulate* or *respond* to the world to achieve that condition.

To be sure, pleasure does involve a critical psychological component, the internalized standards of mind and body. We are "pleased" when the world conforms to those terms. Thus, that pleasure is so commonly associated with bodily movements, psychological fantasies, or other largely "private" indulgences is not surprising. After all, if we wish to achieve ego-mastery—and to discover ascending meaning by placing situations into our own frameworks—then our bodies and minds are surely the regions we can most easily command.

In that context one can contrast the isolationist, self-regarding style of pleasure associated with marginality with the more activist style of pleasure seeking exhibited in the attempt to find positions of privilege. In this latter case, we desire that the world should dance to our own tune. In other words, we do not simply wish to watch what is going on; we wish to "use" the world and, in the process, experience our own powers of transformation. When we are able to transform situations, the pleasure that results is a kind of *satisfaction* that comes from successfully imposing one's will. Still, one can ask as the world dances: is the tune that's being played still challenging or enriching to the conductor?

Said differently, ego-mastery may be a fairly empty experience without worthy external conditions that both challenge and reward us, without the forms and forces of otherness. So "control" is both a process in which we assert ourselves against the strong resistance of the world (and experience excitement) and a more stable condition in which we survey what has been done (and experience contentment). At some point, pleasure requires receptivity to otherness, a feeling that the very forms that we have taunted and challenged have somehow "completed" us. So the runner, the lover, the dancer, the musician, and so forth are rewarded by . the body and mind they have pushed to its limits.

Pleasure can also be gained through other-directed processes of feeling construction. That is, pleasure is frequently an experience of descending meaning, the pattern that features adjustment to external forms and forces. When we say we take pleasure *in*—or enjoy—musical performances, bicycling, long summer nights, and so forth, we are claiming that we find excitement or comfort in the sensations these objects and events provide. To listen to a musical concert or watch a movie is to have the logics of those forms confront us. When we enjoy something in this particular way, we allow ourselves to be manipulated by those forms and to savor the physical and mental responses those patterns produce within us. The pleasure we receive is founded on our willingness to *subordinate* ourselves to the forms before us.

192 ⓘ SELVES, SOCIETIES, AND EMOTIONS

Real-life events usually feature mixes of these polarities—of excitement/satisfaction and self-direction/other-direction—or provide alternations from one extreme to the other. I've emphasized Csikszentmihalyi's analyses of flow and enjoyment because I think they are important commentaries on events in which both ascending and descending meaning are going full throttle, in which claims and counterclaims come as fast as selves and others can handle. Seen in that context, flow is almost "pure" interrelatedness. Selves and others wrap their arms around each other so intensely and intimately that they cannot be separated. At such times there is only the mutuality of endeavor; consciousness of self and other is forgotten. Still, in my view, engagement is only one setting for positive feelings; marginality, subordination, and privilege also offer their own satisfactions.

FOUR PATHWAYS OF BEHAVIOR

Social relationships are not fixed commitments; instead, they feature activity, the movement of people through time and space. Conspicuous among those movements are people's ongoing attempts to establish and comprehend their standings before others. Four distinctive types of standings have been analyzed above. In this section, I discuss some fundamental patterns of activity that people follow to achieve those patterns of self-location. Those four pathways are work, ritual, play, and communitas.

Figure 5 displays the relationship of the four pathways to one another as well as to the four self-standings that were just described.

The first two forms—work and play—are patterns of activity featuring "ascending meaning." The last two forms—communitas and ritual—are orientations dominated by "descending meaning." Just as the four standings can be understood as balances of claims between selves and others, so the four pathways I'm discussing here indicate the relative ability of people to impose their perspectives on the objects of their orientation. Work represents the pattern of interaction in which the self exhibits the clearest control over its environment; ritual is the path that features the most yielding by the self. Play and communitas are patterns that lie between those extremes.

Pathway 1: Work. Work is interaction the willful self dominates. Typically, work is understood to be a task, exercise, or other form of manipulation. Although interaction with the object world may be challenging or interesting, the *experience* of that activity is neither the principal focus of work nor the central motivation for the worker. Instead, work is instrumental behavior in which people seek to accomplish objectives that lie *outside* the boundaries of the event. For the most part, workers focus on products or ends.

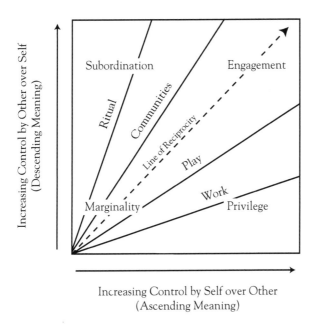

FIGURE 5. **Four Pathways of Expressive Behavior**

Although work is often associated with economic behavior, those ideas are equivalent only if one stretches the definition of "economic" to include all the ways in which people alter the world to promote their own interests. Workers transform the objects of their orientation, such as social and cultural forms, their own bodies, the environment, and their own psychic states. Those changes in otherness, particularly when those changes are thought to have implications beyond the event itself, are the measures of work's success. With ambitions of this sort in mind, we climb stairs, fix a roof, wash and dry dishes, exercise, deliver a sales presentation, prepare a to-do list, and so forth. The vision of an ultimate end-point or goal establishes a logical pattern or progression for the activity, and participants can gauge their progress as a series of somewhat predictable—or at least recognizable—steps forward. In all these ways workers aspire to a standing of dominance or "privilege" with regard to the objects of their orientation. Like Marx's idealized laborers, workers make something of the world and wish both to control that product and benefit from its future uses. None of this is said to deny the fact that real-life examples of work feature all kinds of obligations and compromises that resemble the other four types of relationships described above. However, the principal rationale for work is that people should reshape the world to suit their own interests.

Pathway 2: Play. Like work, play is a showcase for ascending meaning. Although play, as Piaget (1962) emphasized, can be a selfish manipulation of the object world, it tends to be a more interactive and unpredictable activity than work. In other words, play is less an act of control than it is a testing or teasing of the environment. Players try to provoke reactions from objects of their orientation. These reactions then require new responses from the player. When players hop across a room, make puns, wrestle, smear finger paint, tease one another, make goofy facial expressions, and so forth, they effectively challenge other people, their own bodies, and their environments to perform in certain ways. The fascination of play comes from the fact that we cannot predict just how those objects will react or what responses we ourselves will need to come up with to address those reactions.

Critically, the rationale for play differs from that of work. As work focuses on end-products, so play focuses on processes. When play is directed to the attainment of some goal or end—as often occurs in the symbolically organized forms of play called "games"—that ending is important—and meaningful—only within the context of the event itself. Players live inside the moment and their creations—like children's sand castles—have similarly brief lives. When players look outside the event for their motivations, play starts to acquire the qualities of work or, to use Huizinga's (1955) terms, becomes "serious." As patterns of interaction, both work and play are *contestive* in that they oppose and seek to alter the character of otherness. However, players glory in the *unpredictable* whereas workers prefer a more anticipated course.

However appealing or unappealing the above descriptions may be, I would argue that even children know the frames of play and work well enough. They play, as adults do, in ways that respect the magic circle of the event, foster impish creativity within a format of shared rules, and honor the emotional satisfactions of the persons involved. Although everyone plays to see what can be done with the world, they also want the consequences they wreak to surprise or excite them. They survey the changes they have produced—changes that include the willful resistance of the people they have provoked—and then begin again. As displayed in figure 5, players seek positions somewhere between "privilege" and "engagement," between having one's way and having an intensive dialogue with the other.

Pathway 3: Communitas. Like play, communitas is a pattern of interaction that features mutual adjustment between the self and its world. Like play also, communitas is a pathway that pursues "engagement," the balancing of claims and counterclaims. However, as figure 5 indicates, communitas exists on the opposite side of what is described in the figure as the "line-of-reciprocity." That is, in communitas people tend to submit themselves to the forms and forces of otherness. Experience is constructed largely on the basis of those external or "other-directed" formats.

The term "communitas" is surely an unfamiliar and perhaps unwelcome offering to the reader. However, that term is used here because English has few words for participative immersion in social and cultural form. The best-known presentation of communitas is that of anthropologist Victor Turner (1969), who describes how a group of initiates in a sacred ritual are sometimes cut off from the routine support systems of their society, cast into a common predicament, and subjected to the spell of intense feelings of brotherhood or sisterhood. Such feelings of shared commitment—and even transcendence—are also central to Durkheim's descriptions of "collective effervescence" or Collins's "natural rituals." Under the conditions of communitas, people feel themselves to be a part of some collective identity that informs—and frequently transforms—the self. For my part, I use the term in a much broader way, to refer to participative immersion not only in social forms but also in cultural, environmental, bodily, and even psychic forms (see Henricks 2006).

Once again, I would argue that both adults and children know communitas well enough. We know what it means to go to a festival, parade, pageant, fair, picnic, theatrical performance, concert, or sporting event. We know that we will probably be part of a socially united group gathered in a restricted locale and that the setting will, in large measure, determine the pleasures we experience. We also know, like an attendee at one of Simmel's (1971) sociable gatherings, that we must modulate our own interests to sustain the framework of "sociability" that frames the event as a whole. Although we do not get to determine the character of the event to the extent we do in play, this relative lack of control does not bother us. Quite the opposite, the "feel" of the occasion—its sights, sounds, smells, and other sensations—fascinates us. To hear a wonderful musical performance or even to attend a great party is to be heartened by what other people can be and do. To be part of such occasions both satisfies and energizes us.

Like play, communitas is driven not by instrumental purposes but by the desire for satisfying experience. Aside from memories of the event, there is little carry-over into the wider world. In that sense, communitas and play both focus on *consummation*—the sense that experience is completed in the moments of its making. Similar to play as well is the extent to which the event is unpredictable. As developed in Bakhtin's (1981) descriptions of "carnival" as a metaphor for modern life, we wander from one portion of the fairgrounds, dance club, or party to another, not knowing quite what will be offered to us there. To that degree, communitas is not a scripted affair but rather a balancing act between the possibilities inherent to a form (e.g., a roller coaster ride) and our own interest in wringing as much excitement or pleasure from the setting as we can (e.g., by holding our arms in the air during the ride, yelling loudly, etc.). Although we assert ourselves in such ways, we know that external forms and forces largely determine the character of the moment. Against play then, communitas is an acceptance of descending meaning. As play is the contestive experience of otherness, so communitas is its integrative equivalent. At our own choosing we "dive" into the pool, the meal, the crowd, and so forth and find that the experience alters our sensibilities.

Pathway 4: Ritual. I have presented communitas and play as two pathways that move people toward "engagement," although the two pathways lead to that standing from opposite directions. Ritual is the pathway that leads most clearly to "subordination." As noted above, the concept of subordination sits uneasily in the Western mind. How can anyone voluntarily accept a standing of inferiority or dependency within the world or acknowledge gratefully the powers of otherness? However, this is precisely the goal of all ritual forms. In ritual, we surrender ourselves willingly to external direction.

In the social sciences it is customary to think of ritual as a kind of public participation in symbolic order, a socially protected event in which people follow carefully prescribed lines of action. I use the term "ritual" in a much more general way to refer to immersions in both symbolic and physical form. Our lives are filled with little rituals, some socially recognized and others merely personal. Some of these activities follow rules that we can state plainly; most are understood better as "habits," practices that we follow with only the dimmest understandings of their constituent elements and rationales. Most of us, I would guess, go through our morning and evening routines in a personally stylized way. We display characteristic patterns of expression and movement; we enter social arrangements with others that feature sharply demarcated rules and boundaries. All of us seek—and depend on—the orderliness of the world.

Still, ritual is not the same as communitas. The latter form focuses on the *experience* of immersion, the former on its instrumental possibilities. People enter into and rely on rituals to be taken from one condition or situation to the next. We are sleepy in the mornings and need well-worn routines to get us ready for the day. We cannot find our way in life and so require the fortification religious exercise provides. We confront a stranger and depend on established frameworks to help us conduct our business. Thus, we do not enter these patterns for the sheer pleasure of their use but rather to be carried through the activity toward endings we desire. However, in contrast to work, rituals do not aim to change the condition of the world but instead the condition of the participants. Ceremonies of birth, puberty, marriage, and the like are occasions in which the self is transformed through carefully regulated immersion into a publicly acknowledged form. Rituals are not exercises in sociability but rather in "solidarity," understood as the firmer stationing of people in established patterns of life.

To complete the comparison of the four types, rituals are the events most dominated by descending meaning. Like communitas, they are integrative, but they differ from communitas by the degree to which the activity is orderly and predictable. Rituals are well-worn paths leading to clearly anticipated outcomes. They are the vehicles that transport selves through time. Inside those conveyances, the passengers discover experiences not found in the other forms.

EMOTION-SEQUENCES

I've described above some socially recognized "pathways" by which behavior and experience are ordered. When we set out on one of these pathways, we anticipate that we will encounter certain kinds of conditions, and we ready ourselves to respond to those conditions in specialized ways. Children—and adults—know what it means when they are told to "go out and play," to "get to work," to "behave themselves" in a ritualized setting, or even to "relax and enjoy" a special moment. Clearly, much of life is a mixing of these different types. However, I follow Goffman in maintaining that people have a preference for recognizable interaction trajectories. Once we have determined the "kind" of situation we are in, we can move ahead with confidence and bring others along with us. Staying on the appropriate pathway also means that we will not be tramping about in the underbrush of irrelevant activity or otherwise spending energy in unproductive ways. Instead, we can envision beginnings, middles, and ends of our activity and think about the kinds of satisfactions that are to be found at each point of the journey.

In that context, I argue that the four pathways feature somewhat different arrays of emotional possibility. Those patterns of awareness are found at the beginnings of activity (as "feelings of anticipation"), at its middle or interactive stages (as "feelings of the present"), and at its end-points (as "feelings of remembrance"). Taken together, the feelings associated with each pathway constitute what I call an "emotion-sequence"—that is, a relatively predictable pattern of awareness and feeling that reflects one's movement through the event.

The reader will not be surprised to see these matters presented graphically.

In figure 6, various "positive" feelings have been arrayed across a series of time zones described as "anticipation," "the present," and "remembrance." The left side of the figure displays a gradient between two opposite ways of constructing awareness—"other-direction" (corresponding to descending meaning) and "self-direction" (corresponding to ascending meaning). At points along that gradient, the four different behavioral pathways that have been discussed above—and the four different emotion-sequences that are associated with these pathways—are presented. In other words, work, play, communitas, and ritual are described as four relatively distinct—and publicly communicable—formats for personal experience.

Four different feeling-types have been associated with each pathway. Feelings about the future (anticipation) and the past (remembrance) have been discussed in a preceding chapter as being largely "catastemic" (or stability focused) in character and are represented by only one feeling term for each of these forms of awareness. By contrast, feelings of the present are said to be much more dynamic—reflecting the ebb and flow of events—and are represented by two terms. The first of these refers to "feelings of exploration," disorder, or movement (i.e., kinetic feelings) and

	Feelings of Anticipation	Feelings of the Present		Feelings of Remembrance
Ritual	FAITH	ENCHANTMENT	RAPTURE	REVERENCE
Other-Directed Enjoyments (Mystery)				
Communitas	HOPE	DELIGHT	JOY	BLESSEDNESS
Play	CURIOSITY	FUN	EXHILARATION	GRATIFICATION
Self-Directed Enjoyments (Mystery)				
Work	SELF-CONFIDENCE	INTEREST	SATISFACTION	PRIDE
		(Feelings of Exploration/ Disorder)	(Feelings of Restoration/ Order)	

FIGURE 6. Four Sequences of Positive Emotions

the second to "feelings of restoration," order, or stability (i.e., catastemic feelings). Most generally, the purpose of the model is to show how people who move along the four identifiable pathways of events are able to gauge their feelings at four emotional way stations. Those stations are (1) anticipatory feelings, (2) feelings of change and movement, (3) feelings of reaching more stable standings, and (4) feelings of completion and remembrance.

Although few events go forward exactly as planned, two of the pathways—work and ritual—feature relatively straight-ahead movements. That predictability stems from the fact that only one set of standards—either those the self or "the other" provides—dominates the activity. The other two pathways—play and communitas—feature frequently confusing or back-and-forth movements in the present, so that self-standings may be gained and then lost a moment later. With all deference to the complexities of real-life events, I argue that the four pathways produce distinctive (and nameable) feelings that participants can anticipate, experience, and remember—and then communicate to others.

Essentially, the table of emotion-sequences is presented as an "ideal type" that provides an answer to the following question: what feelings would occur if the four pathways were enjoyable at every stage of their development? To be sure, events only sometimes proceed as we wish. Failed experiences—sometimes caused by the high standards we bring to our lives—are commonplace: teenagers find that their prom date does not live up to expectations; worshippers cannot feel the guidance of the sacred at the times they need it most; a work project is ruined; a game was boring rather than fun.

Arguably, the prospect of failure acts as a stimulus to the participant and sweetens any success that may occur. Said more precisely—and to rely on Erikson's (1963, 247–74) famous conception—people's emotional lives move along gradients between successful and failed resolutions of life issues. Feelings of trust—to take one of Erikson's examples—are comprehensible—and cherished—because we "know" mistrust, autonomy stands against shame, initiative against guilt, and so forth. So it is for the terms listed in figure 6. "Interest" pleases us because we can contrast that condition with "disinterest," "blessedness" seems special because it is shadowed by "misfortune," and so forth. When people move down one of the four pathways, they are cognizant of both the emotional rewards and the emotional punishments that can be expected along the way.

I make no claims that the sixteen feeling terms I've chosen are the very "best" choices for the patterns of awareness they represent. Words have many shades of meaning, and, in any case, the English language was not developed with the ambitions of chart makers in mind. For example, the words "confidence" and "pride" have been used here primarily to describe feelings that recognize the powers and skills of the self. There are, I must acknowledge, other—more external—sources of confidence and pride. People can also be "proud" of what their families have accomplished or "confident" because they have powerful relatives who can intercede on their behalf. Nevertheless, I claim that people understand the satisfactions inherent to the four behavioral trajectories in somewhat different ways. With that introduction, I offer a few comments about each of the four emotion-sequences.

The work sequence. The lowest—and most self-directed—sequence of the emotions is preoccupied with the ambitions and satisfactions of "mastery." As noted previously, work tends to feature patterns in which the subject has the situation in hand or at least believes that it will follow a predictable course. Workers normally anticipate what events will transpire and thus approach those events with the expectancy that is termed here "confidence." Of course, workers can also "lack confidence," but even in that case there is a presumption that the person should be able to control her environment and will be judged—by others and by the self—on her ability to do so. In other words, workers operate within a narrative of self-control. They are expected to manipulate the objects of the world to suit their interests and to control themselves in so doing.

Because of the ego's dominance, the resulting experience does not tend to feature high levels of disorder and novelty. However, there are enough degrees of difficulty or resistance to maintain a level of excitement that is termed here "interest"—against "disinterest." Successful completion of the event—which often centers on some technically oriented task—results in feelings of creative success or orderly restoration that are labeled in the figure as "satisfaction." Surveying what has been done, the person may take "pride" in what has been accomplished. Such pride is ultimately an act of self-congratulation, a proclamation of competence.

The play sequence. The second type of emotion-sequence, play, begins with a much less certain, more open-minded orientation that is termed here "curiosity." Lieberman (1977) has described this orientation as "playfulness," a creative, inquisitive disposition that allows some children (more than others) to be able to turn almost any situation into something that stimulates and amuses them. Somewhat against Piaget's (1962) view of play as a repetitive manipulation of objects that builds confidence in personal skills and understandings, most play scholars emphasize that players enter situations just because they are unsure of their abilities to control the elements found therein. They know that they will be asked to control those elements—by testing, teasing, prodding, deforming, and so forth—but they are curious about what will happen when they assert themselves in such ways. Because play tends to be a voluntary—or at least, relatively voluntary—activity, people not possessing this disposition are unlikely to seek or enjoy play.

Once play has begun, the positive feelings associated with that quality of engagement are described here as amusement or "fun." This dialectical pattern, filled with moments of assertion and then adjustment, reaches a culmination in "exhilaration," the sense of being pleasurably spent or even laughed out. Looking back, the participant is "gratified," not only because she is pleased with her own efforts—though this is central to the experience—but also because she is pleased by the challenges the other provided. Critically—and in contradistinction to the patterns to be discussed below—players "make their own fun." That is, they impose their own desires on the world and, in effect, ask it to do their bidding. Players are gratified when otherness "gives them a good game" or otherwise meets their desires for appropriate challenge.

The communitas sequence. The third pathway—communitas—moves deeper into processes of other-direction or "object dependency." In communitas the relevant feeling of anticipation is "hope," that form of wanting that profound uncertainty taints. What the subject hopes for is a turn of events or a change in fortune. She has some understandings of the possible riches or blessings of the world—hence her cautious optimism—but she remains unsure whether those blessings will be bestowed and what she will feel like if they do occur.

When blessings do happen, the appropriate sense of excitement is termed "delight." Exploration is felt as enjoyable confusion, and novelty prevails. But there is also a sense that order is to be found within—and even behind—the disorder. When that recognition of orderliness does come—as in the revelation of a mystery, witnessing a beautiful sunset, or some other perception of worldly coherence, the experience is one of "joy." Joy, in my view, is a feeling that transcends playful excitement or exhilaration. To know joy is to sense that there are spheres of otherness that can effectively engage and then expand the self. In remembrance, one feels fortunate or "blessed" to have been there—and to have participated—in the making of this revelation.

The ritual sequence. The final sequence, ritual, is the most other-directed of the four types. At the other extreme work and play are largely acts of *invention*. People at work and play use their own skills to transform the objects of the world and take satisfaction in what they have created. Those satisfactions can be focused on the implications of that activity for the future (as in the case of work) or on the experience of that activity (as in play). Differently, communitas and ritual are acts of *discovery*. Like work and play, communitas and ritual are forms of encounter with the world; however, in these latter forms what those encounters change is the self. In communitas, people are active agents in that discovery process. They climb the tree of life and marvel at what they can pick from its branches. In ritual, people give themselves more completely to otherness and gratefully receive its lessons.

In the ritual sequence, then, the appropriate mode of anticipation is "faith." To have faith is to banish the uncertainties of hope and curiosity and to replace them with a renewed form of confidence. This confidence is based on a firm belief, not in one's own creative powers, as in the case of work, but instead in the powers of otherness. In rituals one is pulled ahead by well-established, externally based patterns on which the person can rely entirely. In the case of religious ritual, the faithful person believes that she can enter the halls of mystery, receive what is found there, and then can re-enter the wider world as a transformed and more powerful being.

The excitement that accompanies that feeling of transformation is termed here "enchantment." Feelings of novelty, change, and disorder may be prevalent, but these are less a sudden awareness of the curious qualities of the world, as in play or communitas, than a new awareness of self. In ritual one feels herself changed into something else. The most exaggerated form of ritual completion is termed here "ecstasy" or even "rapture." In all the other sequences, one is able to feel their spirits rising. In this latter case there is a sense of being raised or even soaring upward. To know ecstasy is to feel oneself transported into otherness. Looking backward at those moments, there is a feeling of awe or "reverence," a profound respect and gratitude for having been changed in this way. Critically, people do not participate in rituals because they enjoy the experience; that sort of indulgent immersion has been described above as communitas. Rather, they give themselves to these formations because they wish to move on to new stages of their lives.

Once again, the above portraits of work, play, ritual, and communitas have focused only on the happy stations along these pathways. Those pleasant feelings are simply the awareness that events are moving ahead in an idealized or optimal way. All four forms also present possibilities for failure and frustration. Furthermore, although I'm emphasizing the ways in which people transform the world or are transformed by it, I would like to point out that the four pathways can also be forms of desecration. For example, work and play are often acts of demolition, a tearing down of things so that those things can (at least some of the time) be reconstructed. Rituals, as both Durkheim and Goffman emphasized, can be forms of denial or "mortification," formats that destroy current identities and social relationships. These "negative" rites, to recall Durkheim's (1965) term, are usually a prelude to the more "positive" rites that follow. Even communitas, that seemingly happy land of festivity, bonding, and pleasant surprise, can also be understood as a setting apart. Indeed, in Turner's (1969) formulation, people bond so intensely with one another precisely because they find themselves cut off from their ordinary supports and statuses. The joy that comes from those newfound sources of support, like that of "forbidden" lovers who have pushed ahead against every objection of family and friends, arises in a context of loss and sorrow. All this is only to say that the specter of negative feelings makes the positive feelings displayed above meaningful. What makes them positive is the extent to which people have been able to align their actual experiences with their visions of what experience should be.

CONCLUSIONS

This chapter—and this book—has developed the thesis that people seek and then occupy special standings in circumstances and experience distinctive feelings that arise from those locations. Those standings—what I've termed privilege, engagement, subordination, and marginality—enhance the prospect of certain emotions and discourage others. Work, play, communitas, and ritual are the distinctive behavioral formats that people follow when they encounter and interact with otherness. Workers aspire to positions of privilege with regard to the objects of their work; ritualists embrace subordination. People at play or in communitas become dialectically engaged.

These final pages make the point that any one of these formats for self-location or behavior is a specialized way of knowing the world. Ever ingenious, people constantly take account of what kind of situation they are in, what sorts of people they are confronting, and what versions of themselves they wish to present in those settings. They know what they hope to gain from those encounters and what positions they hope to inhabit. That is Goffman's abiding theme, and it is the matter that I have developed in this writing. People who build, teach, write, perform, conduct business, worship, give and receive medical care, love one another, and so forth know that there are many ways of engaging otherness. To pursue those endeavors effectively, all of us seek "frames" that allow us to organize our ambitions, guide our movements within the event, and evaluate what we have done. We need this cultural or public support system to negotiate our relationships with others, but we also need it to make comprehensible to ourselves our own activity.

Each of these formats is a specialized—and therefore partial—way of knowing the world. Societies that celebrate ascending meaning—represented by the formats of work and play—encourage their residents to objectify and control the world. To celebrate the powers and integrity of the individuated self, as many Western societies do, is to extol only acts of manipulation. "Creativity" and "invention" are surely wonderful endeavors, and their counterpart, an elaborately constructed, defended, and possessive self of the sort that William James depicted, is a source of many satisfactions. However, those satisfactions are only of a certain type, and the ultimate consequence of all that inventiveness is only to convince the perpetrators of their own powers to control and recast otherness. The purpose of life—or so it seems—is to adore and decorate the self.

Ideally, work gives people feelings of interest, satisfaction, and pride and builds the self-confidence that leads to future emotions of that sort. In the process people try to banish judgments of their own incompetence, inferiority, guilt, and shame. By contrast, play focuses directly on the experiences of self-induced success. Players want to be excited, exhilarated, and have fun. They want to look back and be pleased about their own role in the merrymaking. What they wish to escape is the possibility that they—rather than the world—can be depicted as being boring, dull, uncool, or otherwise inept in the experience-management process. They want to engage the world, but they want to do this on their own terms.

Against the modern emphasis on ascending meaning, I have tried in this book to show the pertinence of communitas and ritual as alternative pathways for personal experience and social well-being. Such formations teach lessons about the significance of responsibility, respect, and routine. They make plain the point that receptivity to otherness is a practice that expands the self. They celebrate feelings of inclusion, trust, and social support. They counter the perception that people must always be in control of their personal destiny—anticipating every contingency and "risk." They signal the importance of community and interdependence.

Although this book has pointed to the value of descending meaning, I must emphasize again that ritual and communitas possess their own limitations. Just as an independent, scheming self—the focal point of play and work—effectively demystifies the world, so a thoroughly dependent self does service neither to that wider world nor to the person so oriented. Recalling Durkheim's arguments, descending meaning of the forced and fraudulent types is no model for human relationships; instead, communities must be understood as systems of social support for the thoughtful, creative persons who live within them. The older and less reflective styles of being, represented by Weber's affectual and traditional types of action—are inadequate to the challenges of living in an increasingly complicated world. Responsibility does not mean unthinking obedience; rather, it means *being able to respond* in considered ways to external conditions of many types. The modern forms of collective life, however gigantic they become, require critical participation as well as reasoned support.

One can argue, as Aristotle did, that the satisfying and productive life is to be found in a "middle way" between the extremes that have been described above. Instead, I support the visions of Simmel and Goffman that there are distinctive frameworks for human participation; each has its own logic and is valuable in its way. Both writers were well aware of the limitations of their own typologies and metaphors. Just as life cannot be reduced to the tinkering of an artisan's workshop or to the competitive ebullience of a football game, so it is not a festival, party, or religious ritual, where one receives gratefully the bounties of otherness. The lessons learned in all of those settings are important, but each is incomplete.

By making such comments, I do not reject the special insights of the social scientists whose work has been represented in this book; rather, my goal has been to reconsider and reorganize those views and, by that process to remind readers of their continuing importance. When people act in the world, they find themselves in the presence of formations of many types. When we participate in those forms, we seek coherent locations (what I've called "standings") and coherent routes (or "pathways"). Those settings are the foundations of experience. But those participations-in-form raise necessary questions about which involvements are genuine and which are false, which are willing and which are forced, which address the needs of those participants and which do not. Wisdom in the social sciences—as in individual and public life more generally—depends on the difficult and sustained evaluation of these issues.

ACKNOWLEDGMENTS

The influence of human relationships and social circumstances on activity and experience has been the subject of this writing. It is entirely consistent that such matters should account also for the existence of this book. In that context, I wish to recognize my academic institution, Elon University, for its support of my teaching and scholarship. Special thanks are extended to the university's librarians and to its academic staff. Among faculty colleagues, my principal debt is to Larry Basirico for the many conversations we have had about these matters through the years and for his suggestions of new scholarly directions. I also thank Anne Bolin, Lisa Marie Peloquin, and Tom Mould for discussions of these and related themes and for their general encouragement of what appears here.

I also recognize David Heise, Thomas Scheff, Dawn Robinson, Charles Lemert, Randall Collins, and Cecilia Ridgeway for various professional courtesies they have extended me. To say that they have extended me courtesies does not mean that any of them authorizes what has been presented here or even that they vouchsafe my interpretations of their own work; it only means that they are confident enough of their own views to be generous to those with differing approaches. The importance of prominent scholars in this regard is not to be underestimated.

At Paradigm Publishers I am indebted especially to Dean Birkenkamp for his vision of the possibilities of this project and for his subtle guidance. I also thank Jason Barry and the other members of the press for their work in bringing this to its final form. Special thanks go to Kay Mariea, the project editor for this book; and Josephine Moore, the book's copy editor, who enhanced the accuracy and readability of the text; and Sara Eddleman, who prepared the index. Ultimately, gratitude goes to my spouse, Judy Henricks, for making any of this possible; to our children, David and Lizzie, for sharing their knowledge of the emerging electronic world; and to my mother, Sylvia Henricks, for her model of the writer's commitment.

REFERENCES

Abbott, A. 2001. *Chaos of Disciplines.* Chicago: University of Chicago Press.

Amichai-Hamburger, Y., ed. 2005. *The Social Net: Understanding Human Behavior.* New York: Oxford University Press.

Aristotle. 1947. *Introduction to Aristotle.* Edited by R. McKeon. New York: Modern Library.

Bakhtin, M. 1981. *The Dialogic Imagination.* Edited by M. Holquist and V. Liapunov. Translated by V. Liapunov and K. Brostrom. Austin: University of Texas Press.

Baptiza, L. 2003. "Framing and Cognition." In *Goffman's Legacy*, edited by J. Trevino, 197–215. Lanham, MD: Rowman and Littlefield.

Barbalet, J. 1998. *Emotion, Social Theory, and Social Structure.* Cambridge: Cambridge University Press.

Bataille, G. 1986. *Eroticism: Death and Sensuality.* Translated by M. Dalwood. London: Boyars.

Bateson, G. 1972. *Steps to an Ecology of Mind.* New York: Ballantine Books.

Baudrillard, J. 1983. *Simulations.* Translated by P. Beitchman, P. Foss, and P. Patton. New York: Semiotext.

Baumeister, R. 1999. "The Nature and Structure of the Self: An Overview." In *The Self in Social Psychology*, edited by R. Baumeister, 1–24. Ann Arbor, MI: Edwards Borther.

Bell, D. 1976. *The Coming of Post-Industrial Society: A Venture in Social Forecasting.* New York: Basic Books.

———. 1989. "The Third Technological Revolution and its Possible Consequences." *Dissent* 36: 164–76.

Bellah, R. et al. 1985. *Habits of the Heart: Individualism and Commitment in American Life.* Berkeley: University of California Press.

Benjamin, W. 1969. "The Work of Art in the Age of Mechanical Reproduction." In *Illuminations*. Introduced and edited by H. Arendt. Translated by H. Zohn, 217–52. New York: Schocken.

Bertens, H. 1995. *The Idea of the Postmodern: A History.* New York: Routledge.

Blumer, H. 1969. *Symbolic Interactionism: Perspective and Method.* Englewood Cliffs, NJ: Prentice-Hall.

Blumstein, P. 1975. "Identity Bargaining and Self-Conception." *Social Forces* 53, no. 3 (March): 476–85.

Bonica, J. 1979. "The Need of a Taxonomy." *Pain* 6, no. 3 (June): 247–52.

Boorstin, D. 1987. *The Image: A Guide to Pseudo-Events in America.* New York: Atheneum.

Boyer, E. 1990. *Scholarship Reconsidered: Priorities of the Professoriate.* San Francisco: Jossey-Bass.

Branaman, A., ed. 2007. *Self and Society.* Malden, MA: Blackwell.

Briggs, A., and P. Burke. 2005. *A Social History of the Media: From Gutenberg to the Internet.* Malden, MA: Polity.

Brown, N. 1966. *Love's Body.* New York: Vintage.

Buber, M. 1996. *I and Thou.* Introduced and translated by W. Kaufmann. New York: Simon and Schuster.

Burke, P. 1980. "The Self: Measurement Implications from a Symbolic Interactionist Perspective." *Social Psychology Quarterly* 43: 18–29.

———. 1991. "Identity Processes and Social Stress." *American Sociological Review* 56: 836–49.

Cahill, S. 2000. "Toward a Sociology of the Person." In *Erving Goffman*, 4 vols., edited by G. Fine and G. Smith, vol. 3, 17–42. Thousand Oaks, CA: Sage.

Campbell, A. 1981. *The Sense of Well-Being in America: Recent Patterns and Trends.* New York: McGraw-Hill.

Cantor, N. 1997. *The American Century: Varieties of Culture in Modern Times.* New York: Harper and Row.

Carneiro, R. 2003. *Evolutionism in Cultural Anthropology: A Critical History.* Boulder, CO: Westview Press.

Castells, M. 2000. *The Rise of the Network Society*, 2d ed. Malden, MA: Blackwell.

Cheung, C. 2006. "Identity Construction and Self-Presentation on Personal Homepages." In *The Production of Reality*, edited by J. O'Brien. 310–20. Thousand Oaks, CA: Pine Forge.

Cixous, H. 1994. *The Helene Cixous Reader.* Edited by S. Sellers. London: Routledge.

Clark, C. 1997. *Misery and Company: Sympathy in Everyday Life.* Chicago: University of Chicago Press.

Cohen, D. 2008. *Three Lectures on Post-Industrial Society.* Cambridge, MA: MIT Press.

Collins, R. 1981. "On the Microfoundations of Macrosociology." *American Journal of Sociology* 86, no. 5 (March): 984–1014.

———. 2004. *Interaction Ritual Chains.* Princeton, NJ: Princeton University Press.

Consalvo, M. 2007. *Cheating: Gaining Advantage in Videogames.* Cambridge, MA: MIT Press.

Cooley, C. 1962. *Social Organization: A Study of the Larger Mind.* New York: Schocken Books.

———. 1964. *Human Nature and the Social Order.* New York: Schocken Books.

Csikszentmihalyi, M. 1975. *Beyond Boredom and Anxiety: The Experience of Play in Work and Games.* San Francisco: Jossey-Bass.

———. 1991. *Flow: The Psychology of Optimal Experience.* New York: Harper and Row.

Damasio, A. 1994. *Descartes' Error: Emotion, Reason, and the Human Brain.* New York: Grosset-Putnam.

———. 1999. *The Feeling of What Happens: Body and Emotion in the Making of Consciousness.* New York: Harcourt.

Dante. 2003. *The Divine Comedy.* Translated by J. Ciardi. New York: New American Library.

Darwin, C. 1872. *The Expression of the Emotions in Man and Animals.* London: Oxford University Press.

Debord, G. 1977. *The Society of the Spectacle.* Detroit, MI: Black and Red Books.

Deleuze, G., and F. Guattari. 1984. *Anti-Oedipus: Capitalism and Schizophrenia.* Minneapolis: University of Minnesota Press.

Denzin, N. 1977. *Childhood Socialization.* San Francisco: Jossey-Bass.

———. 1984. *On Understanding Emotion.* San Francisco: Jossey-Bass.

Derrida, J. 1981. *Positions.* Translated by A. Bass. Chicago: University of Chicago Press.

Ditton, J., ed. 1980. *The View from Goffman.* New York: St. Martin's.

Domhoff, G. 1998. *Who Rules America: Power and Politics in the Year 2000.* Totowa, NJ: Mayfield Publishing.

Donath, J. 1999. "Identity and Deception in the Virtual Community." In *Communities in Cyberspace,* edited by M. Smith and P. Kollock. 27–58. New York: Routledge.

Dumazedier, J. 1967. *Toward a Society of Leisure.* Glencoe, IL: Free Press.

Duncan, H. D. 1959. "Simmel's Image of Society." In *Georg Simmel, 1858–1918: A Collection of Essays, with Translations and a Biography,* edited by Kurt Wolff, 100–18. Columbus: Ohio State University Press.

Durham, M., and D. Kellner, eds. 2001. *Media and Cultural Studies: Key Works.* New York: Blackwell.

Durkheim, E. 1951. *Suicide: A Study in Sociology.* Translated by J. Spaulding and G. Simpson. New York: Free Press.

———. 1965. *The Elementary Forms of the Religious Life.* Translated by J. Swain. New York: Free Press.

———. 1972: *Emile Durkheim: Selected Writings.* Edited by A. Giddens. New York: Cambridge University Press.

Eco, U. 1984. Postscript to *The Name of the Rose.* New York: Harcourt.

Eisenstadt, S. N., ed. 1970. *Readings in Social Evolution and Development.* Oxford: Pergamon Press.

Ekman, P., ed. 1973. *Darwin and Facial Expression: A Century of Research in Review.* New York: Academic Press.

———. 1994. "All Emotions Are Basic." In *The Nature of Emotion: Fundamental Questions,* edited by P. Ekman and R. Davidson, 15–19. New York: Oxford University Press.

Ekman, P., and R. Davidson, eds. 1994. *The Nature of Emotion: Fundamental Questions.* New York: Oxford University Press.

Eliade, M. 1957. *The Sacred and the Profane: The Nature of Religion.* Translated by W. Trask. New York: Harcourt.

Elias, N. 2000. *The Civilizing Process: Sociogenetic and Psychogenetic Investigations,* rev. ed. Edited by E. Dunning, J. Goudsblom, and S. Mennell. Translated by E. Jephcott. Maldon, MA: Blackwell.

Elias, N., and E. Dunning. 1986. *The Quest for Excitement: Sport and Leisure in the Civilizing Process.* Oxford: Basil Blackwell.

Ellis, C. 1995. *Final Negotiations: A Story of Love, Loss, and Chronic Illness.* Philadelphia, PA: Temple University Press.

Ellsworth, P. 1994. "Some Reasons to Expect Universal Antecedents of Emotions." In *The Nature of Emotion: Fundamental Questions,* edited by P. Ekman and R. Davidson, 150–54. New York: Oxford University Press.

Erikson, E. 1963. *Childhood and Society,* 2d ed. New York: W. W. Norton.

———. 1968. *Identity, Youth and Crisis.* New York: W. W. Norton.

Ewen, S. 1999. *All Consuming Images: The Politics of Style in Contemporary Culture,* rev. ed. New York: Basic Books.

Featherstone, M. 1991. *Consumer Culture and Postmodernism.* Newbury Park, CA: Sage.

———. 1994. "The Heroic Life and Everyday Life." In *Cultural Theory and Cultural Change,* edited by M. Featherstone, 159–82. Newbury Park, CA: Sage.

Featherstone, M., M. Hepworth, and B. Turner, eds. 1991. *The Body: Social Process and Cultural Theory.* Thousand Oaks, CA: Sage.

Fine, G. A. 1983. *Shared Fantasies: Role-Playing Games as Social Worlds.* Chicago: University of Chicago Press.

Fine, G. A., and G. Smith, eds. 2000. *Erving Goffman,* 4 vols. London: Sage.

Fiske, J. 1991. "Postmodernism and Television." In *Mass Media and Society,* edited by J. Curran and M. Gurevitch, 55–67. New York: Edward Arnold.

Forgas, J., ed. 2000. *Feeling and Thinking: The Role of Affect in Social Cognition.* Cambridge: Cambridge University Press.

Foucault, M. 1977. *Discipline and Punish: The Birth of the Prison.* New York: Pantheon Books.

Fredrickson, B. 2003. "The Value of Positive Emotions." *American Scientist* 91: 330–35.

Fredrickson, B., and C. Branigan. 2001. "Positive Emotions." In *Emotions: Current Issues and Future Directions,* edited by T. Mayne and G. Bonanno, 123–51. New York: Guilford.

Freie, J. 1998. *Counterfeit Community: The Exploitation of Our Longings for Connectedness.* New York: Rowman and Littlefield.

Freud, S. 1952. *A General Introduction to Psychoanalysis.* Translated by J. Riviere. New York: Washington Square.

———. 1961. *Civilization and its Discontents.* Edited and translated by J. Strachey. New York: Norton.

———. 1967. *Beyond the Pleasure Principle.* New York: Bantam.

Friedl, J. 1981. *The Human Portrait: Introduction to Cultural Anthropology.* Englewood Cliffs, NJ: Prentice-Hall.

Frijda, N. 1986. *The Emotions.* Cambridge: Cambridge University Press.

———. 1994. "Varieties of Affect: Emotions and Episodes, Moods and Sentiments." In *The Nature of Emotion: Fundamental Questions,* edited by P. Ekman and R. Davidson, 59–67. New York: Oxford University Press.

———. 2000. "The Psychologist's Point of View." In *Handbook of Emotions,* 2nd ed., edited by M. Lewis and J. Haviland-Jones, 59–74. New York: Guilford Press.

Geertz, C. 1983. *Local Knowledge: Further Essays in Interpretive Anthropology.* New York: Basic Books.

Gergen, K. 1991. *The Saturated Self: Dilemmas of Identity in Contemporary Life.* New York: Basic Books.

Giddens, A. 1990. *The Consequences of Modernity.* Stanford, CA: Stanford University Press.

———. 1991. *Modernity and Self-Identity: Self and Society in the Late Modern Age.* Stanford, CA: Stanford University Press.

Gilligan, C. 1982. *In a Different Voice: Psychological Theory and Women's Development.* Cambridge, MA: Harvard University Press.

Glick, R., and S. Bone, eds. 1990. *Pleasure Beyond the Pleasure Principle.* New Haven, CT: Yale University Press.

Goffman, E. 1959. *The Presentation of Self in Everyday Life.* Garden City, NY: Doubleday.

———. 1961a. *Asylums.* Garden City, NY: Doubleday.

———. 1961b. *Encounters: Two Studies in the Sociology of Interaction.* Indianapolis, IN: Bobbs-Merrill.

———. 1963. *Stigma: Notes on the Management of Spoiled Identity.* Englewood Cliffs, NJ: Prentice-Hall.

———. 1967. *Interaction Ritual: Essays on Face-to-Face Behavior.* Garden City, NY: Doubleday Anchor.

———. 1974. *Frame Analysis: An Essay on the Organization of Experience.* Cambridge, MA: Harvard University Press.

———. 1981. *Forms of Talk.* Philadelphia: University of Pennsylvania Press.

———. 1983. "The Interaction Order." *American Sociological Review* 48, no. 1: 1–17.

Goldsmith, H. 1994. "Parsing the Emotional Domain from a Developmental Perspective." In *The Nature of Emotion: Fundamental Questions,* edited by P. Ekman and R. Davidson, 68–73. New York: Oxford University Press.

Gouldner, A. 1970. *The Coming Crisis of Western Sociology.* New York: Basic Books.

Gramsci, A. 1971. *Selections from the Prison Notebooks of Antonio Gramsci.* Edited by Q. Hoare and G. Nowell Smith. New York: International Publishers.

Grice, H. P. 1957. "Meaning." *The Philosophical Review* 66, no. 3: 377–88.

Hall, S. et al., eds. 1997. *Modernity: An Introduction to Modern Societies.* Malden, MA: Blackwell.

Harré, R., and G. Parrott, eds. 1996. *The Emotions: Social, Cultural, and Biological Dimensions.* Thousand Oaks, CA: Sage.

Harvey, D. 1990. *The Condition of Postmodernity: An Inquiry into the Origins of Cultural Change.* Malden, MA: Blackwell.

Havelock, E. 1988. *The Muse Learns to Write: Reflections on Orality and Literacy from Antiquity to the Present.* New Haven, CT: Yale University Press.

Heelas, P. 1986. "Emotion Talk Across Cultures." In *The Social Construction of Emotions,* edited by R. Harré, 234–66. Oxford: Basil Blackwell.

Heidegger, M. 1962. *Being and Time.* Translated by J. Macquarrie and E. Robinson. New York: Harper and Row.

Heise, D. 1979. *Understanding Events: Affect and the Construction of Social Action.* Cambridge: Cambridge University Press.

———. 1989. "Effects of Emotion Displays on Social Identification." *Social Psychology Quarterly* 52, no. 1 (March): 10–21.

———. 2007. *Expressive Order: Confirming Sentiments in Social Actions.* New York: Springer.

Henricks, T. 1991. *Disputed Pleasures: Sport and Society in Preindustrial England.* New York: Greenwood Press.

———. 2006. *Play Reconsidered: Sociological Perspectives on Human Expression.* Urbana: University of Illinois Press.

———. 2010. "Play and Cultural Transformation—Or, What Would Huizinga Think of Video Games?" In *Utopic Dreams and Apocalyptic Fantasies: Critical Approaches to Researching Video Game Play,* edited by T. Wright, D. Embrick, and A. Lukacs, 15–42. Lanham, MD: Lexington Books.

Hewitt, J. 2000. *Self and Society: A Symbolic Interactionist Social Psychology,* 8th ed. Boston: Allyn and Bacon.

Hochschild, A. 1979. "Emotion Work, Feeling Rules, and Social Structure." *American Journal of Sociology* 85, no. 3 (November): 551–75.

———. 1983. *The Managed Heart: Commercialization of Human Feeling.* Berkeley: University of California Press.

———. 2003. *The Commercialization of the Intimate Life: Notes from Home and Work.* Berkeley: University of California Press.

Hoffmeyer, J. 1996. *Signs of Meaning in the Universe.* Bloomington: Indiana University Press.

Homans, G. 1958. "Social Behavior as Exchange." *American Journal of Sociology* 63, no. 6 (May): 597–606.

Horkheimer, M., and T. Adorno. 1972. *The Dialectic of Enlightenment.* Translated by E. Jephcott. New York: Herder and Herder.

Huizinga, J. 1955. *Homo Ludens: A Study of the Play-Element in Culture.* Boston: Beacon.

Irigaray, L. 1985. *The Sex Which Is Not One.* Translated by C. Porter and C. Burke. Ithaca, NY: Cornell University Press.

James, W. 1884. "What Is an Emotion?" *Mind* 19: 188–205.

———. 1952. *The Principles of Psychology.* Chicago: Encyclopedia Britannica.

Jameson, F. 1984. "Postmodernism: Or the Cultural Logic of Late Capitalism." *New Left Review* 146: 53–92.

Jay, M. 1973. *The Dialectical Imagination: A History of the Frankfurt School and the Institute for Social Research, 1923–1950.* Boston: Little, Brown.

Jones, S., ed. 1995. *Cybersociety: Computer-Mediated Communication and Community.* Thousand Oaks, CA: Sage.

Kagan, J. 2007. *What Is Emotion? History, Measures, and Meanings.* New Haven, CT: Yale University Press.

Kahler, E. 1956. *Man the Measure: A New Approach to History.* New York: George Braziller.

Kemper, T. 1978. *A Social Interactional Theory of the Emotions.* New York: Wiley.

———. 1987. "How Many Emotions Are There? Wedding the Social and the Autonomic Components." *American Journal of Sociology* 93, no. 2 (September): 263–89.

———. 1990. "Social Relations and Emotions: A Structural Approach." In *Research Agendas in the Sociology of the Emotions,* edited by T. Kemper, 207–37. Albany: State University of New York Press.

Kemper, T., and R. Collins. 1990. "Dimensions of Microinteraction." *American Journal of Sociology* 96, no. 1 (July): 32–68.

Kunstler, J. 1993. *The Geography of Nowhere: The Rise and Decline of America's Manmade Landscape.* New York: Simon and Schuster.

Kusserow, A. 2004. *American Individualism: Childrearing and Social Class in Three Neighborhoods.* New York: Palgrave Macmillan.

Laird, J. 2007. *Feelings: The Perception of Self.* New York: Oxford University Press.

Lamont, M. 1992. *Money, Morals, and Manners.* Chicago: University of Chicago Press.

Landes, J., ed. 1998. *Feminism, the Public and the Private.* New York: Oxford University Press.

Lawler, E., and J. Yoon. 1996. "Commitment in Exchange Relations: Test of a Theory of Relational Cohesion." *American Sociological Review* 61, no. 1: 89–108.

Lawler, E., S. Thye, and J. Yoon. 2009. *Social Commitments in a Depersonalized World.* Thousand Oaks, CA: Sage.

Lazarus, R. 1994. "Universal Antecedents of the Emotions." In *The Nature of Emotion: Fundamental Questions,* edited by P. Ekman and R. Davidson, 163–71. New York: Oxford University Press.

LeDoux, J. 1996. *The Emotional Brain: The Mysterious Underpinnings of Emotional Life.* New York: Simon and Schuster.

Lemert, C. 1997. "Goffman." In *The Goffman Reader,* edited by C. Lemert and A. Branaman, ix–xlviii. Oxford: Blackwell.

Lenski, G. 2005. *Ecological-Evolutionary Theory: Principles and Applications.* Boulder, CO: Paradigm Publishers.

Levenson, R. 1994. "Human Emotions: A Functional View." In *The Nature of Emotion: Fundamental Questions,* edited by P. Ekman and R. Davidson, 123–26. New York: Oxford University Press.

Lewis, H. 1971. *Shame and Guilt in Neurosis.* New York: International Universities Press.

Lewis, M., J. Haviland-Jones, and L. Barrett, eds. 2008. *Handbook of Emotions*, 3d ed. New York : Guilford.

Lieberman, J. 1977. *Playfulness: Its Relation to Imagination and Creativity.* New York: Academic Press.

Linton, R. 1964. *The Study of Man.* New York: Appleton-Century.

Livingstone, S. 1991. "Audience Reception: The Role of the Viewer in Retelling Romantic Drama." In *Mass Media and Society*, edited by J. Curran and M. Gurevitch, 285–306. New York: Edward Arnold.

Lutz, C. 1988. *Unnatural Emotions: Everyday Sentiments on a Micronesian Atoll and Their Challenge to Western Theory.* Chicago: University of Chicago Press.

Lutz, C., and G. M. White. 1986. "The Anthropology of Emotions." *Annual Review of Anthropology* 15: 405–36.

Lyotard, J. 1986. *The Postmodern Condition: A Report on Knowledge.* Translated by G. Bennington, B. Massumi, and F. Jameson. Manchester: Manchester University Press.

MacKendrick, K. 1999. *Counterpleasures.* Albany: State University of New York Press.

MacKinnon, N. 1994. *Symbolic Interaction as Affect Control.* Albany: State University of New York Press.

Mannheim, K. 1967. *Ideology and Utopia.* Translated by L. Worth and E. Shils. New York: Harvest.

Manning, P. 1992. *Erving Goffman and Modern Sociology.* Stanford, CA: Stanford University Press.

Marx, K. 1964. *Selected Writings in Sociology and Social Philosophy.* Edited and translated by T. Bottomore. New York: McGraw-Hill.

———. 1999. "Economic and Philosophical Manuscripts." Translated by T. Bottomore. In *Marx's Concept of Man*, edited by E. Fromm, 87–196. New York: Continuum.

Mayne, T., and G. Bonanno, eds. 2001. *Emotions: Current and Future Directions.* New York: Guilford Press.

McCall, G., and J. L. Simmons. 1966. *Identities and Interactions.* New York: Free Press.

McGuigan, J. 1992. *Cultural Populism.* London: Routledge.

McLuhan, M. 1964. *Understanding Media: The Extensions of Man.* New York: New American Library.

Mead, G. H. 1964. *On Social Psychology.* Edited by A. Strauss. Chicago: University of Chicago Press.

Michalos, A. 1985. "Multiple Discrepancies Theory (MDT)." *Social Indicators Research* 16, no. 4: 347–413.

Miller, A. 2010. "I Blog, Therefore I Am: Virtual Embodiment and the Self." In *Utopic Dreams and Apocalyptic Fantasies: Critical Approaches to Researching Video Game Play*, edited by T. Wright, D. Embrick, and A. Lukacs, 97–121. New York: Rowman and Littlefield.

Mills, C. W. 1959. *The Sociological Imagination.* New York: Oxford University Press.

Molm, L. 1997. *Coercive Power in Exchange.* Cambridge: Cambridge University Press.

Nisbet, R. 1966. *The Sociological Tradition.* New York: Basic Books.

Oatley, K. 1992. *Best Laid Schemes: The Psychology of Emotions.* Cambridge: Cambridge University Press.

O'Brien, J., ed. 2006. *The Production of Reality: Essays and Readings on Social Interaction,* 4th ed. Thousand Oaks, CA: Pine Forge Press.

Oerlemans, O. 2002. *Romanticism and the Materiality of Nature.* Toronto: University of Toronto Press.

Ogden, C. K., and I. A. Richards. 1923. *The Meaning of Meaning: A Study of the Influence of Language upon Thought and of the Science of Symbolism.* London: Kegan, Paul, Trench, Trubner.

Olds, J., and P. Milner. 1954. "Positive Reinforcement Produced by Electrical Stimulation of Septal Area and Other Areas of Rat Brain." *Journal of Comparative and Physiological Psychology* 47, no. 6 (December): 419–27.

Ong, W. 1982. *Orality and Literacy: The Technologizing of the Word.* New York: Routledge.

Osgood, C, G. Suci, and P. Tannenbaum. 1957. *The Measurement of Meaning.* Urbana: University of Illinois Press.

Papacharissi, Z. 2010. *A Networked Self: Identity, Community, and Culture on Social Network Sites.* New York: Routledge.

Parsons, T. 1966. *Societies: Evolutionary and Comparative Perspectives.* Englewood Cliffs, NJ: Prentice-Hall.

Perinbanayagam, R. 2006. *Games and Sport in Everyday Life: Dialogues and Narratives of the Self.* Boulder, CO: Paradigm Publishers.

Pescosolido, B., and Rubin, B. 2000. "The Web of Group-Affiliations Revisited: Social Life, Postmodernism, and Sociology." *American Sociological Review* 65, no. 1: 52–76.

Piaget, J. 1962. *Play, Dreams, and Imitation in Childhood.* New York: Norton.

Plato. 1963. *The Republic,* Book VII. In *Dialogues of Plato,* edited by J. Caplan, 357–63. New York: Washington Square Press.

Plutchik, R. 2003. *Emotions and Life: Perspectives from Psychology, Biology, and Evolution.* Washington, DC: American Psychological Association.

Poster, M. 2001. "Postmodern Virtualities." In *Media and Cultural Studies: Key Works,* edited by M. Durham and D. Kellner, 611–25. Malden, MA: Blackwell.

Postman, N. 2005. *Amusing Ourselves to Death: Public Discourse in the Age of Show Business,* rev. ed. New York: Penguin.

Putnam, R. 2001. *Bowling Alone: The Collapse and Revival of American Community.* New York: Simon and Schuster.

Radden, J. 2000. *The Nature of Melancholy: From Aristotle to Kristeva.* New York: Oxford University Press.

Rafaeli, S., D. Raban, and Y. Kalman. 2005. "Social Cognition Online." In *The Social Net: Understanding Human Behavior,* edited by Y. Amichai-Hamburger. 57–90. New York: Oxford University Press.

Ridgeway, C., and C. Johnson. 1990. "What Is the Relationship Between Socioemotional Behavior and Status in Task Groups?" *American Journal of Sociology* 95, no. 5 (March): 1189–1212.

Riesman, D., with R. Denney and N. Glazer. 1950. *The Lonely Crowd: A Study in the Changing American Character.* New Haven, CT: Yale University Press.

Ritzer, G. 1994. *The McDonaldization of Society.* Newbury Park, CA: Pine Forge Press.

Robinson, D., and L. Smith-Lovin. 1992. "Selective Interaction as a Strategy for Identity Maintenance: An Affect Control Model." *Social Psychology Quarterly* 55, no. 1 (March): 12–28.

Rose, P. 1996. *They and We: Racial and Ethnic Relations in the United States.* New York: McGraw-Hill.

Rosenau, P. 1992. *Post-Modernism and the Social Sciences: Insights, Inroads, Intrusions.* Princeton, NJ: Princeton University Press.

Rosenberg, M. 1981. "The Self-Concept: Social Product and Social Force." In *Social Psychology: Sociological Perspectives,* edited by M. Rosenberg and R. H. Turner, 593–624. New York: Basic Books.

Ryle, G. 1951. *The Concept of Mind.* New York: Barnes and Noble.

Sartre, J-P. 1948. *The Emotions.* Translated by B. Frechtman. New York: Philosophical Library.

Schachter, S., and J. Singer. 1962. "Cognitive, Social, and Physiological Determinants of Emotional State." *Psychological Review* 65 (September): 379–99.

Scheff, T. 1990. *Microsociology: Discourse, Emotion, and Social Structure.* Chicago: University of Chicago Press.

———. 1997. *Emotions, the Social Bond, and Human Reality: Part/Whole Analysis.* Cambridge: Cambridge University Press.

———. 2006. *Goffman Unbound! A New Paradigm for Social Science.* Boulder, CO: Paradigm Publishers.

Scherer, K. 1994a. "Emotion Serves to Decouple Stimulus and Response." In *The Nature of Emotion: Fundamental Questions,* edited by P. Ekman and R. Davidson, 127–30. New York: Oxford University Press.

———. 1994b. "Toward a Concept of Modal Emotions." In *The Nature of Emotion: Fundamental Questions,* edited by P. Ekman and R. Davidson, 25–31. New York: Oxford University Press.

Schor, J., and D. Holt, eds. 2000. *The Consumer Society Reader.* New York: New Press.

Seiger, J. 2005. *The Idea of the Self: Thought and Experience in Western Europe since the Seventeenth Century.* Cambridge: Cambridge University Press.

Senft, T. 2008. *Camgirls: Celebrity and Community in the Age of Social Networks.* New York: Peter Lang.

Sennett, R., and J. Cobb. 1973. *The Hidden Injuries of Class.* New York: Vintage.

Sharron, A. 2000. "Frame Paralysis: When Time Stands Still." In *Erving Goffman,* 4 vols., edited by G. A. Fine and G. Smith, vol. 3, 94–108. Thousand Oaks, CA: Sage.

Shaver, P., J. Schwartz, D. Kirson, and C. O'Connor. 1987. "Emotion Knowledge: Further Exploration of a Prototype Approach." *Journal of Personality and Social Psychology* 52, no. 6 (June): 1061–86.

Shott, S. 1979. "Emotion and Social Life: A Symbolic Interactionist Analysis." *American Journal of Sociology* 84, no. 6 (May): 1317–34.

Shweder, R. 1994. "'You're Not Just Sick, You're in Love': Emotion as an Interpretive System." In *The Nature of Emotion: Fundamental Questions,* edited by P. Ekman and R. Davidson, 32–44. New York: Oxford University Press.

Sica, A. 2000. "Rationalization and Culture." In *The Cambridge Companion to Weber,* edited by S. Turner, 42–58. Cambridge: Cambridge University Press.

Simmel, G. 1950. *The Sociology of Georg Simmel.* Edited and translated by K. Wolff. New York: Free Press.

———. 1971. *On Individuality and Social Forms.* Edited by D. Levine. Chicago: University of Chicago.

———. 1984. *George Simmel: On Women, Sexuality, and Love.* Translated by Guy Oakes. New Haven, CT: Yale University Press.

Simpson, D. 1995. *The Academic Postmodern and the Rule of Literature.* Chicago: University of Chicago Press.

Smith-Lovin, L., and D. Heise. 1988. *Analyzing Social Interaction: Advances in Affect Control Theory.* New York: Gordon and Breach.

Solomon, R. 2000. "The Philosophy of Emotions." In *Handbook of Emotions,* 2d ed., edited by M. Lewis and J. Haviland-Jones, 3–15. New York: Guilford Press.

Stearns, P. 2008. "History of Emotions: Issues of Change and Impact." In *Handbook of Emotions,* 3d ed., edited by M. Lewis, J. Haviland-Jones, and L. Barrett, 17–31. New York : Guilford.

Strack, F., L. Martin, and S. Stepper. 1988. "Inhibiting and Facilitating Conditions of the Human Smile: A Nonobtrusive Test of the Facial Feedback Hypothesis." *Journal of Personality and Social Psychology* 54, no. 5 (May): 768–77.

Strate, L., R. Jacobson, and S. Gibson, eds. 1996. *Communication and Cyberspace: Social Interaction in an Electronic Environment.* Cresskill, NJ: Hampton.

Stromberg, P. 2009. *Caught in Play: How Entertainment Works on You.* Stanford, CA: Stanford University Press.

Strongman, K. 1996. *The Psychology of Emotion: Theories of Emotion in Perspective,* 4th ed. New York: John Wiley and Sons.

Stryker, S. 1968. "Identity Salience and Role Behavior." *Journal of Marriage and the Family* 30, no. 4 (November): 558–64.

———. 1980. *Symbolic Interactionism: A Social Structural Version.* Menlo Park, CA: Benjamin Cummings.

———. 2004. "Integrating Emotion into Identity Theory." *Advances in Group Processes* 21: 1–23.

Thayer, E., and C. Bing. 2000. *Casey at the Bat: A Ballad of the Republic Sung in the Year 1888.* San Francisco: Chronicle Books.

Thoits, P. 1990. "Emotional Deviance: Research Agendas." In *Research Agendas in the Sociology of the Emotions,* edited by T. Kemper, 180–203. Albany: State University of New York Press.

Toennies, F. 1963. *Community and Society.* Edited and translated by C. Loomis. New York: Harper Torchbook.

Tolstoy, L. 2004. *The Death of Ivan Ilyich and Other Stories.* Translated by C. Garnett. New York: Barnes and Noble.

Tsushima, T., and P. Burke. 1999. "Levels, Agency, and Control in the Parent Identity." *Social Psychology Quarterly* 62, no. 2: 173–89.

Turkle, S. 1995. *Life on Screen: Identity in the Age of the Internet.* New York: Simon and Schuster.

———. 2005. *The Second Self: Computing and the Human Spirit.* Cambridge, MA: MIT Press.

Turner, J. 2000. *On the Origins of the Human Emotions: A Sociological Inquiry into the Origins of Human Affect.* Stanford, CA: Stanford University Press.

Turner, J., and J. Stets. 2005. *The Sociology of Emotions.* Cambridge: Cambridge University Press.

Turner, V. 1969. *The Ritual Process: Structure and Anti-Structure.* Chicago: Aldine.

Wallace, P. 2001. *The Psychology of the Internet.* Cambridge: Cambridge University Press.

Warren, J., ed. 2009. *The Cambridge Companion to Epicureanism.* Cambridge: Cambridge University Press.

Watson, D., and A. Tellegen. 1985. "Toward a Consensual Structure of Mood." *Psychological Bulletin* 98, no. 2 (September): 219–35.

Watson, N. 1998. "Why We Argue about Virtual Community: A Case Study of the Phish.net Fan Community." In *Virtual Culture: Identity and Communication in Cybersociety*, edited by S. Jones. 102–32. Thousand Oaks: CA: Sage.

Weber, M. 1958. *The Protestant Ethic and the Spirit of Capitalism.* Translated by T. Parsons. New York: Charles Scribner's Sons.

———. 1964. *The Theory of Social and Economic Organization.* Edited and translated by T. Parsons. New York: The Free Press.

Weinstein, D., and M. Weinstein. 1993. *Postmodern(ized) Simmel.* New York: Routledge.

Wiley, N. 1994. *The Semiotic Self.* Chicago: University of Chicago Press.

Williams, S. 2001. *Emotion and Social Theory: Corporeal Reflections on the Irrational.* Thousand Oaks, CA: Sage.

Williams, S., and G. Bendelow. 1998. *The Lived Body: Social Themes, Embodied Issues.* London: Routledge.

Wittgenstein, L. 1968. *Philosophical Investigations.* Translated by G. Anscombe. New York: Macmillan.

Wolf. M. ed., 2008. *The Video Game Explosion; A History from Pong to Playstation and Beyond.* Westport, CT: Greenwood.

Wright, T., D. Embrick, and A. Lukacs, eds. 2010. *Utopic Dreams and Apocalyptic Fantasies: Critical Approaches to Researching Video Game Play.* New York: Rowman and Littlefield.

Wrong, D. 1961. "The Oversocialized Conception of Man in Modern Sociology." *American Sociological Review* 26, no. 2 (April): 183–93.

INDEX

221